Bishop Amigo shortly after his Consecration as Bishop

Amigo—Friend of the Poor

Bishop of Southwark
1904-1949

By

Michael Clifton

FOWLER WRIGHT BOOKS LTD
Burgess Street
Leominster
Herefordshire
England

First published in 1987 by
FOWLER WRIGHT BOOKS LTD
Burgess Street
Leominster
Herefordshire
England

.

Typesetting by Print Origination Formby Liverpool L37 8EG

Printed in England by Camelot Press Ltd. Shirley Road Southampton SO9 1WF

Contents

FOREWORD BY ARCHBISHOP MICHAEL BOWEN OF SOUTHWARK

ARCHBISHOP'S HOUSE
ST GEORGE'S ROAD
SOUTHWARK
LONDON SE1 6HX
01-928 5592

September 1986

Peter Amigo was entrusted with the care of the Diocese of Southwark from 1904 until his death in 1949. During that time, there were vast changes in English society and two world wars. Despite all the problems this brought, the Diocese, which then covered the whole of Surrey and Sussex as well as its present area, saw great expansion and a growing contribution by the Church to the life of these islands, despite some old suspicions which still lingered on.

At the forefront of all this was the subject of this book. He was a larger than life figure, unafraid of controversy, yet whose every action was imbued with a great priestly zeal. We all owe a debt of gratitude to Father Michael Clifton for his interesting and lively study of a devoted and caring pastor.

Michael Bowen
Archbishop of Southwark

Acknowledgments

I should like to acknowledge the help I have received in preparing this text from Miss Elizabeth Poyser the archivist of the Archdiocese of Westminster, particularly with regard to the early years of the Archbishop and the differences between Cardinal Bourne and himself. Also I wish to thank those priests who sent in reminiscenses of the Archbishop in particular his last secretary, Mgr. Anthony Reynolds, Father Charles Tritschler, Canon Edward Mitchinson, Mgr. Humphrey Wilson (Nottingham) and Father Richard Hickey. I must thank also Canon Edward Mahoney OBE for assistance with the chapter on Education. Finally I would like to thank Mrs. Searle of Mitcham for typing out the final copy for the printers.

DEDICATION.

TO ARCHBISHOP MICHAEL BOWEN, THE SECOND
ARCHBISHOP OF SOUTHWARK TO BE BORN ON THE
ROCK OF GIBRALTAR.

Preface

Archbishop Amigo was Bishop of the Diocese of Southwark for forty-five years and his episcopate covered the period of both world wars. He was a Gibraltarian and never entirely lost a slight Spanish accent. However this did not stop him from becoming one of the greatest Bishops of the first half of this century. He did not limit his attentions merely to the diocese he controlled but sought at all times to play a role in national and international affairs if he considered the interests of the Catholics were at stake. If Catholics were being oppressed or persecuted and he could help them, then he would leave no stone unturned to obtain justice. I have called this biography 'Amigo—Friend of the Poor' and I use the word 'poor' in the widest sense to cover those who were oppressed and persecuted. The Archbishop's role in securing aid for the oppressed shows itself best in his intervention in Irish affairs in 1921 and his assistance to Belgian refugees in the first war and Gibraltarian refugees in the second world war.

The Archbishop had a genuine and lasting affection for the poor of London, the East-Enders, whom he had served at Commercial Road before coming to Southwark. As Bishop also he took especial interest in the welfare of the poor. The Parishes most visited by him were those with the poorest people.

His phenomenal memory for names and faces meant that he could establish a close rapport with everyone he met. He had a solid old-fashioned piety and expected the very best from his priests. He knew well the weaknesses of human nature and that people are liable to grow luke-warm in their religious observances. To counter this he established the practice of regular general missions in every parish and would often visit such missions even up to the last week of his life. He was always a keen supporter of the various guilds and confraternities, particularly the Men's Guilds.

Of course, he was not without faults. At times he could be very abrupt and even blunt. He had a strange, almost perverse sense of humour and was inclined to be hasty if anything went wrong at major ceremonies.

Perhaps the most serious mistakes were his acceptance of his Chapter's refusal to greet Cardinal Bourne after he had been created Cardinal in 1911 and his continued backing for Mussolini in the 1930's even after the invasion of Abyssinia. I understand that the word 'Fascist' was daubed on the walls of Archbishop's House at that time.

In spite of these faults he was greatly loved and revered by both priests and people. His greatest grief was the loss of his Cathedral in 1941, but early on in his episcopate he felt greatly the loss of friendship of Cardinal Bourne who had done so much to place him as Bishop of Southwark. The causes of this disagreement are analysed in Chapter 5.

It was the intention of the Archbishop to ask the well known historian Fr. Gordon Albion to prepare his biography. For a short while, Fr. Albion acted as the Archbishop's secretary. Even after he left Bishop's House, he was helped by the resident archivist, Fr. Herbert Rochford. Fr. Rochford sorted through many of the letters and documents relating to the most controversial elements of the Archbishop's episcopate. Yet after the Archbishop's death nothing further was done and the papers were left in their boxes until I started work on them about four years ago.

Much of this biography is based on the records kept at the Southwark Archives. There is a vast amount of material available, enough to produce a separate book for each of the major topics. There is however very little material indeed on the early life of the Archbishop and the period of his priesthood in Westminster Diocese.

In order not to slow down the narrative I have thought it best to add several supplements or appendices to the work, including the long letter of R. A. Butler on Education and the Bishop's own article for the 'Dublin Review' on Spain. This work is intended for the general reader with the historian of the period in mind also. To this end I have not added notes to the text, but at the back of the book there will be found a detailed list of the sources used for each chapter, together with a Bibliography. The index does not pretend to be exhaustive but covers the main topics dealt with and the most interesting personalities involved.

Chapter 1
Early Life

A thunderstorm was breaking over the Rock of Gibraltar on the morning of May 26th 1864. It was the feast of Corpus Christi. At the Amigo household in Waterport Street (now Main Street), Mr. Peter Amigo waited for the doctor to attend the birth of their ninth child. Four of their children had died in infancy including three boys. One of these boys also called Peter had died the day after his birth. Now again it was a question of premature delivery. For the first time in his life, Mr. Amigo had to miss Mass on a Day of Obligation in order to be with his wife. But just before noon, Emily Savignon Amigo was safely delivered of a son. The baby was tiny and premature so Mr. Amigo called on the priest at the nearby Cathedral of St. Mary the Crowned to come round at once to baptise the new arrival. He was duly christened Peter Emmanuel and the parents prayed that this time they would have a son who would survive the dangers of infancy. On June 8th both mother and baby were well enough to attend the Cathedral Church where Fr. Narcissus Pallares completed the ceremonies of the baptism he had performed at the house. Eventually the family comprised three sons and five daughters—Peter Emmanuel was the eldest of the three boys who survived infancy.

Peter Lawrence Amigo was a native of Gibraltar and was born there in August 1825. His parents had come to Gibraltar from Varazze about $1\frac{1}{2}$ miles from Genoa. They came during the Napoleonic troubles at a time many immigrants from Italy were arriving. Emily Savignon (sometimes spelt Sabinon) was also a native of Gibraltar having been born there in 1827. Her father came from Puerto Real near Cadiz while her mother came from Mahon, the capital of Minorca in the Balearics. The Savignon family are still to be found in Gibraltar.

The future Bishop's parents were married at St. Mary the Crowned

1

on the 30th June 1851. Mr. Amigo carried on a very successful business as a trader in flour and flour based products including Semola and Maccaroni. To start with they lived in Waterport Street, at what is now 114 Main Street. Soon after Peter's birth they moved to a fine large house in George's Lane. The Gibralter Register for 1877 carries the following advertisement.

> "The Steam Flour Mill, 4 George's Lane, Bakery and Vermicelli Manufactory. Flour, Semola, Bran, Bread, Biscuits, Vermicelli and Maccaroni can always be had fresh and good in this establishment on the most favourable terms."

By 1882 they were able to afford to buy the property next door in George's Lane and until recently a plaque was to be seen on the door of No. 12 (the numbers have been altered) carrying Mr. Peter Amigo's name. At this time also Mr. Amigo obtained a property in City Mill Lane for the elder daughters.

Mr. Amigo was a founder member of the "Exchange and Commercial Library" the one and only trade organisation in the town for many years. In 1876 this organisation came into conflict with Bishop Scandella, Vicar Apostolic of Gibraltar. It seems that the Spanish government were irritated by the growth of the tobacco trade and in particular tobacco smuggling in the town. Their own trade was suffering. So the British government drafted a bill to ban tobacco trading in the town. Bishop Scandella called the members of the Exchange and Commercial to meet him but these members including Mr. Amigo refused to agree to the Bishop's suggestions and told him not to interfere. The Bishop went to London to lobby members of Parliament to have the measure withdrawn. The Exchange and Commercial sent their own delegation to the Manchester Chamber of Commerce where they found little support. They then wrote back to Gibraltar saying that the Bishop's activities were hampering their cause. This led to serious antagonism against the Bishop and a rise of anticlericalism amongst the citizens of the Rock. The Bishop was forced to abandon his plans to return by ship and in the event slipped quietly over the land frontier. Although the trouble died down, the flame of hatred was still lingering below the surface.

In 1880 Bishop Scandella died and was succeeded by his secretary, Bishop Gonzalo Canilla. Fr. Canilla had accompanied Bishop Scandella to London and the old hatred was stirred up again. The members of the Exchange and Commercial stopped him from entering his own Cathedral for over a year. However it must be said that Mr. Amigo was not amongst those who opposed Bishop Canilla and took no part in this second round of trouble. This story is told here because in a strange way it affected the life of Peter Amigo the future Bishop.

Bishop Canilla died in 1898 and the name of Father Peter Amigo by now a priest of Westminster Diocese was put forward as his successor. It would seem that the only reason he was not in fact appointed was because of his father's involvement with the Exchange and Commercial Library. Gibraltar's loss was to be Southwark's gain.

To return to the family, it must be admitted that we know very little of Peter's life as a young boy in Gibraltar. In accordance with practice of the time he made his first Holy Communion at the age of 11 on 13th December 1875 and was confirmed the same day by Bishop Scandella. As to his early schooling we have but scant information. It seems likely that as an infant he attended a Mr. Aitken's "collegiate" school while later he was a pupil at St. Bernard's College, a diocesan foundation. This school had been run by the Irish Christian brothers up to 1838 and Bishop Scandella eventually persuaded them to return it in 1878. Among the brothers was a young man, Edward Murnane, later to become a Priest of Southwark where his former pupil would become his Bishop. Archbishop Amigo in later life also recounted that he had learnt French from a very old man in the town who had been a drummer boy in the French army of Napoleon at Austerlitz.

At the age of 14 Mr. Amigo sent his son to St. Edmunds Ware with a view to a career in law. He was not particularly bright, especially when compared with his brother Joseph, nearly two years younger than Peter, who had already been at St. Edmunds one year when Peter arrived. Peter and Joseph were actually in the same class at St. Edmunds, Upper Rudiments. St. Edmunds at the time was in effect both a public school and a Seminary. Students for the priesthood continued with the study of philosophy after completing the course of humanities and then went on to St. Thomas's Hammersmith to complete theology. St. Edmunds was not a large community. There were only 13 students in each class at the time. Young Peter however had not entered as a Church student.

As far as life at the college was concerned however there was almost no distinction between Church students and lay boys. The only major difference was that the lay boys rose 20 minutes after the "divines" and were not obliged to attend meditation before Mass. The order of day was as follows. Rise 6.00 am. Meditation 6.30 am. Community morning prayer 6.50 am. Mass 7.00 am followed by short time for reading.

Breakfast at 8.00 am. Lectures or classes from 8.45 to 12.45. Lunch at 1.00 pm then recreation. Drill or Music from 3.00 pm to 4.00 pm. Study from 4.00 pm to 5.00 pm followed by tea at 5.00 pm. Prep time from 5.30 to 7.15 pm followed by visit to the Blessed Sacrament and spiritual reading. Supper followed at 7.35 pm followed by recreation and night prayers at 9.00 pm. Prayers were usually said in the dormitory before the boys came down in the morning. The morning offering, Our Father, Hail Mary, I Confess and Apostles Creed.

There were games three afternoons a week. Students over the age of 14 were allowed a bicycle. The usual punishments of the time were "lock up" (Detention), Lines to learn or write, Extra Drill and a speciality of St. Edmunds "The gallery walk." For serious offences a thrashing could be administered by the general prefect of discipline.

The fees for tuition were thirty guineas a year to start with later rising to forty guineas. In addition there were special charges for games equipment and books. Boarders like the Amigo boys would only return home from the Summer holidays so extra allowance had to be paid for their accommodation during the other holidays spent at the college. Mr. Amigo allowed Joseph and Peter the sum of one shilling per week pocket money, but after the fees went up and Fernando came to the college, Peter received one shilling per week but Fernando only sixpence. The sum of 24 shillings was allotted for their return home by steamer in the Summer.

The St. Edmunds archives for the period contain a full list of exam results for the period of the Amigo boys stay. Thus it is possible to chart Peter's progress. For the first eighteen months or so his results were disappointing. But by the start of 1880 he begins to appear as one of the brightest boys in his group.

The archives at Southwark provide a possible clue to his remarkable progress. He started to receive a monthly magazine called "Cassell's Home Educator." This was a work intended for adults who lacked formal education but who wished to "better themselves" and contained instruction in all the basic subjects up to what we would term today 'O' Level standard. It was probably at this time too that Peter acquired his astonishing ability to remember everything photographically so that he could recall facts about people he had met only once or twice many years afterwards.

Perhaps also he was not too happy with the general standard of education at St. Edmunds at that period. There were frequent changes of the President (as the Rector was called). When Peter first arrived the

President was Mgr. J. L. Patterson an Oxford convert who later became assistant to Cardinal Manning as titular Bishop of Emmaus. In 1880 he was succeeded by Fr. Akers (later Canon Akers who was to be parish priest of Commercial Road when Fr. Amigo came there as curate). Finally came Fr. Patrick Fenton who later became an auxiliary Bishop to Cardinal Bourne.

Some time during 1881 Peter decided he would try his vocation to the Priesthood. In his "Memoirs", Fr. Philip Fletcher who attended St. Edmunds as a mature student in 1878 to 1879 recounts how he used to chat with two younger students about his aspirations for the priesthood. These two students were Peter Amigo and Francis Bourne. It is perhaps rather strange that they should have met at all for according to the rules prevalent at the time the younger boys did not mix at all with the seniors or "First Division" as they were known. However it was almost certainly then that the idea of a vocation to the priesthood first came to young Peter.

The First Division consisted of the classes of Poetry, Rhetoric and Philosophy. (Roughly speaking the sixth form of a school today plus the Philosophy). In September 1881 Peter had entered the First Division. Francis Bourne had only studied one year at St. Edmunds, but in the year 1881 to 1882 there were many other students who would be well known to Peter later on as Priest and Bishop. One year below him was Arthur Doubleday, later to become Rector of the Seminary of Wonersh and later still 2nd Bishop of Brentwood. A mature student of that year was Edward St. John, nephew of Cardinal Newman's friend. At the end of that year his positions in the various subjects were as follows. Latin, French, History, Natural Philosophy and Chemistry . . . all 1st in class. English and Euclid (Geometry) 2nd. Arithmetic/Algebra 4th. In the special class on Catechism of the Council of Trent which was jointly held for the entire First Division he came 12th out of 39 students. Edward St. John failed dismally with 39 marks. He accused the Rector Father Akers of incompetence. Father Akers was so upset he resigned and Edward St. John was withdrawn to study privately for the priesthood before going on to St. Thomas's Hammersmith.

In 1883 Peter received the tonsure, the first important step on the road to the Priesthood from Bishop Weathers, Rector of St. Thomas Seminary, Hammersmith, and auxiliary Bishop to Cardinal Manning. This same Bishop conferred all subsequent minor and major orders on the future Bishop. He received the orders of reader and lector at St. Edmunds on 14th April 1884. Having matriculated with success at St.

Edmunds he was transferred to St. Thomas's Hammersmith in January 1885 and received the orders of exorcist and acolyte there in February 1885. Here he completed his theological studies and was ordained subdeacon on 20th March 1886, deacon on 5th March 1887 and finally was ordained priest on February 25th 1888 at Our Lady of Victories, Kensington, then pro-cathedral for the diocese of Westminster for which diocese he was ordained.

Once again we know very little of his time at Hammersmith. One of his fellow students was William Francis Brown, later to become his Vicar General at Southwark and then Auxiliary Bishop. He relates in his memoirs "Through Windows of Memory" that the students found the Canon Law lectures from Fr. Surmont difficult to follow as he spoke Latin with a strong Belgian accent. Another fellow student for a while was Edward St. John who was dean of studies for a while, and we do know that while at Hammersmith Peter was able to renew his friendship with Fr. Francis Bourne then currently curate at Mortlake just over the river from Hammersmith. It is clear too that the young theological student had the highest regard for the rector of St. Thomas's, Dr. Weathers. He called him later 'an undoubted Saint'. He was known for the austerity of his life coupled with a great regard for the students under his care. Later on Bishop Amigo would seek to copy his old Rector in his own personal lifestyle.

Chapter 2
Priest of Westminster Diocese,
Vicar General in Southwark

When Father Peter Amigo was ordained, the diocese of Westminster was administered by the great Cardinal Manning. As young Father Peter had shown such great talent as a student he was earmarked to become a professor at St. Edmunds Ware. His first temporary appointment however was as assistant to Father Ethelred Taunton of the Church of Our Lady of Good Counsel in Stoke Newington. Fr. Taunton was something of an authority on Canon Law and had published a small work on the subject, the first in English since the Reformation. When Fr. Amigo joined him however, he was a sick man. After a short holiday in August 1884 he joined the staff at St. Edmunds where he taught Classics, Church History and Scripture mainly to the Junior classes. He could already speak French and Spanish fluently and later on was to master Italian. Unfortunately we know little of these years at St. Edmunds. One or two former pupils wrote later to congratulate him on becoming Bishop but that is all. For a while he was Regent of the Junior House it seems.

Following the accession of Archbishop Vaughan to Westminster in 1892, Father Peter was appointed as assistant to Fr. Alfred White at the Church of Holy Trinity, Brook Green, Hammersmith. At that time this was quite a mixed Parish, comprising both the wealthy and the poor. Southwark Archives possess his visitation books from this time, and they show his assiduous attention to the duties of Parish visiting. He was already becoming known as a particularly zealous priest.

In 1896 Cardinal Vaughan wrote to Canon Akers outlining a scheme to raise the missionary and religious spirit of the clergy especially in the first year of their ordination. He proposed that Canon Akers should open a house of Pastoral Theology at St. Mary's and St. Michael's Commercial Road. All young priests would spend a period of time at Commercial Road and receive spiritual training and exercise in preaching before being sent out to various missions. He would give Canon Akers one of his best priests to assist him in the new work. This priest was Father Peter Amigo. And so in June 1896 Father Amigo was transferred to Commercial Road. This area was one of the toughest in London. Cardinal Vaughan's scheme had little chance of success there. Canon Akers was not well and most of the responsibility fell on Fr. Amigo. He proved himself a very hard worker. He developed a skill in outdoor preaching and was rewarded for his troubles by being pelted at times with stones and eggs. He attended to the sick at the London Hospital and continued his assiduous visiting. He raised funds to extend the elementary schools in the Parish. He won the hearts of all the people and there were some present at his funeral sixty years later who still remembered his days in the East End.

However in October 1897 Francis Bourne now Bishop of Southwark wrote to Cardinal Vaughan requesting that Fr. Amigo be transferred to Southwark. Why did he take this step? It seems that when Fr. Bourne was Curate at Mortlake he had discussed with Peter Amigo, then a student, a scheme to form an association of secular priests. He knew that Cardinal Vaughan's scheme at Commercial Road was not working out and knew that Fr. Amigo would support him with his own scheme. When Cardinal Vaughan refused to release Fr. Amigo, Bishop Bourne wrote back (13 Jan 1898) "God's will is always best and there is nothing else worth living for."

Meanwhile at Commercial Road, Canon Akers was getting weaker and weaker and eventually died on 14th August 1899. Fr. Amigo was appointed Parish Priest in his place. When he eventually left in 1901 to enter Southwark there was a deputation to the Cardinal to plead against his removal.

In February 1901, Bishop Bourne again renewed his pleas for the release of Fr. Amigo to help start the association of secular Priests and this time Cardinal Vaughan agreed to part with Fr. Amigo for five years. After that time the matter was to be re-examined. If the scheme was a success it would be extended to other dioceses. The proposed association was to be run according to the Sulpician model and Bishop Bourne wished Fr. Amigo to spend some time with the Sulpicians at Issy and St. Sulpice. The plan was for the society to be a purely voluntary association. One of Bishop Bourne's ideas was that a strong bond of brotherly union be set up between those who work on the mission and those who are at the Seminary. All the first members should have been brought in contact with the Sulpicians. The Spirit was to be purely ecclesiastical founded on the teaching of the Church in her Canon Law and liturgy, and yet in no way was it to be an imitation of religious life.

The archives retain a copy of the rules of the proposed association. They are as follows.

1. Convinced that to sanctify others, we must begin with ourselves. We shall take care about our preparation for Mass, and our Thanksgiving after Mass, about our Meditation, Spiritual reading, Office, Rosary and Sacred Study, and Visit to the Blessed Sacrament. Also if possible we shall set aside one day each month for recollection and make our retreat year by year.
2. To help us to lead a life of sacrifice, we shall place all our offerings for Christmas and Easter, our Salaries, our Stipends for Mass, our stole fees, into a common fund. From this we shall have fifty pounds every year, and the surplus after each priest has had his quarter's money will be disposed of at the meeting of the Association which will be held at the end of each quarter.
3. As an act of atonement to God for the sins of drunkenness we shall abstain from the use of ardent spirits.
4. We shall pray to God for ourselves and other priests, saying Mass once a year at least for the Secular Clergy. We recommend also the Missa pro Populo to invoke God's blessing on our work.

Fr. Amigo was officially notified of the move to Southwark on April 5th 1901. About one week later Bishop Bourne told Fr. Amigo of his plans. They were to go together to Paris and Fr. Amigo was to spend May and June at the Sulpician Solitude at Issy, he would then have a break in Gibraltar in July and start his work in Southwark by taking charge of the Parish of Walworth in South London. This had already been agreed upon with the then Parish Priest, Fr. Doubleday (later Bishop). At Walworth Fr. Amigo was to start up the proposed Association of Priests and as it turned out later to begin the work of training for the priesthood men with late vocations still working in business.

However the strain of leaving Commercial Road brought on a temporary illness for Fr. Amigo and on 15th April Bishop Bourne wrote to say that this would alter their plans. He now wished Fr. Amigo to accept the nuns invitation to recuperate at Isleworth. Fr. Amigo quickly recovered and went to stay with the Sulpicians at Issy in May 1901. While at Issy Fr. Amigo wrote to Bishop Bourne suggesting that some younger priests and young men aspiring to the Priesthood should live a common life together. While at Issy Fr. Amigo had in fact gathered information on various places where priests were already leading some kind of community life. One of the problems for the proposed Association was a considerable difference of opinion on the method of pooling resources and the objects for which the surplus, if any, should be allocated. Another problem was that of priests being able to concentrate in specific areas and it was sometimes impossible to have more than a single priest serving a particular district. The aim however was always to have two priests at least, working together if it was practicable and Fr. Amigo when later he became Bishop seems consistently to have pressed this policy.

Fr. Amigo took up his duties as Rector of Walworth on 28th June 1901. The First Rector of Walworth was Fr. Joseph Reeks who later became Parish Priest of Woolwich and died there. He started living in the Parish having worked the area from the Cathedral parish earlier. That was in 1890. The Parish then had new schools opened the same year, but no Church.

The debt on the schools was paid off in 1899 but a new debt of £2,000 existed on the site of the new Church. Then there was an estimated £6,000 for the building of the Church. The foundation stone was laid on February 15th 1902 by Bishop Bourne. The prayers of the congregation were earnestly solicited and before the end of the year one large gift of £1,200 had already been received, quickly followed by another gift of £1,500. These gifts seemed to have been in response to special novenas. In the early summer of 1903 the Church was practically ready for use and was to be opened by Bishop Bourne on August 15th that year. However the opening had to be postponed for other events had superimposed themselves on the lives of both men.

After Fr. Amigo had been in the diocese for 18 months as Rector of Walworth, he was appointed as 2nd Vicar General in addition to Canon Johnston who was now unequal for the task and lived too far from London to be in full communication with the Bishop. Bishop Bourne expressed the hope in his letter that Our Blessed Lady and St. Edmund, under whose protection they first met, would enable them to do much together for the honour of God and the salvation of souls. There was a slight difficulty at the start however. Canon Surmont of Westminster wrote to Fr. Amigo stating the he doubted if Bishop Bourne had power to appoint two Vicars General. Canon Surmont informed Cardinal Vaughan who contacted Mgr. Merry del Val in Rome. The good Monsignor replied that all was in order. He received many letters of congratulation. Fr. Roderick Grant at Brook Green wrote to say he would not congratulate him unless he wished it since a Vicar General is like a Bishop in being a "Signum cui contradicetur in Ecclesia" ... but sent his best wishes and prayers for complete success and that he might weather all storms. Fr. James Driscoll wrote that he was personally delighted but hoped he would not get too proud and look down on poor struggling curates!

In practice Fr. Amigo did all the work of Vicar General for the few months that intervened before Bishop Bourne's appointment to Westminster. In January Bishop Bourne went to Rome to try and settle a problem to do with Chaplains and their responsibilities to their Bishops. The Bishops of Southwark had, since the time of Bishop Grant, undertaken the work of liaising with the authorities over the appointment of military chaplains as there was no forces Bishop in those days. Bishop Bourne determined to stay in Rome until he received a favourable reply. His return was delayed several times and he finally arrived back on May 16th 1903. On 18th April he wrote to Fr. Amigo that it was a great comfort to him in his prolonged absence that he had appointed him Vicar General as he felt that he (Amigo) would neither allow business to get above him nor commit him (Bourne) to any decision of which he might not approve.

Bishop Bourne had barely returned from Rome when Cardinal Vaughan died on 19th June. The following month saw the demise of Pope Leo XIII on the 20th July while on August 4th came the election of the new Pope St. Pius X. The announcement of the elevation of Bishop Bourne to Westminster came on the 28th August. The circumstances by which so young a Bishop as Bourne came to be appointed to Westminster are related by Shane Leslie in his memoir on Cardinal Gasquet. It appears that Gasquet missed out by one vote in the final selection made in Rome by the consultors after the intervention of Cardinal Moran of Sydney who was fiercely anti-Benedictine and had just ousted this order from Australia.

However on his appointment to Westminster there took place a very strange event in which Fr. Amigo played a leading role. It seems that Bishop Bourne was none too popular with his Chapter. They objected to his officious manner and the fact that he refused to consult them over business connected with the Seminary. Their strongest complaint however was that he refused them any knowledge of the finances of the diocese. Before his time under Bishop Butt there had been a small advisory committee on finance but this ceased under Bishop Bourne and the finances were then fully under the control of the Financial Secretary Canon Edward St. John and his lay adviser W. H. Bishop.

As soon as news broke of the appointment of Bishop Bourne to Westminster he spoke of his desire to be Administrator of Southwark until the appointment of a new Bishop of Southwark was made. When Mgr. Fenton, the Vicar Capitular of Westminster, officially announced the appointment of Bishop Bourne on the strength of authentic information from Rome that the Holy Father had made Bishop Bourne Archbishop of Westminster, the Southwark Chapter assumed that he had received his Brief. They decided to meet at once to elect a Vicar Capitular for they feared that if they did not do so within the eight days required by law, Bishop Bourne would exercise his right of appointment and secure the position of Administration during the vacancy. When Bourne heard that the Chapter were going to meet the following day to appoint a Vicar Capitular he discussed the matter with his Secretary, Mgr. Charles Coote and at the latter's suggestion drew up a writ of excommunication against the entire Chapter. The wording states that they would be excommunicated should they meet before the Brief was received. Mgr. Johnston got to hear of this scheme. He then went to see his fellow Vicar General, Fr. Amigo and they agreed that great damage might result to the Archbishop if the excommunication were fulminated. He went directly from Walworth to Hyde House, Clapham Park, where the new Archbishop was staying and after much hesitation he agreed that the fatal document be handed over to Fr. Amigo. So the following day when the Chapter were due to meet. Fr. Amigo went to the Cathedral and met first with Canons Keatinge and Connolly. He persuaded the two Canons to advise the Chapter not to meet and thus the danger of any resort to extreme measures was averted. After the Brief had arrived the Chapter duly met and elected Provost Moore as the Vicar Capitular. With this appointment Fr. Amigo ceased to be Vicar General and for a while remained simply as the Parish Priest of Walworth.

Chapter 3

The Appointment as Bishop of Southwark

Five months elapsed before the announcement of the new Bishop was declared. This period known as an "Interregnum" was a period of considerable stress for Fr. Amigo as he found himself unwittingly at the centre of a very unpleasant controversy.

The Southwark Chapter met on September 21st 1903 to appoint a Vicar Capitular, this time with the consent of Archbishop Bourne. On the 1st October they met again to decide on the "Terna", the three names to be sent to Rome as possible choices for the new Bishop. The Canons selected Mgr. Patrick Fenton of Westminster one time Rector of St. Edmunds Ware as their first choice, with Canon James Keatinge and Dr. Thomas Scannell as the second and third choice. Although the names of those selected were supposed to be kept secret, they were in fact published in the press shortly afterwards. Meanwhile the English Bishops met and approved the choices on 6th October. But rumours were already flying around. It was said that the succession was already 'fixed' and the choice of the Archbishop was for Fr. Amigo. The rumours appear to have started from Father Coote, the Archbishop's Secretary. On the 8th October Fr. Amigo wrote to Provost Moore, the Vicar Capitular.

"I should like to see all this unpleasant business settled. It is a pity to let the Archbishop leave the diocese in such a manner. I wish to do all in my power to bring about peace. I have questioned Dr. Coote as to the statement which he is supposed to have made, and he most emphatically denies that he ever said that the succession was settled last April. The most he may have said when asked was that he would wish me to succeed. I am absolutely certain that the same is the most

13

the Archbishop has said. The whole affair is very painful. It shows how easily words may be twisted about and mischief made which is not intended. As for myself I can assure you that I had no idea that my name would even be mentioned. The honour attached to the episcopate has no attraction whatever for me and I know enough of the responsibility to make me shrink from desiring such a burden . . . but if I am to become Bishop, I trust that the Chapter will put more confidence in me than they have done in the late Bishop and that God will give me the grace to do my duty to priests and people."

The Archbishop left for Rome to collect the Pallium on the 26th October accompanied by Fr. Coote and Canon St. John. The rumours however continued to spread. At the beginning of November Canon O'Halloran, Parish Priest of Greenwich, Our Lady Star of the Sea, acting on his own, arranged to send a representative to Rome to act for the Chapter. The priest chosen, Fr. James Warwick of Balham, was not a member of the Chapter. When Canon O'Halloran told Provost Moore of this arrangement, the Provost at once dissociated himself from Canon O'Halloran's action. Canon O'Halloran wrote to Provost Moore on November 13th.

"Father Fleming (an English speaking Consultor in Rome) whom I consulted two or three times about the defence of the Terna, insisted that we must have a representative in Rome to answer questions and write for information and interview persons of influence . . . I felt obliged to act on my own responsibility to save time and send out someone at once, never doubting that the majority who elected the Terna would gladly sanction what had been done in defence of the Common Cause."

The magazine of the Southwark Catholic Children's Society, *'The Shield'*, which was in effect a diocesan magazine reported the existence of "various rumours" and added (December 1903) "Father Warwick of Balham is also taking a quiet holiday in the Eternal City."

At the end of November Propaganda in Rome at length considered the problem of the Southwark Succession but referred the matter back to the Bishops again who dealt with the new situation at a meeting on December 22nd. Once again the rumours flared up anew. Why was it necessary to have this second meeting of Bishops? The *'Shield'* for January 1904 spent two pages explaining events. The Archbishop put out a public statement explaining the situation. (*Shield*, January 1904 page 4).

"They (Bishops) have moreover never hesitated to suggest other names if they judged well to do so. In the present instance however, as their right to mention other candidates had been called in question, they contented themselves with forwarding their report to Rome, but abstained from suggesting additional names as they would have done under ordinary circumstances, and remitted the whole question to the judgement of the Holy See . . . . The matter now rests with the Holy See . . . .the Holy See only desires to select the best man and welcomes the fullest information from the most authoritative source."

At the second meeting of Bishops, Archbishop Bourne added the names of Fr. Amigo and Canon St. John to the Terna. One can deduce from the letter above that he would have done so earlier but for the rumours circulating already in early October. It can also be deduced that he persuaded Propaganda to refer the succession back to the Bishops again in order that he could add the names of Fr. Amigo and Canon St. John for the final selection meeting of Propaganda.

Fr. Warwick who had returned from Rome in December was now hurriedly dispatched again. While in Rome he wrote two letters to Fr. Amigo in which he states that he is still pressing for Mgr. Fenton as the choice of the Chapter, and that his main preoccupation was to stop the election of Canon St. John whom he felt lacked the qualification for the post, having never spent any time on strictly pastoral activities. (He had spent his entire priestly career as Financial Secretary to the previous two Bishops and also ran the Southwark Rescue Society for Orphans).

The names of Fr. Amigo and Canon St. John however were included in the final deliberations of Propaganda and after many delays on February 24th 1904, the news was given to the public that Father Peter Amigo was indeed to be the new Bishop of Southwark.

When the news came that indeed Fr. Peter Amigo would be the next Bishop, he received many letters of congratulations, most of which are preserved in the Southwark Archives. Some in particular were marked by the Bishop "keep". The first of these was from an old friend from Seminary days, Father Charles Kuypers of Hertford. This contained a prophetic note which as we shall see was soon to bear fruit in the first years of Bishop Peter's episcopate. Fr. Kuypers in his letter deals mainly with the finances of a diocese.

"From the late Pope (Leo XIII) hoarding his millions in secret cupboards down to the average priest keeping his so-called accounts in a washing book, there is an utter lack of any sense of financial integrity. Bishops are doing every month acts for which laymen are arraigned at the Old Bailey on criminal charges. It is inevitable that such breaches of trust should take place so long as individual ecclesiastics are left to their own responsibility in dealing with money. The consequence is that enlightened laymen are utterly mistrustful. They have no sort of guarantee that their charitable bequests will be respected... The only remedy so far as I see, lies in an act of self-effacement on the part of bishops by the appointment of a council of responsible laymen, not mere dummy nominees, for each diocese, and the publication of detailed accounts properly audited and certified. I am confident that any bishop who had the courage and honesty to take the Catholic laity into his confidence and give them a share in the administration of monies with a guarantee of integrity, would very soon find his financial embarrassments reduced.... If you will do something to restore confidence along these lines, I shall be able to congratulate Southwark as well your prospective Lordship."

The second letter comes from Fr. George Newton at Rotherhithe. This saintly priest was later appointed as spiritual director of the students at Wonersh Seminary.

"As I have known you so long and so well it seems to me the natural result and supernatural crowning of a life that has always been unflinchingly devoted to duty and God's service. A life that has aimed at perfect ideals, which if not attained, at any rate which has been directed and moved without swerving to the right or left at the ideal priesthood. You know my dear Peter, that the one devotion of your life for yourself always and for others at St. Edmunds and since you have been on the Mission has been a perfect priesthood. And so anyone who knows you as well as I think I do, must look upon your higher vocation to the fullness of the Priesthood as God's seal and reward upon this one main devotion of your life.... To me like yourself who has always tried to be (I use this phrase to preserve your humility) 'a faithful and wise servant', responsibility means two things, first a closer more constant and more perfect co-operation with Almighty God in his work for souls. Above this responsibility is one side of the balance which is weighed down on the other by grace, merit and reward; so as responsibilities become greater, the other side will more than overbalance them with privileges here and nearness to God hereafter."

Some letters came from old priest friends he had known at St. Edmunds and give a little insight into those earlier days. Father Edward Watson wrote from Brentwood.

"God will bless your pure motives and your hard work, your infinite capacity for taking pains and the other faculties he has given you which are necessary and sufficient for your high office."

Father James Driscoll wrote from Westminster Cathedral.

"It is indeed with heartfelt pleasure for me to know that my old dormitory master at St. Edmunds and one who has always been a true friend to me when I needed help and advice has been raised to so great a dignity. These feelings I am sure I share with many others who have experienced your kindness in the past. Although the cheeky young-ster of the past must mend his manners in the future, believe me his old feelings of friendship and gratitude are ever present."

Father Carol Tate wrote from Bellingham, Northumberland.

"It must be nearly 13 years since we met, and I can hardly venture to hope that you have a very vivid recollection of me, but for my part I remember the grave young professor of those philosophy days, who so faithfully acted up to the apostolic injunction, 'Argue, obsecra, increpa' very well. I thought you did the 'increpa' part very well 'in omni patientia'."

After all the controversy surrounding his appointment it is hearten-ing to note that Provost Moore on behalf of the Chapter wrote this note to the new Bishop after a Chapter meeting.

"The Canons and clergy here were all delighted with our meeting today. Confidence and ease on both sides promises well for the future. All have expressed themselves as highly pleased. I am so glad, and I think you will have an easy and happy fortune."

The last sentence was somewhat wide of the mark but in spite of the fears expressed earlier by some of the clergy and particularly by the Chapter, it is true to say that 90% of the clergy gave Bishop Peter Amigo their full support from the start. The Chapter in particular showed themselves most loyal allies in the battles ahead.

Bishop Peter Amigo was consecrated on March 25th, the Feast of the Annunciation at St. George's Cathedral. The event was reported in the Daily Press. The most poetic description is that of the '*Daily Chronicle*'.

"The consecration and enthronement of the Right Reverend Peter Amigo as Bishop of Southwark—one of the most stately and impressive ceremonies in the Roman Catholic Church—in succession to Dr. Bourne, now Archbishop of Westminster, took place yesterday at St. George's Cathedral, Southwark.

Seldom has Pugin's fine Church, his only one in London, been seen to such advantage. The building was ablaze with light while two red canopied thrones, the varied vestments of the clergy, the grandeur of the ritual, and the vastness of the congregation, drawn from every part of the metropolis, combined to complete a scene that will not readily be forgotten. The Archbishop was received in state at the western doors by the Chapter and Bishops and conducted to the sanctuary where, vested for Mass and wearing the pall, he took his seat in front of the altar. The Bishop-Elect clad in white cope and biretta, with two assistant Bishops coped and mitred, was presented to Dr. Bourne and took the oath of fidelity to the Pope, a special clause stating that nothing in this vow was opposed to the allegiance due to the King.

A formal examination as to faith and practice followed and then the Mass of Consecration was begun. Prostrate, the Bishop-elect lay on the floor of the sanctuary while prayers were offered for his guidance and help. The sonorous Latin rolled forth majestically, and towards the end the Metropolitan rose and turned towards the prostrate figure with a thrice-repeated appeal for divine blessing. Then the Bishop-elect knelt before the Archbishop, who delivered the charge and afterwards to the chanting of the 'Veni Creator' anointed the hands and head of the new Bishop and handed to him the pastoral staff and ring. Subsequently the newly-consecrated Bishop knelt before the Metropolitan who with the assisting Bishops (The Bishops of Portsmouth and Newport) placed on his head a mitre gleaming with gold and precious stones and in his hands the gloves that form a part of the pontifical attire. Thus fully vested he was placed upon the vacant throne after which while the 'Te Deum' was being rendered he proceeded round the church bestowing his blessing upon the worshippers.

At the conclusion of the Mass his lordship seated on his throne, received the homage of the clergy and imparted the Papal benediction.

After the ceremony Bishop Amigo entertained the prelates, clergy and his personal friends at a luncheon in St. George's Hall."

The account given in the *'Times'* adds the little detail that at the luncheon Archbishop Bourne spoke and said "He had desired Dr. Amigo to be his successor in Southwark, because he believed that he of all men would continue and develop his work."

The new Bishop lost no time in getting down to work. His first duty was to rearrange the schedule of confirmations and visitations that had been held over since the translation of Archbishop Bourne. He spent several days at the seminary at Wonersh interviewing all the professors and students. He found it necessary to make only one change. Fr. Charles Dessoulavy the Professor of Philosophy, was appointed as Assistant Priest at Greenwich. It had become clear that he was deeply imbued with modernist principles. He re-appears later in this account of the Bishop's life in connection with the death of Fr. Tyrell.

During July and August Bishop Amigo visited as many convents as possible and he did not take a holiday or break of any kind until October when he visited both Rome and Gibraltar.

He arrived in Gibraltar on 26th October 1904 and received a wonderful reception. Various commissions went on board his ship to greet him. On landing he received an address of welcome from the one public representative body then existing, 'The Exchange and Commercial Library'. The bells of the city churches were all rung and a procession was formed to the Cathedral where he was received by the Bishop and a solemn 'Te Deum' sung. He remained in the town until 23rd November when he left for Rome. There were various celebrations during his stay, the most interesting items being that he sang Pontifical High Mass in the Cathedral on All Saints Day, an event surrounded by extraordinary solemnity according to local press reports, and that on the 19th November he was the recipient of a handsome presentation by the townspeople. This took the form of a gold chalice adorned with precious stones and a silver episcopal ewer and basin purchased by public subscription. He used the chalice for the first time in a public Mass celebrated in the Cathedral on the 22nd November, the morning before he left.

Before moving on to deal with his life as Bishop of Southwark it would be well to look at the Diocese as he found it on its accession.

The Diocese consisted then of the County of London south of the Thames together with the counties of Kent, Surrey and Sussex. When the Dioceses of England and Wales were created in 1850 the diocese had also included Hampshire, the Isle of Wight and the Channel Islands. These areas however were cut off to form the Diocese of Portsmouth in

1884. The Diocese was still large enough and indeed growing rapidly. The introduction of the electric tram is often said to be responsible for the growth of the inner London suburbs in the years before the First World War, and likewise the electrification of the railway routes of the old Southern Railway in the years after the First World War caused another phase of expansion in the 1920's, particularly in the outer suburbs.

When the Bishop took over the diocese the real wealth was concentrated in the country parts. The newly emerging town missions were generally very poor and saddled with large debts. In many cases it was difficult for these new missions to keep up interest payments on their debts. Wherever possible the policy had been (and continued to be) to build Catholic Schools as soon as possible in new missions. This increased the burden of debt. The position was eased slightly by the generous benefactions of certain very wealthy individuals. Mention must be made of a certain Miss Ellis whose benefactions included the provision of money and or sites for Churches in 38 different locations. The Churches known still as Ellis Churches were usually of a very simple plain design but many of them are still doing the duty for which they were first erected. Unfortunately the terms of her benefactions did not extend to the building of accompanying schools.

The Bishop set himself the task of visiting and confirming in every mission of the diocese once every three years. This programme he carried out to the very end of his life through both world wars and except for the last few years of his life, using public transport. He consistently refused to accept gifts of cars on the grounds that most of his people did not have cars, so why should he.

Again right from the start of his episcopate he made a point of meeting as many people as possible. With his phenomenal powers of memory he was able to recall their names even if it were many years later when he met them again. He was particularly fond of talking with children and visiting schools.

As to the number of missions and priests the new Bishop was responsible for, the figures are that at the time of his accession there were 210 secular priests in the Diocese together with 159 regular priests (of religious orders). There were 170 public Chapels and Churches and a further 110 Chapels of religious communities. The Diocese had its own Seminary at Wonersh near Guildford, opened in 1891 with Father Bourne (the new Archbishop of Westminster) as first Rector. When Bishop of Southwark, Bishop Bourne had also undertaken a vast extension of the work of care of orphans under the auspices of the Southwark Rescue Society.

This expansion in particular had created a serious debt problem in the diocese which as we shall see later was itself to create serious differences between the Archbishop and Bishop Amigo.

Bishop Amigo soon won the affection of all his clergy and the first two years of his episcopate passed off relatively quietly. The difficulties started in 1907 with a crisis at the Seminary, followed quickly by the modernist crisis and the financial troubles. We can turn our attention first to the modernist difficulties centred mainly but not entirely on the well known Fr. George Tyrell SJ.

Chapter 4
Bishop Amigo and the Modernist Crisis

Bishop Amigo had only been Bishop for a few months when he was confronted with a series of problems that would have broken the back of many lesser mortals. These were the Modernist Crisis, difficulties at the Seminary, an acute financial crisis and most serious difficulties with Archbishop Bourne. In this chapter I shall consider the problems which arose in connection with the modernist crisis which affected the whole Church in the first years of the 20th century.

Modernism as a heresy is very difficult to define. Perhaps it is easier to understand by considering what the modernists were trying to do, that is to blend together the findings of modern science with Catholic theology and Biblical scholarship. Such an effort can be most praiseworthy, but many of these who were condemned fell into the trap of putting scientific method ahead of the beliefs of our faith. They usually ended up as regarding God as immanent in creation rather than transcendental, consequently tending very much to a form of pantheism. They also tended to deny that there was very much that could be called real history in the New Testament, hence leading to a denial of the real basis of our faith in Holy Scripture. In England the modernists were led by Fr. George Tyrell SJ, who was asked to resign from the Jesuit order as a result of his teachings. As he ended his days as a subject of Bishop Amigo it will be necessary to consider his case in some detail.

To return however to the early days of the Episcopate, the first problems arose at the Seminary. The Rector of the Seminary was Fr. Joseph Butt, a nephew of Bishop Butt former Bishop of Southwark.

The Seminary covered both the Junior and Senior sides, so that a young boy could enter Wonersh at the age of 14 and emerge at the age of

24 as a Priest, having spent his entire training in the one establishment. The Juniors were kept apart to some extent but clearly it was impossible to keep the two parts entirely separate. The Juniors had their own superior known as the Regent of the Junior House. Dr. Thomas Hooley was appointed to this position in 1899 shortly after his ordination. However Dr. Hooley and Fr. Butt did not see eye to eye on how Wonersh should be run, and the differences were known to the students. To start with however the differences between the two superiors were overshadowed by the problems caused by modernism. Quite early on Bishop Amigo was forced to dismiss Dr. Dessoulavy and Fr. Fowell from the staff because their teachings were affected by modernist ideas. Writing much later on to Fr. Doubleday then Rector of the Seminary, Fr. Ernest Corbishley (later to become the first Rector of the separate Junior Seminary at Mark Cross), described his own days at the Seminary during this difficult period. He describes how the students formed little groups known as the Loisyites and the Tyrellites (after the Abbe Loisy and Fr. Tyrell, the two leading modernists). He wrote as follows (January 6 1912).

> " . . . I heard such remarks as 'that is just the loop hole in the Church'; that all truth is relative, that if you argue the authenticity of the Scriptures from tradition you get an officious (vicious) circle; that God is infinite, man finite, therefore we cannot know anything certain apart from revelation.' Now some of these arguments were just from one student . . . . I know students argued a good deal about these matters as I had overheard now and again scraps of arguments. I think it was the age of arguments at Wonersh. I once heard a student on my group say he did not know much about Tyrell etc etc but that he had heard some say that the existence of hell, purgatory etc could not be directly proved from Holy Scripture as it was not mentioned in the Scriptures . . . . "

Such was the power of rumour and gossip in these days that suspicion of modernism was cast upon the Rector of the Seminary, Fr. Butt and the eminent theologian Mgr. Banfi who served Bishop Amigo so loyally through all the years.

One story current at the time which was still going the rounds a few years ago, was that Bishop Amigo had accused Archbishop Bourne of fostering modernism at the Seminary. Also that this report was responsible for the long delay before Archbishop Bourne received the honour of the cardinalate which always goes with the Archbishopric of

Westminster. This story deserves to be told in full, first to scotch the libel on both the Archbishop and Bishop Amigo and secondly to illustrate how rumour and gossip can almost ruin careers even when ill-founded.

The story begins in a long letter of Bishop Cahill of Portsmouth to Bishop Amigo (24 May 1909). He writes as follows.

"When I went to London for the Bishops meeting on the 14th I was told the following story; one of the priests of Westminster Cathedral had come in a great state of agitation and indignation to the Archbishop's House, and he stated that while the priests of the Clergy House were talking with Dom Bede Camm O.S.B. the conversation turned upon the sermon preached by Fr. McNabb (Fr. Vincent McNabb O.P.) which it was said the Archbishop had praised (though this appears now not to have been the case). Dom Bede Camm he reported, had said that there was nothing wonderful in this, for the Archbishop was known to be favourable to advanced opinions and then he went on to say . . . that Fr. Denis Shiel, Provost of Birmingham Oratory, had lately returned from Rome where he had been in intimate relation with Cardinal Merry del Val and that he had learned from him that whereas in March last there was established a great cordiality between the Cardinal and the Archbishop of Westminster, now the whole understanding was at an end, for a letter had been written by the Bishop of Southwark to somebody and conveyed to the Cardinal asking advice as to the closing of Wonersh because the tone young priests who had come from that Seminary was quite Modernist and the priests themselves were unmanageable. Finally he said Archbishop Bourne would never be made Cardinal while Pius X lived. I am given to understand that the priest who brought this news used the strongest language about the Bishop of Southwark . . . .

I have come to the conclusion that as a priest of the Archbishop who in the circumstances could hardly defend himself effectively if he were supposed to be fighting for the Cardinalate I ought to ask Mgr. Butt to obtain from Cardinal Merry del Val himself correct information . . . as the one who ought really to defend himself was not the Archbishop who had left the Seminary some eleven years ago but Mgr. Butt himself, who until recently was responsible for the Seminary . . . . Only last summer I received in Rome a newspaper cutting purporting to come as a telegram from Rome and saying this very thing that he was to lose the Cardinal's hat because he did not deal firmly with Modernism . . . what is at the bottom of these reports? Who is the real author? Now a definite statement is made giving the groundwork of the reports and coupling your name with it. Whatever others may think, I cannot believe that you intentionally started this present accusation. But as the credit of the Archbishop is at stake, you ought to refute absolutely the statements which have been made. . . . For the moment I am able to keep my judgement in suspense . . . ."

Bishop Amigo was rightly furious for the effect of this rumour was not only to discredit Archbishop Bourne, but also Mgr. Butt and himself. It was entirely mischievous. He replied on 28th May.

"I own that I am very indignant. I thought you knew me better than to accept on the authority of Westminster gossip such a gross charge against me . . . . I have not written to Cardinal Merry del Val directly or indirectly about the Seminary. Reports have been about for a long time and I knew more than 18 months ago that they had reached Rome. They were not sent by me nor approved by me and in order to defend the Archbishop against them Abbott Bergh (retired Abbott of Ramsgate Abbey) drew up for me the Report ordered by 'Pascendi' (the 1907 encyclical of St. Pius X on modernism) in which he distinctly refuted the accusation of Modernism in the Seminary. Dom Bede Camm seems to have been most imprudent. I know that Fr. Sheil has not been in Rome for months and the Cardinal is not likely to have written to him on such subjects. I am sorry that anyone should pain the Archbishop by such reports but I think that I have even more reason to be angry because my name should be associated with such a charge . . . I shall write to the Cardinal not only denying the statement attributed to me but also praising Mgr. Butt for his actions at the Seminary in regard to Modernism."

Mgr. Butt was at the time the Rector of the Beda College in Rome and he saw Cardinal Merry del Val on June 2nd. He then wrote to Bishop Amigo on the 3rd.

"I wanted to ascertain his Eminence's attitude and if necessary rectify any misunderstanding both as regards the Seminary and your own feeling towards it. I was careful to make it quite clear to him that I was defending myself and others not against you but against the chatterers. As I was (for once) in possession of names I could really do something effective in shutting up the gossips and putting the Cardinal on his guard against them . . . ."

Father Bede Camm wrote to Bishop Amigo in November (9th).

"I enclose a copy of a letter which I have written to his Grace. Father Denis Sheil has also written to him denying that he ever heard or said anything of the sort. The Cardinal did tell him that Mgr. Butt had been to him to say that he was NOT a modernist as Father Denis had reported him to be and the Cardinal appears to have been rather amused at the whole affair and to have treated it very lightly . . . . You may believe me when I assure you that whenever I have spoken of you it has been with the utmost respect and affection and the only thing that troubles me about this silly story is that it has caused pain to one who has always treated me with such unmerited kindness and who must have more than enough worries of his own."

Clearly the effects of gossip here caused great pain to three innocent parties, and it may be true that the effects of the story did indeed cause a delay in Archbishop Bourne receiving the Red Hat.

Bishop Amigo is however best remembered in connection with modernism over the funeral of Fr. George Tyrell SJ. Father Tyrell had received the notice dismissing him from the Jesuits on 19th February 1906. He then had no ecclesiastical superior and was forbidden to say Mass. He tried in vain to find a Bishop who would accept him and on 7th January 1907 he applied to Bishop Amigo for a *celebret*. (Letter authorising a priest to say Mass). Bishop Amigo entrusted the reply to Mgr. Banfi, a professor at Wonersh who notified Tyrell that the papers would have to be sent to Rome first. In the spring of 1907 Tyrell came to live permanently at Storrington near Arundel inside the diocese of Southwark as then constituted. He stayed first at the Norbertine Priory and later with his close friend Miss Maud Petre. While he was making efforts to obtain the celebret the encyclical "Pascendi" of Pope St. Pius X was published on the 8th September and Tyrell replied with a lengthy attack published in the '*Times*' for 30th September and 1st October 1907.

The tone of these articles is in general sneering and sarcastic at the obscurantist Pope who condemns everything that does not fall in line with ancient scholasticism. Speaking of the authority of the document itself Tyrell wrote.

"The new theory of quasi infallible utterances claiming all the force and none of the responsibilities of ecumenical decisions demanding absolute inward assent to avowedly reversible propositions is of no

account with the 'modernist' on whom therefore the 'Roma locuta
Est' of the journalists falls flat. As for censure and excummunication
they belong to the logic of the position and he will expect them as a
matter of course . . . . They were the portion of his spiritual ancestors
who in past ages so often saved the Church sick unto death with the
pedantries of scholastric rationalism and the 'rabies theologorum.'
. . . His faith is not something that can be annihilated in a moment
by the word of an angry Bishop. Much as he prizes the sacramental
bread of life, he prizes still more the unleavened bread of sincerity
and truth . . . . What he will most deeply regret is the loss of one of the
Church's greatest opportunities of proving herself the saviour of
nations . . . . Protestanism in its best thinkers and representatives had
grown dissatisfied with its rude antithesis to Catholicism and was
beginning to wonder if Rome too had not grown dissatisfied with her
rigid medievalism. The 'modernist' movement had quickened a
thousand dim dreams of reunion into enthusiastic hopes . . . when Lo!
Pius X comes forward with a stone in one hand and a scorpion in the
other."

In the same article Fr. Tyrell made a very prophetic remark.

"Should the repressive measures of the Encyclical be successfully
carried out which is rather difficult to imagine, it is to be feared that
modernism to whose astounding energy, versatility and diffusion the
Encyclical bears reluctant testimony, will be simply driven underground to the catacombs there to grow and strengthen and organise
itself against the not distant day when it shall be able to break forth
again with gathered impetus."

Tyrell might well have preferred living in the Catholic Church in the
years following Vatican II.
However this was 1907 and the mood was very different. On October
12th Bishop Amigo wrote to Rome to report the article.

"Many Catholics are scandalised and will be more so when they learn
that he receives holy communion each morning in my diocese."

The Bishop, writing in French, goes on to say that he cannot act
without consulting the Holy See and is ready to carry out any instructions he may receive.
Cardinal Merry del Val replied on 17th October.

"His Holiness having given his attention to what your Lordship explained has given me the task of signifying to you that it is His will that you intimate to the aforesaid M. Tyrell, the privation of the partaking of the Sacraments and make known to him at the same time that the case is reserved to the Holy See."

Notifying Tyrell of this decision by Rome, Bishop Amigo added.

"I earnestly hope that you will humbly accept this decision of the Sovereign Pontiff and that you will promptly by God's grace make your submission to the Vicar of Christ. All your friends will join with me in prayer that this our wish may soon be realised."

Father Tyrell died at Storrington on 15th July 1909. The events surrounding his death have been described by many writers in particular by Maud Petre herself in her "Life of Fr. Tyrell." However nearly all the accounts depict Bishop Amigo as some kind of cruel monster unwilling to let a dead man rest in peace.

The Southwark Archives help to resolve this problem by showing that the Bishop acted with the utmost fairness throughout and that the refusal of a Catholic burial was inevitable in the circumstances.

During the final week of Tyrell's life as he lay dying in a semi coma, he was visited by many friends. The first priest visitor was Fr. Dessoulavy (who had been dismissed from his post at Wonersh for his modernism). Fr. Dessoulavy wrote an account of his visit to Storrington on July 16th the day after Tyrell's death. Dessoulavy had come to visit Tyrell on July 10th.

"... I took the precaution of asking the advice of a priest of experience with the result that we agreed a manner of proceeding in the two alternative hypotheses of the patient being conscious or unconscious. In the former case I was to suggest some sort of general act of regret and submission to the Church to be assented to by the patient, in the latter case I was to presume to administer the last rites. In the event after I had been a short time with Fr. Tyrell, he was aroused and recognised and greeted me and seemed to be aware of the reason of my attendance, though he immediately began to relapse into the previous state of coma. As he was evidently dying. I thereupon thought right to act as pre-arranged. As however he did not seem to me to be actually at the very point of death, and as according to medical opinion ... there was a chance of the patient rallying to some extent and recovering his senses before death, I also decided to delay the administration of Extreme Unction believing that Fr. Tyrell would prefer to receive the sacrament when conscious."

Two days later Maud Petre was forced to call the Prior of Storrington (who had previously been warned off from coming near the house) as Fr. Tyrell was evidently dying. The Prior administered the last rites. He was told that Fr. Dessoulavy had previously absolved him. However by now Fr. Tyrell was totally unconscious. The Prior wrote to Bishop Amigo to describe his actions.

"He could neither speak nor show any sign, but he heard and understood so they said. (This seems unlikely). After having directed his mind like a friend to serenity and trust in God, and to complete abandonment of his entire being to Divine Pity, Miss Petre was there holding the dying man's head, I said the Acts of Faith, Hope, Charity and Contrition, especially the act of Faith; I urged him to a total acquiescence of his mind and his will to the teachings of the Church . . . . I urged him to contrition for all his faults, of all his errors, past and present. In short I did my best to bring a ray of light, of faith, of hope, of love, of repentance to his soul. Finally I gave him the Sacrament of Extreme Unction . . . I said to him 'I will come to see you again at 1 o'clock, would you like that?' But there was no sign."

The Prior was not able to return as Fr. Tyrell's friends, including Fr. Dessoulavy, Baron von Hugel and Fr. Bremond had now come. Fr. Bremond gave the dying man conditional absolution.

The day after Tyrell died, Maud Petre published an obituary notice for the *'Times'* newspaper. In this she said that Fr. Tyrell "would not wish to receive the sacraments at the cost of a retraction of what he had said or written in all sincerity and still considered to be the truth." When Bishop Amigo saw this article, he sent a telegram to the Prior of Storrington (who showed it to Miss Petre). It read "No Catholic Funeral unless evidence of definite retraction." Miss Petre wired back at once.

"Think my duty respectfully warn your Lordship scandal of your refusal will be enormous to numbers in and outside the Church where you ask the impossible in case of speechless and weak man. Canonical right to burial since received sacraments. Should spare nothing to explain all in press if refusal maintained."

The Bishop wrote at once at 5.30 pm the same day.

"I am very sorry to hear of the death of Fr. Tyrell especially under such circumstances as your letter to 'The Times' reveals. Unless Fr. Bremond or Fr. Dessoulavy can assure me in writing that Fr. Tyrell made a definite retraction, I cannot allow his being buried with Catholic rites. I do hope that in the midst of this sorrow, all his friends will have the knowledge and the consolation of knowing that he repented of his disobedience to the Holy See."

The following day the Bishop added another telegram.

"If Baron von Hugel's statement in your letter to papers is correct Catholic Burial impossible unless Tyrell made some verbal or written retraction which can be published."

Immediately Miss Petre replied with the following telegram.

"Your telegram received condition of sick man rendered your condition utterly impossible am now announcing funeral arrangements and leaving Your Lordship responsible for open scandal that will ensue."

In the following few days before the funeral, Bishop Amigo received many more pleas to allow Tyrell a Catholic funeral to which he gave the same reply that he could not do so unless there were evidence of retraction. Meanwhile the Prior of Storrington in an interview with Miss Petre (relayed by letter to the Bishop) asked about the part of the letter to the Times which stated that Tyrell would never have retracted. He told Miss Petre that he thought Tyrell had already confessed and retracted before he gave him the last rites. Miss Petre stared at him and replied 'Tyrell did not have any retraction to make.'

Tyrell was buried in the Anglican cemetery at Storrington and a burial service was conducted at the graveside by Fr. Bremond who preached a short sermon. When he heard about this service the Bishop told the Prior not to allow Fr. Bremond to say Mass in the diocese. The Bishop then wrote to Cardinal Merry del Val in Rome, who replied.

"I have communicated all to the Holy Father and we do not see how you could have acted differently. It is all very sad. The scandal, the real scandal, doing terrible harm to souls would have been far greater had you given way, nor could you have found an explanation consistent with principle. I feel that you must have gone through a very trying moment when so much pressure was brought to bear on you in order to force your hand...."

Given all the circumstances one can but agree with this verdict. Tyrell had given much scandal by his writings in general but the particular point on which he was asked to retract was in fact his attack on the Holy Father in the '*Times*' which cost him the excommunication. It is clear from what he himself wrote, that he considered the excommunication worthless and would never have retracted his statements.

However the saga did not end with Fr. Tyrell's death. There was still the question of Miss Petre herself. Even before Tyrell's death there had been a question of asking her to refrain from going up to Communion. On 16th November 1908 Cardinal Merry del Val had written to the Bishop that if Miss Petre continued to protect Fr. Tyrell she cannot be allowed to receive the Sacraments. However the Bishop thought it better to take no action.

The question was raised again by the Prior of Storrington on 23rd November 1909. He told the Bishop that none of the Fathers there wish to give Communion to Miss Petre. They judge that they cannot do so any longer in conscience. The Bishop replied on 27th November that he would like to place the Prior's difficulties before the Vigilance Committee (set up in many dioceses to combat modernism). The Bishop said he cannot order any of the Fathers to go against his conscience. The Prior then replied that they would hold to their decision unless the Vigilance Committee ordered to the contrary.

Now in retrospect one can see the Prior was in the wrong here. When the Bishop said he could not order any of the Fathers to go against their conscience he was tactfully saying to them to take no action until the Committee had reported back. But what happened next forced the Bishop's hand. Miss Petre herself describes what happened on the morning of the 2nd December. She entered Church as usual for Mass when the Prior rushed in and said that he was no longer prepared to give her Holy Communion.

When Bishop Amigo heard of this development he consulted Abbot Bergh and drafted a letter to Miss Petre suggesting that if she would send a declaration in writing that she submits to the Holy See in the matter of the Encyclical Pascendi, and Lamentabili, then this would help solve the difficulty. On the 8th December 1909 Miss Petre replied to the Bishop refusing his terms and making further criticism of 'Lamentabili' and 'Pascendi'. In August 1910 the Prior complained to Bishop Amigo that Miss Petre simply went to Communion in other Churches instead of at the Priory. In response to this the Bishop wrote to Cardinal Rampolla in Rome informing him about the conduct of Miss Petre. He replied in Latin as follows.

"His perpensis mandat Suprema Hoc Congregatio ut tramquam ex te parochus admoneas ne ipsam mulierem ad Sacram Communionem admittant tamquam publicam peccatricem."

(By these instructions this congregation orders that the Parish Priest must warn the said lady, as if the order was from you, that she is not to be admitted to Holy Communion being considered a public Sinner).

This falls short of direct excommunication and in practice Miss Petre used to communicate in other Churches but generally outside the diocese to the end of her life. When the Bishop wrote to inform her of the Roman decision he stated the prohibition would be removed if she were to answer him that she were not a modernist and also to make a profession of faith before him. On 14th October Miss Petre wrote a long letter to the effect that she would submit if the Bishop would assure her on his episcopal authority that every condemnation or proposition from the two documents without a single exception is DE FIDE now and will always be in the same sense DE FIDE.

The Bishop consulted four different theologians but in the end sent no reply as Miss Petre published yet another letter in the 'Times' and circulated the parishioners of Storrington with an account of the actions taken against her.

The ban against Miss Petre in Southwark remained to the end of her life in 1944. However in 1924 she did write quite a kind letter to him when he was very ill. In 1934 her brother-in-law Captain Clutton had pleaded in her favour and in response she wrote again to the Bishop pleading her good character but she would not make any statement on her modernism. Bishop Amigo replied on 5th October 1934.

"It would be a great pleasure if your religious position could be freed from all ambiguity, so that you could receive the Sacraments again, which I know you desire to do, as in the old days before the trouble occurred. In your letter you write 'I know that you would not want me to say anything I do not mean, to repudiate past actions which I still feel to have been *in the main* right, whatever fauts there were in manner or conduct.'

In the same way I am sure that you do not expect me to revoke the prohibition which I put upon you as to receiving Holy Communion in my Diocese on account of your Modernistic opinions, without being certain that you no longer hold such views about Religion and are prepared to declare so plainly. It will give great joy to your many friends if you assure me of this. God will hear our prayers."

There is no record in the Southwark Archives of any later correspondence direct with Miss Petre. Not everyone agreed with the actions of Bishop Amigo on this issue. The Bishop of Portsmouth and the Bishop of Newport both considered the judgement too harsh. Canon Scannell, an eminent theologian, also objected that the treatment was too harsh. "She is a woman and therefore not a fit subject for persecution at the hands of men."

On this point I think the judgement of history may go against the Bishop. There is a certain stubbornness about his attitude which he showed to good effect on other issues but which was surely out of place here. Baron von Hugel was in a similar position in the Diocese of Westminster and no action was taken against him.

The problems of Modernism were by no means confined to Fr. Tyrell and Maud Petre. Southwark had an active Vigilance Committee ordered to be set up in every diocese by Pope St. Pius X in 1907. The Southwark Committee met 23 times between 1907 and the final meeting in 1914. Besides discussing Fr. Tyrell and Miss Petre, they had to deal with other errant individuals. The most public case was that of Fr. William Hammersley. He was a young priest who was acting as a Diocesan Inspector of Schools. He had come under the influence of Dr. Dessoulavy at Wonersh and openly advowed his modernism but said he would never preach the theories in public. He was denounced to the Committee by a priest who overheard his remarks. The case was brought to the attention of the Committee in June 1908. It was agreed that he should be called to appear before a subcommittee. However he failed to appear and when summoned by the Bishop also failed to come. Naturally he was suspended "A Divinis", but instead of fading away gently from the scene he chose to make the whole business public. He produced printed sheets widely circulated possibly with the help of Baron von Hugel, in which he gives his side of the story, and he published the correspondence between himself and the Bishop. The Committee arranged for its Secretary, Fr. James Warwick of Balham, to make a public reply and this in turn was widely circulated. This round of letters ended when Hammersley published a second "letter to Friends" on 19th November 1908. Fr. Hammersley then applied for leave to practice as an Anglican Vicar under the auspices of the Archbishop of Canterbury and married shortly afterwards.

He developed cerebral palsy a few years later and retired to Burton Bradstock in Dorset where he died early in 1944 still unreconciled.

A frequent topic of conversation at the committee was the attitude of

Dr. Dessoulavy. At the time there existed in Southwark and the surrounding counties, a clergy magazine called "Pastoralia" edited by Fr. Edward Murnane. This was a direct forerunner of the "Clergy Review". Considering the mood of the times the articles were surprisingly daring. Dr. Dessoulavy contributed articles under the pen name 'Cyon'. In the issue of February 1908 he wrote an article entitled "The Descent into Hell". Fr. Warwick adjudged that this article gave a purely human origin to the article of faith in the Creed in that it stated "the rise of the belief expressed in the 5th article of the Creed comes from the Gospel of Nicodemus in the 4th century." The committee censured Canon Murnane and Fr. Warwick for allowing the article to appear. Fr. Warwick informed Dr. Dessoulavy, who sent a most sarcastic letter in reply.

> "Will you at your convenience offer my condolence to the responsible editor who was reprobate, rash or sleepy enough to allow such an abomination to sully the spotless reputation of so orthodox a journal?"

Father Dessoulavy did in fact take the anti-modernist oath and after the death of Tyrell nothing further is found on his modernist views.

Two priests of the Diocese besides Fr. Hammersley seem not to have been willing to sign the anti-modernist oath. Fr. Wallace then a curate at Blackheath, refused several times to sign and eventually retired to Brighton, but he did not leave the Church or the Priesthood. Fr. George Hitchcock, a convert Anglican Clergyman, ordained in 1910, had problems over modernism from the start. After he preached in local Anglican Churches in the Croydon area, he was suspended from priestly faculties but he then left the Church. That was in 1914.

The only other priest to come before the committee was Fr. Duggan, of Slindon. He had the dubious privilege of having two books written by him, placed on the Index of Forbidden Books. In 1908 he wrote to the *Tablet* (March 7th).

> "History has no pronouncement to make with regard to the existence of God, for the simple reason that the matter does not belong to its domain, any more than to geography or geometry. Why should it undertake to make any pronouncement as to the Divinity of Christ?"

The Vigilance Committee merely cautioned him that time, but in 1914 he was very nearly deprived of his Parish following reports of his conversation and sermons. The points raised against him make interesting reading as they indicate the nature of what might be called "Practical Modernism" ... not the theories of Tyrell or Loisy, but Modernism in the sermons to the people. The statements alleged were.

'That Christ did not institute Baptism nor Penance, nor did He make Matrimony a Sacrament.'

'That neither the Sacraments nor any form of dogma is essential to salvation.'

'That faith in the Incarnation or in the Sacraments is not essential to the Christian Religion.'

'That Christ's Resurrection is not historical.'

'That the Church is not a divine institution.'

'That Christ's words are not to be believed except after close Scrutiny.'

It was perhaps as a result of these experiences Bishop Amigo was always extremely firm on the question of imparting orthodox teaching. He seems in general to have been rather suspicious of 'higher learning', though it must be admitted that he was on very good terms indeed with priests like Fr. Banfi and Dr. Scannell, both of whom helped him with writing his pastoral letters.

Chapter 5

The Differences Between Cardinal Bourne and the Bishop

The differences between Cardinal Bourne and Bishop Amigo put a cloud over the first part of Bishop Amigo's episcopate. In the long run the reader will probably agree that there was here a clash between two very strong personalities. It is necessary to understand how the troubles came about and the origin of the difficulties lay in the Seminary at Wonersh.

Bishop Butt had commissioned Fr. Bourne as he then was to be the first Rector of the new Seminary at Wonersh and even after he became Bishop he spent much of his time there. Nor was the Bishop very popular among the senior priests of the diocese. He had a certain autocratic manner and had dissolved his Commission of Financial Advisers and was forever at loggerheads with his Chapter over their rights on diocesan finances and the administration of the Seminary.

As Seminary Rector and Bishop it was Frances Bourne's policy to appoint young newly ordained priests to the staff at Wonersh where this was possible.

The Juniors and Seniors occupied the same building but had quite different rules. The head of the Seminary was Bishop Butt's nephew who later became an auxiliary in Westminster. The Juniors were headed by Fr. Thomas Hooley. The two priests did not hit it off together and both kept on seeking the advice of Bourne with whom both were friendly.

In 1907 things came to a head and seeing the staff were so against him, Butt resigned. The circumstances that led to this resignation and the subsequent appointment of Father (later Bishop) Doubleday are very important for this history.

A key meeting between Bourne and Amigo took place at Westminster on March 25 1907. According to Bourne, Amigo said that if Bourne obtained the resignation of Butt, then Amigo gave his word he would appoint Hooley to replace him.

Bishop Amigo's account differs. "I told you that though I felt Dr. Hooley was not ready for the Rectorship, I should not appoint any outsider provided Mgr. Butt kept on." The following day Mgr. Butt called on the Archbishop and was persuaded to offer his resignation to Bishop Amigo. (A professors' meeting had effectively indicated no confidence in him). The two Bishops met again and Bourne pressed Amigo to appoint Dr. Hooley. Amigo reports "I felt ready to do so not through being convinced but because it came upon me suddenly and I had not time to think." About two days later Amigo wrote to Bourne telling him he could not in conscience appoint Dr. Hooley because he was too young (31) and the staff were against him. He would appoint Doubleday.

At this point (9th May) Archbishop Bourne in a letter now lost or destroyed intimated that they could no longer be considered as friends because Amigo had gone back on his word. A week later Bourne wrote "I beseech you be on your guard against any action which would injure Bishop Butt's work for the maintenance and continuity of which alone, I procured your appointment as my successor in Southwark, at a cost to myself which evidently you are unable to fully appreciate."

From that time on (until 1924) the letters to Bishop Amigo are stiff and formal, while on the other hand Bishop Amigo usually continued to sign off "Yours affectionately."

We have however shot ahead in time for a serious financial crisis had already risen.

For many years the finances of the Diocese were in the hands of Fr. Edward St. John, nephew of the famous Oratorian friend of Newman's. He was a late vocation and had worked for five years as a bank clerk.

On the strength of his financial acumen he was appointed Finance Secretary by Bishop Butt and continued in office until his resignation in 1909. It was a time of great progress in the Diocese, missions were being developed in the London Suburbs, and large institutions built to deal with children (orphans) under the Poor Laws (Orpington). All this was entrusted to Canon St. John. The Diocese had never been in a strong financial situation since the division of Portsmouth from Southwark. (The division of funds was entirely in favour of Portsmouth). To build up missions, benefactors were sought out and where they were lacking money was borrowed. First older missions with money invested were told that their investments would be changed into property development and the interest on lettings would be higher than that obtained on the market. This never happened because Canon St. John had used a certain William Romaine as Director of Buildings and he was simply a cockney con man who made a quick profit on every stage of the operations. He left suddenly in 1908 when financial matters were at their worst.

To make up any remaining sums, Canon St. John mortgaged off mission houses when built and even the very churches themselves (effectively the land they stood on) to raise fresh capital and with a constant cash flow everything looked rosy.

However even before the crash of 1905, back in 1901 Bishop Bourne had had to ask the Duke of Norfolk for £4,000 to bolster the flagging fortunes of the Diocese. (Multiply all sums by 45 to obtain equivalent values today). Just at an opportune time a certain wealthy individual, Mr. Charles Dawes, died and left the Diocese the sum of £86,000 for new missions. This money was in the form of a Trust and the Trustees were Bourne, Amigo, St. John and Canon Murnane. When Bourne moved to Westminster his name was not removed from any Trust or Account whatever because of the cost that such a move would involve the Diocese in.

However the Trustees hardly ever met, and the accounts were never properly audited. The Trustees did not verify the securities held by them for the Trust. They left this to Canon St. John and the Diocesan Financial Adviser since 1870, Mr. W. H. Bishop.

Canon St. John had implicit trust in both Romaine and Mr. Bishop. However, unbeknown to Canon St. John, Mr. Bishop had abused this confidence and started speculating with Diocesan money on the Stock Exchange. Canon St. John on 5th September 1905 issued contract notes for the purchase of Stock with Dawes fund money, but in the end most of the money involved (about £13,000 on this transaction) was lost because the Stocks were not delivered. Constantly Mr. Bishop made excuses. In October Mr. Bishop's clerk, Mr. Chandler, told Canon Murnane that Mr. Bishop was squandering the assets of the Diocese. Chandler had just been dismissed by Mr. Bishop for drunkenness. Canon Murnane told Canon St. John but Mr. Bishop told him that Chandler was a liar. This was on 26th October and the September Stock had not been delivered.

Canon St. John failed to inform the Diocesan Solicitors, Fooks of

Arnold Fooks and Chadwick, and on December 23rd the crash came; Mr. Bishop declared himself bankrupt. The whole affair was made public in the magazine *Truth* and allegations made particularly against Archbishop Bourne for mismanagement.

This is all recorded in Oldmeadow's Life of Cardinal Bourne. What is not recorded however is the sequel. The examination of Mr. Bishop's affairs took two years and at the start of 1908 the Charity Commissioners informed the Attorney General of the Breach of Trust by the Trustees and the Attorney General's office decided to prosecute. However a concerted effort persuaded the Attorney General that this would cause untold scandal and damage to the Church for years to come. So the Attorney General referred the matter for the Charity Commissioners to re-arrange. The Commissioners came up with a scheme in 1911 whereby the Trustees lost much of their freedom of action with regard to the investments.

Returning now to 1906 onwards, the position of the Diocesan Finances grew worse. The accumulated debts of the Diocese to the missions, private lenders and Law Union Rock (Insurance firm who lent them money against properties) now came to over £300,000 (round about £14 million at today's values). Not only was it proving difficult to find the interest to pay the lenders but the full effects of Romaine's double dealing in property were being felt. The properties he obtained were not worth the money he paid, and very little money could be earned from letting them. Some had to be sold for less than they cost. Worse still thanks to the articles in 'Truth', people were not inclined to lend money to the Diocese at all and some with loans outstanding began asking awkward questions. there was a general loss of confidence.

Following the referral of the Dawes losses to the Attorney General in 1908, the Trustees of the Southwark Rescue Society met in the Autumn and discussed the idea of inviting some of the leading laity of the Diocese to a meeting to inform them of the state of affairs. On 23rd November a group of forty met consisting of senior priests with the Bishop and leading laity led by the Duke of Norfolk. Originally the meeting had been held to consider merely the debts on the orphanages but the Duke argued that the laity should be made aware of the total Diocesan debts. Many members spoke out and said the laity should be taken into the Bishop's confidence.

This meeting resolved to appeal at once for the institutions and the meeting terminated on the understanding that His Lordship would take steps a little later to take the leading laity into his confidence. Accordingly on 15th December 1908 the Bishop invited seven leading lights together, including the Duke of Norfolk, James Hope (First Baron Rankeillour) and Sir John Knill (later Lord Mayor of London) with a view to setting up a Commission. The Chapter suggested that some of its members be invited as members together with the Vicar General, Fr. Brown of Vauxhall.

Their written Mandate (and this is very important) was "To investigate the general financial position of the Diocese, to have access to all accounts and documents and the assistance if necessary of Chartered Accountants. To ascertain the cause of excess of expenditure over income and to make such recommendations as they think fit."

The work of drawing up a Statement of Accounts was entrusted to Canon St. John and submitted to Chartered Accountants. However although the Statement was quickly drawn up it did not give a full and correct account of the financial position of the various properties managed by Mr. Romaine. The Accountants were then forced to reassess the position; the properties managed formerly by Mr. Romaine had to be "devalued". The general tenor of the Report remained unaltered however ... that the Diocese needed to raise an extra £2,600 a year, that no investments be made in property and that a Finanacial Committee be set up again.

In preparing the reports however it was agreed to omit the Balance Sheet which might frighten people from giving further aid to the Diocese (on the advice of Mr. Fooks).

While all this was going on during the early months of 1909, the Bishop was also considering what to do about Canon St. John. It was clear that he was undertaking too much work, and he had himself at times suggested he might like a lighter burden. At the end of February 1909 the Bishop proposed informally that St. John should have care of the Rescue Society but a separate Financial Secretary should be appointed. St. John offered his resignation but at the time the whole matter was dropped while the Norfolk Committee proceeded. However by June it was clear that St. John had made very serious errors in his accounting. Bishop Amigo decided to implement his February scheme. Canon St. John was furious and resigned from both Rescue work and the Finance Office. He continued to serve on the Norfolk Committee and to retain his Canonry in the Chapter but from then on he became an implacable opponent of the Bishop. The Bishop offered him several good appointments in the Diocese but he refused and by 1911 he was living with

Cardinal Bourne. (He later became Prison Chaplain at Walton Jail).

It was this break with Bishop Amigo that led to the really serious difficulties with Archbishop Bourne.

I have already mentioned that the Archbishop's name was on many Trusts and Deeds of the Diocese. The Bishop had decided that it would be better for the Archbishop to come out of Trusts but that this would have to be done gently so as not to make people lose confidence. This on the advice of Mr. Fooks.

On January 7th 1910 Mr. Fooks wrote to St. John to ask him to sign some new Deeds and Warrants. He refused to do so. On the 28th January a letter was sent to the Archbishop requesting his signature (which had always been given up to this point) on certain documents. The Archbishop refused to sign until justice was done to Canon St. John, and he personally was cleared of the charge of mismanagement.

For the next two months letters flowed to and fro between Westminster and Southwark but always to the same effect that the Archbishop would not sign until he was certain his own administration was not under attack, and that he failed to see any urgency in signing.

However on April 9th he did in fact return the Deeds now signed.

Matters were quiet until June when a Committee Meeting of the Rescue Society was held. A new Committee had been set up but on the 24th June the Archbishop wrote stating that the meeting had been irregular. (It must be pointed out that it was no business whatever of his to write about this topic).

The Bishop replied that Canon St. John could not be re-appointed to the Committee and that he, the Bishop, should always be the undisputed master in his own Diocese (letter 26th June 1919 No. 127). Another furious round of letter exchange followed and on 12th July the Archbishop refused to sign another Trust Deed. Round about the 20th July the Archbishop sent another letter, now lost, indicating he would again refuse to sign Deeds unless justice was done over Canon St. John. At this the Bishop convened his Chapter and they decided that there was no option but to take the case to Rome. He wrote to Merry del Val on 28th July and he replied on 1st August telling him to put all facts before Cardinal de Lai at the Consistorial Congregation. Del Val agreed in general with Bishop Amigo but the other side must be heard. At the beginning of September Bishop Amigo sent a priest delegate to represent his case. None other than Fr. Hinsley (later Cardinal).

At first all went well. On October 7th Cardinal de Lai wrote to Archbishop Bourne ordering him to leave Bishop Amigo free in the administration and government of Southwark. One might have hoped that would be the end of the affair but Archbishop Bourne still refused to leave the Trusts. He intimated to Rome that the only way to solve the problem was to arrange that Bishop Amigo be moved to another Diocese. Accordingly on 29th January 1911 Cardinal de Lai offered him the Diocese of Plymouth (the procedure seemed somewhat irregular to put it mildly). Of course this kind offer was declined. Fr. Sheahan now joined Dr. Hinsley in Rome to prepare a detailed report. The Memorandum together with Bourne's own objections and the replies to these objections were marked 'sub secreto' and I am not using them here.

The Memorandum was handed in on April 4th 1911. The final judgement in Bishop Amigo's favour was not given until 16th December 1912 because by then the financial troubles had been overtaken by a long hard-fought battle on the question of the possible Division of the Diocese of Southwark.

To illustrate that Bishop Amigo did not let the troubles upset his basic affection for the Archbishop I should like to quote this letter sent on 23rd March 1911.

"My dear Lord Archbishop. Let me congratulate you on the Golden Jubilee of your birth and I wish you most heartily many happy returns on your birthday and I have not forgotten you in my Mass today. I cannot agree with you about your actions over the Trust Deeds of Southwark and supporting Canon St. John against me, but differences of opinion do not affect my friendship towards you. With every best wish. Yours affectionately. Peter."

Meanwhile in Rome the Consistorial Congregation were considering the Memorandum and they decided to send out one of their members, Fr. Lepicier (later Cardinal Lepicier and Protector of the English College Rome) on an Apostolic Visitation to Southwark and Westminster. It appears they were mightily puzzled at this strange dispute.

During these months the Consistorial was preparing the plan to break the English Dioceses down into provinces. The document setting up the provinces is known by the title "Si Qua Est" and was finally issued on October 28th 1911. The Decree sets up Westminster, Liverpool and Birmingham as Metropolitan Sees. It makes hints about further divisions yet to come. According to Oldmeadow, Cardinal Bourne strongly denied ever being responsible for the idea of fresh divisions. This is perhaps surprising for Cardinal Gasquet wrote to Bishop Amigo in April 1917 telling him that fresh divisions of the

English Dioceses had been discussed since 1901. The plan suggested by the Consistorial in the Spring of 1911 and quoted by Oldmeadow was curious. Brighton would have been the seat of a new Province and the Diocese of Brighton would have included Surrey and Kent. The Province would have included Portsmouth, Plymouth and Clifton, while London would have become one Diocese. Many other changes were recommended. Now Archbishop Bourne was indeed only too anxious to see London as one Diocese under his control. He also wanted to have Surrey so that he could control Wonersh once again. From the Spring of 1911 he promoted the idea of London as one Diocese consistently. He argued that London was one big administrative area under the London County Council and that in discussions with this huge local authority it was better to have only one Diocese covering the area. He argued also that the world's major cities had only one Diocese each.

It is quite likely that the idea of seeking the whole of London as one Diocese originated from Canon St. John. He had had many years of dealing with the London County Council.

In answer to the arguments put forward by the Archbishop in the years to come, Bishop Amigo put forward the following points. London was not the only city to be in two Dioceses. New York had a fellow Diocese in Brooklyn. The debts of his own Diocese were enormous and any division would create enormous problems over responsibility for these debts. The Bishop stated he had all his priests behind him in wishing to preserve Southwark as one entity though he said that if the debts were cleared and the Catholic population increased, then he would have no objection to a further division of his own Diocese in years ahead. Such a division was eventually made in 1966 when the Diocese of Arundel and Brighton was created by cutting off Surrey and Sussex from Southwark. The Bishop always argued also that any division of any kind should only follow after the matter had been aired fully by the hierarchy as a whole and the wishes of individual Bishops had been respected.

To return to the story of the troubles. To confirm that Bourne was already anxious to gather up Southwark into Westminster there exists a letter of Fr. Hinsley to Mgr. Doubleday at Wonersh dated March 1911 which states that quite apart from the financial business, Dr. Bidwell (auxiliary Bishop of Westminster) had been in touch with the Holy See with a view to Westminster absorbing Southwark. There is also a memorandum handed in to Fr. Lepicier by Bourne in August 1911 stating the need to have London as one Diocese with Southwark somehow retaining a 'separate identity' and its own Chapter. On July

11th Bishop Amigo had told Lepicier that he did not favour a division without further consultation.

There is also in the Southwark files a document from the Consistorial Congregation dated 7th August 1911 from Cardinal De Lai, head of the Congregation. The effect of this letter is that Archbishop Bourne was to resign from the Trusts. When the new Diocese of Brighton is created then Bishop Amigo will have charge until the new Bishop is appointed. Brighton will be in Westminster Province and Oxfordshire is to be merged into Portsmouth.

Archbishop Bourne had a private meeting with Bishop Amigo on August 21st 1911. The Bishop wrote an account of their get-together. They disagreed again over what had happened in 1907 to break their friendship. Bourne said that the idea of Amigo going to Plymouth was purely that of Cardinal de Lai and the presenting of the Memorandum had only started off the Consistorial on a plan to re-divide England.

At the end of the year Archbishop Bourne was created Cardinal and the events are described by Oldmeadow in his biography. The actions of Bishop Amigo here must be criticised. The Southwark Chapter withdrew its speech of welcome to the new Cardinal on his arrival in England because in Rome, Bourne had hinted at division of Dioceses. The Chapter's action had the approval of the Bishop. Furthermore the whole affair was widely reported in the Catholic and National Press. Mgr. Brown called a meeting at St. George's Hall, attended by over 2,000 people, to protest at the new Cardinal's takeover plans. To back up the protest he sent out a letter to all the clergy asking for their signature to a petition to Rome not to divide the Diocese. Only six priests refused to sign. The most interesting 'absentee' was Fr. Philip Hallett, who later on became Rector of Wonersh. The Bishop sent a letter to the rebellious six asking if they were really loyal to him. This again must be judged a mistake as the request for support was not official.

At the start of 1912 came the appointment of a Commission in England of certain Bishops to look into the possibility of dividing Dioceses and considering also the financial problems. The members of this Commission were the Bishops of Westminster, Southwark, Liverpool, Northampton, Newport, assisted by four lay counsellors.

The Commission met in February but it appears that their meeting was not Minuted and the Holy See did not accept the verbal report given. I have no record nor has Westminster of this first meeting. However Westminster has a record of part of the second meeting which took place in July. Their Lordships were to discuss the following plan of Cardinal de Lai.

The scheme was A NEW DIOCESE OF LONDON London Middlesex, Hertfordshire, whose Bishop would be termed Apostolic Administrator of Southwark.

A NEW DIOCESE OF BRIGHTON which could be an Apostolic Vicariate.

A NEW DIOCESE OF CAMBRIDGE including Norfolk, Suffolk, Cambridge.

(Northampton would be given Oxfordshire to make up for its losses).

When their Lordships came to give their 'Votums' on 7th October 1912 only Liverpool sided with Cardinal Bourne. All the rest agreed that cutting off Sussex would create immense financial problems over fund divisions . . . as all the wealth lay in Sussex and the rest of the Diocese could not face the interest charges . . . .

On 5th November the Southwark Chapter suggested a separate Provincial Status for Southwark ahead of any divisions. Later that month Cardinal Bourne went to Rome to attend a Consistorial meeting to put his case again. Mgr. Brown represented Bishop Amigo. The Votum's of the Bishops were handed in.

The decision in favour of no division was received on 16th December. Basically the decision was that there would be no division of Southwark unless the matter was mutually agreed and the priests had been consulted. One might have thought the matter was closed. But by no means. First of all there was a humorous incident.

The Catholic Directory for 1913 was sent as ever to each Bishop ahead of the normal distribution to the rest of the public. Archbishop Ilsley of Birmingham opened his copy only to find that the map showing the location of Churches had been replaced by a special map showing London as all one Diocese with the Churches numbered throughout from 1 to 190. This was of course because Bourne was quite certain he would win his case. The Archbishop got in touch with Bishop Amigo who then proceeded at once, it is said to the publishers and ordered them to delete all the maps from copies for distribution to the public. This action was in fact taken. The Archbishop had also heard that his own Diocese was to be divided off in yet another way.

Bourne had changed his mind on the scheme outlined in January 1912 and now wanted to combine Oxford and Cambridge into one Diocese

(Diocese of Oxbridge) and in fact place Father Bede Jarrett OP as Bishop of the new set up. Father Bede was barely 31 at the time.

Matters were fairly quiet in 1913. In 1914 Cardinal Bourne made a long speech at Cardiff about the prospect of further divisions, which may have prompted Bishop Amigo to visit Rome in the summer. The Bishop's Diary records an outline of the conversation with Pope St. Pius X. The important section reads as follows.

> "I mentioned that I went to meet His Eminence on public occasions and that by degrees I hoped that he would be reconciled and that I thought he never realised Southwark's debts. He then mentioned the remark about His Eminence wanting to be Primate and his own desire to have three Archbishops so that he may have restricted powers as he ought to be kept under."

The advent of the new Holy Father Benedict XV and the Great War did nothing to dampen the ardour of Cardinal Bourne for divisions and he again pressed his demands. At the Consistory itself he obtained a loose agreement that Sussex should be a Diocese and Kent a Vicariate while Surrey and London should be united to Westminster. He claimed he had a large sum of money available to solve the debt problem of Southwark. However nothing happened until 1916. In the meantime another cause of friction had sprung up, as Bishop Peter and most of the hierarchy were in favour of having a Bishop in charge of Forces Chaplains and Cardinal Bourne was absolutely against the scheme. Not until near the end of the war was the matter decided against the Cardinal.

At the end of 1916 Bourne made a big attempt to push his schemes through. By determined effort he insisted on becoming a full member of the Consistorial Congregation. Cardinal Gasquet informed Amigo of this on December 31st 1916. It was, he said, in order to get his way over army chaplaincies. His action had mightily displeased Cardinal de Lai and many others in the Congregation. He informed the Bishop that Bourne had again seen the Holy Father to press for divisions of Dioceses but the Holy Father was against this during the war and anyway Bishops would have to be consulted separately. Cardinal Bourne however stayed on in Rome and his persistence was rewarded when on 20th February 1917 Cardinal de Lai wrote to Amigo to inform him that the Congregation had decided that the process of division of Dioceses should be expedited. This however was only to take place after hearing the views of those affected. Cardinal Bourne had agreed to relinquish control of

Essex. Would Bishop Amigo consider likewise relinquishing Kent? The Cardinal had found a rich and pious man who would offer a mensal fund of £5,000 for at least two years. The Holy Father would be willing to nominate Mgr. Brown to the new See.

On the 7th March Bishop Amigo, in response, called an unofficial meeting of the Suffragan Bishops of the Westminster Province. Their view was that all Bishops should be consulted first. He then wrote to the other Archbishops and arranged that a special meeting be called for the following week.

In the continued absence of Cardinal Bourne, the Archbishop of Birmingham (whose Diocese was threatened with dismemberment) called this meeting. It took place at Oscott on 15th March and they agreed to send a letter to Rome expressing their views.

On the 22nd March Bourne wrote back objecting strongly to this meeting which took place without his permission and on the same date the official Decree setting up Brentwood was announced.

On the 10th April the Suffragans replied to the Cardinal that they had every right to meet in his absence privately.

Meanwhile just before the Low Week meeting at which Bourne actually presided after his long sojourn in Rome, an article appeared in the *Tablet* which purported to be a translation of a document received by Cardinal Bourne. This seemed to state that the Holy Father had appealed for consent to the Division of Dioceses. Everything however hinged on the translation of the words in the Latin original UTINAM QUEAT. Amigo contacted Gasquet on the 14th and received the following on the 18th from Gasquet.

"I saw the Holy Father who said the translation was wrong. What he meant was 'would that circumstances would allow the Bishops to think Divisions useful and possible.' He went on to say that the Holy See would always allow the Bishops to consider whether circumstances favoured the divisions or not and would not proceed to dismember Dioceses in opposition to the wishes of the Bishops."

Two days earlier Gasquet had written "The Low Week meeting should be of interest and may give occasion for the Police to be summoned." It should be noted that the 1917 Low Week meeting was the first time that the entire Hierarchy had even been asked to consider divisions of dioceses. In the event Bourne published an apology in the *Tablet* and the Low Week meeting went decisively against the Cardinal.

Matters were still not finished. There were two further "scares" in

1921 and 1925. A letter on 18th February 1921 to Hinsley in Rome suggests that there had been mooted the idea of making Amigo an Archbishop in either Liverpool or Birmingham. He would refuse the position because he would never be accepted by the clergy there as a complete outsider. He remembers his own struggles against certain clergy during the first three years of his reign.

On March 6th 1921 Gasquet informed Amigo that Bourne had been in Rome to press Division of Dioceses. On the way he had lost his baggage. Two rumours were circulating in Rome, one that the I.R.A. had seized his private papers and secondly that Amigo had been arrested on the Swiss border carrying the Cardinal's small bags!

On 25th August the Consistorial sent him a formal request to consider the setting up again of a Brighton Vicariate with a detailed Notulae ... of the division of funds. He was asked however to make "declarations, observations and advices" as to how quickly and easily the work could be done.

He replied in detail on 17th October with eight pages of "observations" giving detailed reasons why such a scheme was not necessary. I must in fairness however point out that he did not reject the idea of future divisions, but pointed out that the time was not ripe then as the new Vicariate had not developed enough (in population growth) to warrant the division. He would welcome a division if such growth took place.

In 1925 Bourne tried again for the last time as far as I can see seriously, with Pius XI this time. About the middle of June rumours circulated that a new Diocese would be created. The Daily Telegraph for the 19th June carried the story taken from the *'Catholic Herald'* ...."A new Diocese has been determined upon by the Holy See. The probable area will be the county of Sussex, and the seat of the bishopric, Brighton. The name of a well known ecclesiastic is mentioned in connection with the proposed new Diocese."

Bishop Amigo again wrote to the Consistorial on the basis of the Catholic Herald report and the final letter in the file from the Consistorial signed by De Lai reads "Be Tranquil, the rumours you have heard are without foundation, and although we cannot know what God alone knows for the future, you know that no decision will be taken without consulting yourself."

Bishop Amigo took every care now to restore good relations with the Cardinal. After two priests had found the burden of being Seminary Rector at Wonersh too much for them, he consulted with Bourne and appointed Mgr. Philip Hallett as Rector, one of the ardent Bournites.

In 1926 the Hierarchy reopened the matter of the Canonisation of Martyrs including Sts. John Fisher and Thomas More. Bishop Amigo was put in charge in this work and it was confirmed in 1930 when their causes were formally re-introduced. Mgr. Hallett was appointed to promote the cause in this country.

There were even then a few little hiccups in the relationship but the Bishop sent a charming letter as the Cardinal lay dying.

It seems likely that it was Amigo who persuaded Pius XI to appoint Hinsley to Westminster knowing very well there would never be any further problem about Southwark with an Archbishop who as a priest had served him so well as his agent in the troubles with Cardinal Bourne.

As soon as Archbishop Hinsley was appointed he went personally to inspect the Consistorial files on the Division of Dioceses and wrote at once to Bishop Amigo that the matter was now at an end and they had far more important matters to attend to.

Chapter 6

Silver Jubilee of Ordination and the First World War

On 25th February 1913 Bishop Amigo celebrated the 25th anniversary of his ordination to the Priesthood. The Bishop let it be known that he would not accept any personal presentation in view of the large Diocesan debts, so the Duke of Norfolk started the "Bishop Amigo Jubilee Fund" with the aim of raising £100,000 towards reducing the debts. The prospectus issued in his name gives a good idea of the progress of the Diocese and the problems faced.

"It is well known that in the work for souls, debts have had to be contracted to provide Churches, schools and presbyteries for many of the Missions in South London where Catholics are numerous but for the most part very poor . . . . In consequence however of the large and increasing number of their parishioners, they have been forced to provide large elementary schools to receive the numerous catholic children of their districts and being unable to provide the cost of these and other buildings from their own resources they have been compelled to raise loans for the purpose. . . . It should be added that these poor missions are for the most part in South London, stretching from Battersea down the river to Plumstead; that their congregations owing to the migration of the better-off are much poorer (though more populous) than they were . . . that nearly all of them have their schools quite full of Catholic children; and that they are a standing witness to the work of the Church amongst the poorest of the poor."

The Archives of the Diocese have preserved records of nearly all the contributions to this fund which continued long after the year 1913 until the required sum was reached.

51

Naturally the Bishop received many letters of congratulation, of which two perhaps stand out. The first was from Fr. Edward Murnane of Bermondsey. The Bishop had been one of Fr. Murnane's pupils as a boy in Gibraltar before he became a priest.

"It is a great joy in writing to you for your Silver Jubilee to feel that I am writing as one of your oldest, if not the very oldest of your friends in England. It is over forty years since we first met on the Rock, and it is a great consolation and delight that as an old Master I am spared to see this great day in your life and that our friendship of over 40 years has never been overshadowed.

And it will add to the joy of your Jubilee for yourself, your Priests and people, that it comes by a loving dispensation of God, to crown a long period of anxiety and trial, patiently borne. . . . All the Priests here are saying Mass for you tomorrow morning and nearly all the children and many of the congregation are going to Holy Communion . . . . May our Masses and Communions and prayers win for you countless graces and blessings, and Begging a Jubilee blessing for us all. Affectionately and respectfully yours . . . . E. Murnane."

The second letter came from Fr. John Rory Fletcher, Parish Priest of Streatham Hill. Fr. Fletcher was a convert who had given up work as a surgeon at Charing Cross Hospital to become a Priest, shortly after his conversion.

" . . . If I may, I should like to congratulate your Lordship on being the first Bishop as far as my knowledge goes, who has thought it worthwhile to take into his confidence, the priests of his Diocese. The air of mystery which for many years has surrounded the financial affairs of the Diocese and the suspicious attitude adopted towards the clergy has had a very bad effect on the relations between Headquarters and the clergy. I do not say the Bishop and the clergy, though naturally he could not escape being involved. It does not seem to have occurred to those in authority that Bishop and Priests should be a corporate body, that all members should have a personal interest in the Diocese and should be knit together by esprit de corps. . . . Nothing was a greater mystery to me when I became a cleric than the absence of this esprit de corps. I could not find it in the Seminary, nor in St. John's Association (Wonersh 'old boys') nor among the priests of the Diocese, with the experience of two English Public Schools, a Medical School and an English Regiment in all of which esprit de corps amounts almost to a religion and persists among its members for life, it is still a subject of wonder to me that any body the members of which are bound not only by natural but also by spiritual ties, should lack it.

There is nothing in our religion which should militate against this close feeling of kinship and loyalty, and I could only put it down to want of union and mutual confidence among the clergy of the Diocese. A Bishop years ago said to me 'The Clergy think that when a priest becomes a Bishop he ceases to be honest' There has been a feeling among the clergy that they were mere pawns on the diocesan chess board to be moved ad nutum episcopi (at the nod of the Bishop). I feel sure ... that each priest will feel that Southwark is *his* Diocese and that *he* has an interest and responsibility in all its concerns.

My Lord, I am an old man—else should I not have dared to say what I have—an ordinary priest, a spectator at the bottom of the hill and it is well that sometimes you who sit at the top should know the view as it appears to the man below. Asking your Lordship's Blessing, Yours Sincerely, John Fletcher."

The Bishop had a great regard for Fr. Fletcher, who later became a Canon in the Diocese, archivist, and a great worker for the cause of the beatification of the English and Welsh Martyrs. In retirement he worked on the history of the Brigittine nuns (now of South Brent, Devon, and the oldest community of nuns in England).

The joys of the Jubilee were short-lived however as war clouds began to gather over Europe. In August 1914 the great conflict started which was to change the face of Britain. For Bishop Amigo it marked the start of his work on the national stage. Up to this point his episcopate had been marked mainly by the unfortunate troubles with the Cardinal, but all this was soon to change. During the war he was to undertake work for the British Government, particularly with regard to Spain.

Before dealing with Spain it might be well to look at some of the other concerns of the Bishop at this momentous time. Shortly after the outbreak of war Pope St. Pius X died and on his way back from the conclava Cardinal Mercier, Archbishop of Malines stopped off in London to elicit support for the Belgian refugees who were beginning to arrive in great numbers as their country was being overwhelmed by the German forces. There was a special link with Southwark here because since 1835 St. George's Cathedral had been regarded as the Church of the Belgian Legation in Britain. Cardinal Mercier sang High Mass on Sunday 13th September in St. George's. Arrangements were then made whereby one of his auxiliaries, Mgr. Dewachter came to stay at Bishop's House to look after the spiritual needs of the exiles. Bishop Amigo took a great personal interest in the exiles and was rewarded by the Belgian Government at the end of the war. One could note that this marks the beginning of Bishop Amigo's special interest in groups that were being persecuted. This interest can be seen later in regard to the Royalists in Spain, Catholics in Malta and particularly in Ireland, and Gibraltarians during the Second World War.

There was of course a pressing need for Chaplains to the Forces and Southwark provided no fewer than 25 priests to act as Chaplains for at least some part of the war. Two of these, Frs. John Carden and Bernard Walsh, were awarded the Military Cross. No Southwark Secular priest was killed during the conflict but two religious, Fr. Denis Doyle SJ from Roehampton and Fr. Bernard Kavanagh CSSR from the Redemptorist House at Clapham were killed in action. The appointment of Chaplains was in the hands of Cardinal Bourne. The work of liaison with the War Department had previously been in the hands of the Bishops of Southwark, but when Bishop Bourne was transferred to Westminster he continued the work from Westminster. However, right from the start of the war many members of the English Hierarchy thought that it would be better if a Bishop could be appointed who would be in charge of the Chaplains. Bishop Amigo was most anxious that such an appointment should be made and pressed the case in Rome. Eventually the first Chaplain General to the Forces was appointed. This was Rt. Rev. William Keatinge, himself a Southwark Priest who had served throughout the Boer War where he had the honour of special mention in dispatches and was awarded the C.M.G. and the Cross of the Legion of Honour.

One of the features of the First World War in Great Britain was the sudden mushrooming of a number of societies pledged to some form of relief work either for those who remained at home or for the forces serving abroad, or for refugees. This is an area which merits more research. As far as Bishop Amigo was concerned it meant that he was asked to serve on a number of committees or actively sponsor a large number of new groupings. The archives show that he took a great personal interest in the Borough of Southwark Emergency Committee of the National Relief Fund. This was set up to deal with cases of hardship, often among women whose husbands were at the front. The

Bishop actually served in person on the Committee. The reports of meetings seem rather humorous today. From the report of 16th December 1914 we read.

Gifts "We have to report the receipt of the various gifts of cheese, salmon, flour and potatoes, specimens of which are exhibited on the table ... it is suggested that all recipients of relief should, during Xmas week, participate in these gifts, to be recommended by the sub-committee."

Short weight was evidently still a problem though.

"*Potatoes* I understand should be 90 lbs per sack, upon checking this weight, the average was 86 lbs per sack."

The aim was to provide work if possible rather than straight relief. A scheme was suggested by the Committee for sweeping the streets.

"The road, pavements etc would be swept, the refuse collected into barrows and emptied into a dustcart conveniently placed. At intervals a driver and horse would come round and take the cart to the depot and return it. Thus the maximum of labour and minimum of horse traction would be required."

A full list of the organisations which requested support from the Bishop will be found in an appendix to this chapter. Not all the groups found the support they sought. Thus the "Queen's Work for Women" sought to collect funds from children attending Sunday Schools to help unemployed women. The Bishop pointed out that the children in his Diocese were already contributing to various other funds. The Bishop declined to be a patron of a flag day for victims of Poland as he considered a more senior Bishop would be better to head their lists.

More controversy surrounded the "Guild of the Pope's Peace". The Guild was founded by a group of Catholics including Francis Meynell and E. I. Watkin. Their prospectus quoted from the various messages of Pope Benedict XV asking for an end to the fighting and a conference. In July 1915 he had called on the fighting nations to lay down their arms "You bear before God and men the terrible responsibility of peace and war . . . . Blessed is he who first shall raise the olive branch and give his right hand to the enemy, offering reasonable conditions of peace . . . we invite all the friends of peace in the world to help us in hastening the end of the war." (Letter to the Peoples now at War and to their Rulers, July 28th 1915).

The prospectus for the Guild contained the following words.

"The proposals themselves demand the support of every rational being who feels that nations should know for what causes they are so torturing each other; of every patriotic Christian; and more than all of every Catholic."

Now these sentiments, very fine in themselves, were seen by many in Britain as little better than appeasement.

The C.T.S. had circulated the prospectus with every copy of its "Book Notes" for April 1916. Bishop Amigo wrote to Fr. Paine of the Committee of the C.T.S. on 13th April 1916.

"I think you still preside at the Committee Meetings of the CTS. My attention has already been called to the circular about the Guild of the Pope's Peace which has been sent round with the last number of the Book Notes. While realising the purity of the sentiments of Catholic devotion and loyalty to the Holy See, which animate the promoters of such a Guild, I think that this Notice, considering the temper of the Country at the present time, is likely to arouse the gravest misunderstandings, and I am sorry that it seems to come out with the approval of the authorities of this Diocese when I have not been consulted. I am sure that you will agree with me in regretting its being issued."

One rather interesting enterprise that sprang up during the war was the "Catholic Huts Council". This group was pledged to provide huts for the use of Soldiers and Sailors at their Home bases and camps. The Bishop was a member of the committee. These huts would provide not only shelter but act as sales points, so they were closely allied to the modern N.A.A.F.I. In the Diocese of Southwark they were to be found at Dover, Lydd, Woking and, rather strangely, in the Church Hall at Anerley in South London. They were staffed mainly by members of the Catholic Women's League. The Chairman of the organisation was Alderman O'Bryen, Mayor of Hampstead, and the Vice-Chairman was the Duke of Norfolk's daughter Mrs. James Hope. After a short time difficulties arose and Mrs. Hope withdrew the C.W.L. members from the council, calling the Mayor 'hopeless' as an organiser, and stating that opportunities were being lost. The C.W.L. then set up some huts of its own.

The Bishop himself regarded the war as the opportunity for extra penance in the way of self-denial. The National War Savings Committee had asked him to obtain the support of all his clergy by having them

preach a special sermon to support their appeal. In his own letter to the
clergy the Bishop wrote.

"I hope that all the clergy, while asking the people to join with the
rest of the nation in acts of self-denial, will point out that God wants
us to atone for our sins and that we shall bring down His Blessing
upon us and upon the Country by acts of mortification and self-
sacrifice. The time of war is a time of special penance."

The Bishop was a total realist in regard to the war. He realised that
appeasement would never work. Besides the sad affair of the Guild of
the Pope's Peace there exists a letter he wrote to the Mayor of
Southwark on 3rd August 1917.

" .... I unite myself with you all in the earnest desire to secure that
the rights and liberties of the Empire and of our Allies be permanently secured. This cannot be done by peace at the present moment. We
must pray that God will give us soon that victory which we have so
much at heart . . . ."

However, Bishop Amigo surely secured his right to a place in the
history books through his involvement with the British Government in
securing the neutrality of Spain during the War.

The story of Bishop Amigo starts in June 1915. The Bishop offered
his services to the Government in order to help in the work of securing
Spanish neutrality during the war. There was a strong pro-German
element in the country, particularly among the clergy who disliked the
anti-clerical regime in France and considered that the Kaiser and his
forces represented the strength of Christianity against the errors of
atheism. This nonsense was propagated by German agents in Spain and
some of them went as far as to say that the Kaiser would promise them
Tangiers and Gibraltar if they entered on the side of Germany. The
King Alfonso XIII was in a difficult personal position as his wife
Victoria Eugenie (Ena) was a grand-daughter of Queen Victoria, while
his mother was Austrian. The position was further complicated by the
presence of a substantial number of republicans and extreme socialists
who sided with France and who later on would create the difficulties
that led to Alfonso's abdication.

Sir Claude Schuster at the Ministry of Information wrote to the
Bishop on 30th June 1915.

"I have talked over with the Foreign Office the question of the very generous and patriotic offer which you made to me yesterday and as I anticipated would be the case, the Foreign Office are heartily in agreement with the proposal which you make. I am exceedingly glad of this for as I told you yesterday I expect that great good will result from your visit to Spain . . . . I understood from you yesterday that you wish to bear your own travelling expenses but if you should be of another mind we should consider it a pleasure to do so. I am, My Lord, Yours faithfully, Claude Schuster."

On the 26th July Bishop Amigo wrote back to Sir Claude to say he would pay his own expenses but asking that the government pay the expenses of his Secretary who would travel with him. He told Sir Claude that his idea was to visit the Bishops and other influential Catholics to remove the strong prejudice against the Allies. He would also take some pamphlets with him explaining the allied cause. The Bishop left England on 2nd September 1915, returning on 7th October. While in Spain he visited San Sebastian, Bilbao, Valladolid, Madrid, Saragossa, Barcelona, Loyola, Toledo and El Escorial. Afterwards he made a confidential report to Sir Claude Schuster but he then wrote an account of the journey for the Dublin Review of April 1916. This article will be found as an appendix to this volume. However, the article, for diplomatic reasons, omits the detail of the Bishop's visit to the Spanish Royal Family. The Archives of Southwark give the Bishop's own account of their meeting.

The King started by saying that he had great sympathy for the Allied cause. Spain was unsuited to German rule. He would be afraid to drop cigarette ends in the street under the Germans. He had lost many English friends at the Yser and in the Dardanelles, and at the supreme moment he would have liked to have been with them. Thanks to his promise of neutrality the French were able to take their troops away from the border. He spoke of his personal problem in having an English wife but an Austrian mother. The Bishop told him that the Austrians had been deceived by the Germans. The King said the Germans had been clever in making promises about Gibraltar and Tangier that they could never keep. The Allies could help allay Spanish fears by promising something themselves. He told the Bishop that no submarines had been sheltered in Spain except in one case. He was sure that Britain would win but it was a pity from a military point of view that she had no proper army before the conflict started. He mentioned that two Spanish priests had been killed at Louvain in Belgium. The Spanish Bishops thought they must have deserved their fate but he had made personal representations to the Germans which were not backed up by the Bishops. The report to Sir Claude Schuster adds the detail that the Bishop then had an interview with the Queen Mother who lamented that there should be war between Britain and Austria and hoped that these two countries would not actually fight one another. At the end of the confidential report the Bishop made certain positive suggestions. These were that the cinemas should produce pictures which would promote our cause, and that papers should interest themselves in the British case, that the English and Scottish colleges at Valladolid could be used for sending out circulars and articles as propaganda, that France should establish diplomatic relations with the Vatican and that perhaps Britain could make some kind of promise to Spain. Finally he suggested that the British Press should take the opportunity of praising Spain, particularly if this could be done by a Government Minister. The Spanish have the idea that the British rather despise them and they like recognition. There had been misunderstandings in the past.

The Bishop knew that with regard to those who opposed the British viewpoint there must be a "softly softly" approach and he was much upset when the *'Tablet'* on 6th November 1915 published a summary of an article by the Abbe Lugan. The article strongly attacked those in Spain, including certain members of the clergy, who were taking a pro-German stance. Bishop Amigo decided to counter the damage done by writing directly to the *'Times'* which printed the letter on 23rd November. Here are some of the salient points made by the Bishop in this letter.

"In judging the situation, however, we must not forget that it is not merely a question of being in our favour or against us. Politics play an important part. The Carlist movement has been revived lately to some extent and the dread of a revolution has to be reckoned with. When Lerroux (socialist revolutionary) and his friends are on our side, it is not difficult to understand that those who love the Monarchy should fear to have a Republic in Spain if the Allies are victorious . . . . It would however be an easy matter to have the whole Spanish nation completely on our side if only we acknowledge mistakes of the past and try to understand Spain better, not despising the many sterling qualities which the Spaniards have . . . . The number of pro-Germans is in reality small, and will be found chiefly among the military, who admire German methods of training soldiers and also among the clergy. Let us not irritate by hurting the most tender feelings of a nation which has excellent traditions of which it is proud, and let us not expect them to look at everything in the same way as we do here."

At this time the Bishop was proposing to go and see the Holy Father and give an account of his journey to Rome. He proposed to Charles Masterman that he should take with him an official letter signed by Sir Edward Grey addressed to himself (Bishop Amigo) stating how much the Government were pleased with the visit. The letter could not be to the Vatican unless it were written by the King.

All was still in prospect on 25th November when Mr. Masterman wrote:

"I have been in communication with the Foreign Office; they do not see any reason at all why everything should not be arranged and you be able to get away on Tuesday next . . . all the letters from Sir Edward Grey etc. will be ready for you . . . ."

On the 27th November however Mr. Masterman wrote back:

"I am exceedingly sorry to say that there seems to be a hitch at the Foreign Office at least for the time . . . I cannot quite ascertain the nature of the hitch, but it is something to do I gather with the complicated politics of Rome and with the present general position in Europe concerning peace overtures."

Why was the official visit cancelled? It seems that there was a Consistory in Rome at the time at which Cardinal Bourne was present. In the course of the Consistory Pope Benedict XV condemned in very clear terms the barbarous conduct of the Germans and Austrians in the matter of Belgian deportations and the bombardment of open cities. At the same time there were certain peace overtures in progress as mentioned in the letter and there was a special mission being prepared by Sir Henry Howard. The Bishop finally decided to visit Rome in a private capacity in January 1916. Mr. Masterman wrote to him on the 5th January 1916.

" . . . You will understand that I could do little in this matter without the Foreign Office actually seeing you and consulting you about your scheme. It is evident from what your letter states that they are afraid of some jealousy or confusion in connection with Sir Henry Howard's mission. I am glad however that you are going yourself to Rome, and I am sure you will do everything that is possible for our cause. The enemy seem to have gained renewed strength and vigour in the last few months.... I should be very glad to hear from you from Rome ... and in any case I should be glad if you could call on me when you come back. With every kind wish for the New Year and all such happiness and prosperity as is possible when the world is falling to pieces."

There can be no doubt that the Bishop's visit did in fact help maintain Spanish neutrality. This is confirmed by a letter to the '*Times*' from Count Albiz in Madrid on 11th December 1915, backed up by a letter of the Spanish Ambassador to Britain (Count Merry del Val) on 12th December. "The Bishop's kind action has evidently produced a wide and excellent impression in Spain." John Walter of the '*Times*' went in person to Spain in late December and his report of the journey in the '*Times*' speaks well of the efforts of Bishop Amigo in gaining the goodwill of Spanish Catholics for the *Entente*.

In July 1916 a group of 500 leading Spanish figures published "An Address by Spanish Catholics to Belgium" totally in sympathy with the Allied cause. This prompted the Bishop and the Government to send out propaganda leaflets to the Spanish episcopate. The material sent included a "Collective letter of the Belgian Bishops to the Bishops of Germany, Bavaria, and Austria", a Pastoral of Cardinal Mercier and a covering letter from Bishop Amigo.

By October, however, pro-German feeling was running high again in the Peninsular. Mr. Walter published an article in the '*Times*' on the 5th October stating that our best allies in Spain were to be found among those who are profoundly dissatisfied with the present state of affairs in Spain (i.e. Republicans). This prompted a sharp retort from Bishop Amigo saying it was a mistake to show ourselves the admirers of the opponents of the clergy, the aristocracy and the military. As Cardinal Mercier published an important "allocutio" on 26th November, the Bishop thought it wise to circulate this document to the Spanish Bishops and at the suggestion of Mr. Koppel of the Ministry of Information this letter was sent not only to the Bishops of Spain but also to the Spanish speaking Bishops in Central and South America, Cuba and the Philippines. The archives preserve some of their replies. In general they are polite if non-commital but the reply from the Bishop of Buenos Aires was very critical.

"As Your Lordship has taken the liberty to write to me, I also take the liberty of giving you some advice. Instead of troubling the peace of our America with the Horrors of war (which does not end through the fault of your countrymen), you ought to employ your time in converting the people of your Diocese who were, when I visited them, nearly all steeped in materialism and Protestantism. The time Your Lordship spends in any other employment is lamentably lost."

In 1918 the Spanish learned quickly the true nature of the German onslaught when their own shipping was attacked. The Government of Alfonso continually protested but little account was taken of their protest. In August Bishop Amigo was invited to attend the first "Mariano and Montfortiano" National Congress in Barcelona. The Bishop decided to combine this with a visit to the celebrations at Covadonga, near Oviedo on 8th September. This day is chosen by the Spanish to commemorate the battle won in 718 by Pelayo against the Moors, the initial victory of the "Reconquista" which continued until the fall of Granada in 1492. It was in effect the 12th centenary of the Spanish Monarchy, for Alfonso XIII was the lineal descendant of that Asturian Chief who was victorious at Covadonga. The celebrations consisted of a High Mass sung by the Cardinal Primate of Toledo in the presence of the King and Queen and after Mass the coronation of the old venerated Statue of Our Lady with a special jewelled crown.

The Bishop set off in good faith but when he arrived in Paris he discovered that Cardinal Guisasola (the Primate of Spain) had made a difficulty about the Bishop's going to Covadonga. There would be no room for him in the town's hotels. They were fully booked some time ago. The Bishop visited the Spanish Embassy in France where a representative of the Ambassador told him to go ahead as the King would be offended if he did not arrive for the celebrations. What happened next was little short of disaster, but it had its humorous side also.

The Bishop arrived by hired car together with his travelling companion, a Franciscan Priest, quite late in the evening of 6th September. He attempted to book in at the Hotel Pelayo but there was no room at the inn. It looked for a while as though the two divines would have to spend the night "sub Divo" (in the open air), but they were met by a Mr. Mackenzie, an English Engineer, director of a local mine, and an honorary Vice-Consul. Mr. Mackenzie had been informed of the visit and had himself informed the Abbot of the local monastery. The next day they presented themselves at the residence of the Bishop of Oviedo shortly before the hour fixed for a special ceremony of presenting the colours to the Covadonga regiment. Here he found assembled not only the bishop of Oviedo but four other local Bishops and Cardinal Guisasola. The Bishop moved up to greet the Cardinal at one end of the grand reception Hall. He was received extremely rudely by the Cardinal and the remaining Bishops retreated to the other end of the Hall where they could still hear the loud and angry tone of the Cardinal's voice. He told the Bishop in no uncertain terms that he was not welcome, that the occasion was distinctly national and the presence of a foreign prelate was most imprudent without an invitation. He implied that the Bishop was an emissary of the British Government. Bishop Amigo said he had come on his own account, but the Cardinal continued that the best thing he could do now was to take a car and leave. The Bishop spoke quite firmly in reply "Without doubt you forget that I am a Catholic Bishop just as you are and that my Diocese is more extensive than yours." The Cardinal then told him that he should take off his episcopal insignia and he was not to join with the other Bishops in the ceremony but merely to look on as a private spectator. In the event Mr. Mackenzie obtained a place for him in the "Diputacion Provincial" where he was sufficiently prominent to be seen by all, both on that day and the following, when the main ceremonies were held. A nobleman deputed by the newspaper '*Epoca*' came to see him after the ceremony and the Bishop gave him the story of what happened.

When the tale was told in that worthy journal the Bishop was described as the 'Bishop of Gibraltar'. Bishop Amigo travelled soon after the ceremonies to San Sebastian where he met the King and Queen of Spain. The King had read the report in 'Epoca' and remarked laughingly to the Bishop that his presence at Covadonga was a reminder to everyone that all Spain had now been reconquered except Europa Point (Gibraltar). In his report to the Government following the visit, the Bishop remarked that he was quite sure that the trip to Covadonga was quite inappropriate.

On his return to England the Bishop discovered that the '*Manchester Guardian*' had quoted from the Republican Paper "*El Pais*" an account of the discourteous reception of the Bishop by the Cardinal Primate. There was a risk here that the Republicans might make their own propaganda over a split between the esteemed clerics, so Bishop Amigo replied to the Manchester Guardian.

"I fear that your note on Pro-Germanism in Spain may alienate some of our many friends in that country and will not win those whom we wish to have on our side. The report in *'El Pais'* is certainly wrong in many respects and I am very sorry that the paper should have mentioned the incident at all. Cardinal Guisasola does not necessari-. ly represent the opinions of Spanish Catholics but did not consider it prudent at a very critical time for an Allied Bishop to be present at a function to which only the Bishops of the provinces of Asturias had been invited. I assisted at all the celebrations and any misunderstanding was completely removed by the gracious kindness of the Sovereign and by many expressions of good will towards us from all quarters."

When the war had ended the *'Times'* started attacking the monarchy saying it was too detached from the people. The policy was for open support of the Republicans. After a hostile leader on the 5th March 1919, Bishop Amigo wrote to the *'Times'*.

"It was with very great interest that I read this morning your leading article on Spain as I have twice been to that country during the last four years. I know that Spain was quite unprepared for war and if she had joined us serious troubles would have arisen there without any real service to us. But though she kept out of the war, she helped us in manifold ways and we ought to appreciate this assistance. We should aim at bettering relations between Spain and England instead of making the separation greater. Both countries will benefit by being brought into contact . . . . You say in today's issue that some members of the American House of Representatives contended in regard to the Irish question that the internal affairs of Great Britain were not the concern of the people of the United States and would they not have more reason to maintain that the Catalonian problem (Republican stronghold) is one for the Spaniards themselves?"

The Spanish Ambassador, Count Merry del Val, wrote to thank the Bishop on 8th March. Part of his lengthy letter reads:

"I have just received your note of today's date. It is only natural that you should receive congratulations for your witty letter to the *'Times'* on Spain. I am sending it to my Government with the praise it deserves . . . . Thanking you again for all you do for Spain. I remain sincerely and gratefully yours. A. Merry del Val."

It only remains to say here that on Friday 13th August at 12.00 noon

Bishop Amigo gave a lecture on "The Catholic Church in Spain" to the Local Lectures Summer Meeting of the University of Cambridge. The lecture was part of a series on various aspects of Spain's literary and artistic history.

Bishop Amigo's interest in Spanish affairs continued and it will be necessary to return to the topic of the Spanish Civil War later.

One result of the help given to the British Government on Spain was that the Government employed him on certain other business connected with the war.

His services were taken advantage of by the Military Permit Office in getting him to advise them as to the fitness or bonafides of applicants for travel to the Continent. The class of applicants was chiefly Irish Church students, secular and regular, who were to take up burses at Rome or Genoa. This entailed a good deal of letter writing with both the applicants and the British Government Permit Office. The Bishop had also to advise on many cases of nuns who wished to go abroad for their novitiate or for other purposes. Permissions were not easy to obtain as facilities for travel by civilians were very restricted in the war zones. Hence much work was thrown on the Bishop through interviews as well as writing. The archive correspondence shows that the Bishop's efforts were much appreciated by all concerned. A typical case would be that of a certain Charles Matthews, an Irish student of the Bishop of Kilmore. On the 3rd November 1917 Bishop Amigo wrote to the Bishop of Kilmore:

"I have just had a visit from one of your students, Charles Matthews aged 20 who is being sent out to the Irish College Rome by your Lordship. The Military Permit Officials have communicated with me and told me that they do not wish him to go . . . . I have some friends at the Permit Office who have promised me that they will allow those strongly recommended by me . . . . If your Lordship can arrange for Matthews to study in Ireland the Permit authorities will be most grateful. If however you do not see your way, kindly write a strong letter to me urging his being allowed to go to Rome, and I shall do my utmost to help your Lordship. This case will be more difficult for me to pass as they have definitely told me that they do not want Matthews to go. They formed the opinion of him that he was too uneducated to profit by a University course and I suppose they did not believe him. He had no papers on him to show he was really a Church student beginning his philosophy."

Evidently the story had a happy ending for a permit was duly obtained.

Bishop Amigo was also asked to assist the Government in Middle Eastern affairs. On 10th May 1916 Lord Onslow wrote to the Bishop asking for information and advice about the Christian denominations in Syria (that is modern Lebanon and Syria together). He then sent the Bishop an extract from an Egyptian newspaper called '*Mohattan*' which detailed the appalling sufferings of both Christians and Arabs under the Turkish rule. The Bishop decided to enlist the help of the French Jesuits based at Ore Place, Hastings. They had missionaries working in Syria. The idea was that these missionaries could give first hand accounts of the Turkish regime and then help to counter the German propaganda in neutral countries by circulating the realities of the Turkish misdeeds. There was an important link with the Spanish work here because there was much pro-German feeling among the Spanish Jesuits at that time. Admiral John Fisher from the War Office sent the Bishop a copy of an article "Turkish Tyranny and the Famine in Syria" which was written by a French Jesuit who had just left the country in which he describes an appalling famine which stretched over the country from Aleppo to Jerusalem itself. Meanwhile the Jesuits at Ore Place made translations of various documents and letters from Arabic into English for the Government. The Superior, Fr. LeClerc SJ, also asked the Bishop to use his influence with the Military Permit Office to allow their six Hungarian and Austrian Novices to remain at Ore Place and not be interned. This permission was duly granted, but in a further letter of 17th September 1916 Fr. LeClerc said that their conditions of residence were stricter than if they had been prisoners of war. They were not allowed either to leave the house or to write letters.

Just after the war ended Bishop Amigo attempted to use his influence with the Government to let Cardinal Mercier represent the Vatican at the Peace Conference. The Pope had been excluded by the Secret Treaty of London. The Bishop wrote the following to Charles Dormer at the Foreign Office:

"You know that I have done my best to help the cause of the Allies during the war. A few months after my first visit to Spain, I went to Rome in February 1916, and there Cardinal Granite di Belmonte told me that at the Vatican they could not trust the British Government because they were aware that in the secret Pact of London it had been decided to exclude the Pope from the Peace Conference. I replied that I was certain that our Government would not do anything so mean, especially as a Mission had been sent to the Vatican, showing our belief in the influence of the Pope. The Cardinal repeated his statement and remarked that the sending of a Minister under the circumstances only made matters worse. On my return to England, I spoke to Mr. Masterman who was then at the head of the propaganda work, and I wrote to the Cardinal that my opinion had been confirmed by one who had been in the Cabinet when the Treaty was supposed to have been signed. Events in Russia later on showed that the Vatican's information had been correct all along, though the secret here had been exceedingly well kept.

The Pope set his heart on being represented at the Peace Conference, and he will consider it an insult if he is left out. Apart from what we Catholics think of his position, the Pope is the greatest moral power and his influence extends to every nation. The Germans realise this fully, and my two visits to Spain have shown me how they try to win favour among Catholics by pretending to be the friends of the Pope. Erzberger is a Catholic and will do his best to make out that the Germans wanted the Pope to be represented and that the Allies refused. It will be a pity to have any divisions among the Allies when union is so important.

Cannot we checkmate the Germans by suggesting through Count de Salis that Cardinal Mercier should be sent to the Conference on behalf of the Vatican? Even the Italians must admire this heroic figure of the War and he would certainly be a favourite in the other Allied Countries. We should undo our enemies in Germany and greatly please the Pope by having this distinguished ecclesiastic at the approaching Conference.

You have the privilege of meeting Mr. Balfour frequently. Will you put this suggestion of mine before him?"

Dormer acknowledged this letter on 26th November but the Allies had of course made a firm arrangement to exclude the Vatican.

Finally, on a happier note, the Belgian Government determined to reward the Bishop for his services to their country in the work of looking after the interests of Belgian Refugees. He was awarded the Decoration of "Commander of the Order Of Leopold II" on 3rd February 1918. Even at this happy hour British officialdom showed up. The wearing of a decoration awarded by a foreign government requires the permission of the Crown. So on 8th March 1919 the Bishop received the following letter from the Home Office, signed by Mr. A.J. Eagleston.

"Rt. Rev. Sir, I am directed by the Secretary of State to inform you that a Warrant is about to be submitted to His Majesty for signature authorizing you to wear the Insignia of Commander of the Order of Leopold II conferred upon you by His Majesty the King of the Belgians and that the document will be forwarded to you when it has been impressed with a 10/- stamp, as required by the Stamp Act, 1891 (54 and 55 Vict., c 39).

I am to request that you will be so good as to forward the sum of 10/- to this Department, in the form of a money order or postal order made payable to me, in order that the Warrant may be completed and despatched, in the ordinary course through the Foreign Office.

P.S. Will you kindly be good to furnish your second Christian name."

The Royal Warrant permitting the Bishop to wear the insignia of the Order was signed on 10th April 1919 by King George V. The Warrant is far more impressive than the Decree awarding the honour from Albert, King of the Belgians.

"George the Fifth, by the Grace of God, of the United Kingdom of Great Britain and Ireland and of the British Dominions beyond the Seas, King, Defender of the Faith, to Our Trusty and Well-Beloved the Right Reverend Bishop Peter Emmanuel Amigo, Greeting. Whereas His Majesty the King of the Belgians has been pleased to confer upon you the Cross of Commander of the Order of Leopold II in recognition of valuable services rendered by you in the allied cause, and We being graciously pleased to approve thereof; Know ye that of Our Special Favour have given and granted and do by these Presents give and grant, unto you the said Peter Emmanuel Amigo, Our Royal Licence and Authority that you may avail yourself of the said mark of His Majesty's Favour and wear the Cross of Commander of the Order of Leopold II and that you may enjoy all the Rights and Privileges thereunto belonging; Given at our Court at Saint James, the 10th Day of April 1919 in the Ninth year of Our Reign; by His Majesty's Command."

The document is signed on the front by the King and at the end by Sir Edward Shortt.

The Bishop and the King were soon to have further communication on the troubles in Ireland.

Supplement to This Chapter

A List of Organisations which appealed for support to Bishop Amigo during the war:

St. Elizabeth's Fund (for Vestments in Churches destroyed in Belgium)
National Committee for Relief in Belgium
Polish Victims Relief Fund
Armenian Relief Fund
Belgian Soldiers Comforts Fund
Montenegrin Red Cross and Relief Fund
War Savings Fund
Red Cross
Food Economy Campaign (1917)
Committee of War Damage
Vice Lieutenants (Kent) Comforts Fund (for prisoners of war)
Queen's Royal West Surrey Regiment and East Surrey Regiment Prisoners of War Relief Fund
Catholic Huts Council (An early type of NAAFI)
London New Army Battalion Fund (for new Battalion formed 1915)
Prince of Wales National Relief Fund (for soldiers dependants)
Queen's Work for Women Fund
Women's After Care Hostel
League of Perpetual Prayer in War Time (organised by Lady Mary Howard for continuous prayer in convents)
Guild of the Pope's Peace
National Relief Fund—Southwark Emergency Committee
Tobacco Fund

Chapter 7

Bishop Amigo and Ireland

Bishop Amigo's active involvement in Irish politics dates from the start of the First World War. He was on holiday in Ireland when war broke out. He involved the Irish Nationalist leader, Mr. John Redmond, in a meeting with Cardinal Mercier a few weeks later, to gain Irish sympathy for the plight of the Belgian Refugees.

In 1916 he was approached by Gavin Duffy, Counsel for the imprisoned Irish patriot Sir Roger Casement to let him be visited by an Irish Priest instead of the regular Chaplain at Brixton who was English. After the Irish uprising of 1916 many leading Sinn Feiners were imprisoned in Portland prison. A false rumour was spread about that Bishop Amigo had somehow banned them from going to Mass. This is all the more surprising when one considers that Portland was not even in the Diocese of Southwark. On the 23rd August 1917 the Chaplain at the prison, Fr. O'Loughlin, sent a long account of the incident which led to the rumour. The Sinn Feiners at Portland hoped to gain recognition for their case by being considered "belligerents" and thus entitled to a place at the Peace Conference at the end of the war. On Whit Monday they mutinied at the prison and said they would not work or co-operate with the authorities unless they were made prisoners of war. They were ordered to their cells pending a decision of the Home Office. The Chaplain asked the Governor if they could attend Mass on Sunday and permission was given provided they agreed to come and go to the chapel in an orderly way. When Fr. O'Loughlin spoke to them on the Saturday they refused to give this undertaking. So the Chaplain then went to Mr. De Valera who was being kept in solitary confinement there and he said that he would order the men to give the undertaking by shouting from his window, but the undertaking was to be given only to the Priest. Fr. O'Loughlin refused to accept this arrangement and De Valera told him

71

that it would mean no Mass. But returning to see the others he discovered a note from the Irish Leader saying that the prisoners after Mass were to refuse to re-enter the cells and smash the locks. This notice had been secretly circulated among the prisoners before the Chaplain's visit to Mr. De Valera. As no Mass was said, trouble had been averted, and De Valera had not on this occasion been able to exercise his authority over the prisoners. Further trouble was avoided with the release of many of the prisoners.

The real nature of the Bishop's feelings for Ireland became apparent in 1918. The 'Catholic Union' meeting on 30th April that year passed a resolution appealing to the Pope against the decision of the Irish Bishops to resist compulsory national service for Irish citizens. The wording of the last part of the appeal is as follows:

> "The Catholic Union desires emphatically to dissociate itself from a movement which cannot fail to hamper the full development of the military forces of the Allies, and thereby endanger the cause of humanity."

This meeting followed directly from a letter sent by one of the most prominent members of the Union, the Earl of Denbigh, to the *'Times'* arguing in the same way. Bishop Amigo wrote to the Earl on the 29th April.

> "I was very sorry to read your Lordship's letter in the 'Times' this morning, because I fear that the very object which you must have had in view will be hindered by it rather than furthered. ... When nearly thirty Bishops in Ireland with their clergy and people are all of one mind at present, there must be a good deal to be said for their point of view, even if we do not understand it .... Why should we find fault with a Hierarchy which numbers such holy and learned men and which alone can use a restraining influence in stopping most serious evils in Ireland? Your Lordship agrees that mistakes have been made in our treatment of Ireland ... we are rightly proud of the English sense of justice. Ulster has been allowed to do what Catholic Ireland claims to do now. We have to pray most earnestly that God may guide our rulers in these critical days."

The Bishop then wrote to Mr. Walter of the *'Times'* asking him to use his influence to stop the attacks on the Irish Bishops in that paper. He also wrote to the War Office and finally on 28th May to the Prime Minister, Mr. Lloyd George.

"I must say at the very outset that I have no Irish blood in me. My sympathy and love for the Irish began by my working among the poor in the East End of London, and since then I have been honoured by the friendship of many Irish Bishops, priests and laypeople. (later) ... The appointment of Sir Edward Carson as Attorney General in spite of his preparations for resistance to law in 1914 had a disastrous effect on the Irish. There was little or no sympathy with the Easter Rebellion but the way in which the Sinn Feiners were dealt with aroused the sympathy of an emotional race. ... It is in your power now to do what will secure you the warm appreciation of the present and of future generations of Irish people. The Irish can be won, but never driven. You would have all the soldiers you need without any conscription, if the Irish could be made to trust British politicians, but every man and every woman in Ireland will resist conscription. The deportations of the Sinn Fein leaders will not help our cause .... You are going to have disaster and we shall lose the war unless the Irish question is settled once and for all. You know that the Irish character is altogether different from the English. Why not try to rule Ireland accordingly? The presence of so many soldiers in Ireland now; their guarding bridges etc. all these circumstances are helping to excite the Irish people. The Irish Bishops have been able to restrain them up to now. Their influence is very powerful but if care is not taken by the Government the young people will be beyond restraint soon. While we boast that we are out to protect small nationalities, we are alienating the splendid Irish race ...."

This letter received the barest one line acknowledgement from the Prime Minister's Secretary. One can but reflect on what might have been if the Bishop's advice had been heeded.

During 1919 the situation in Ireland deteriorated and the English used ever more repressive measures to control the situation. Archbishop Mannix of Melbourne was forbidden to enter Ireland because of his well known sympathy for Irish independence. Bishop Amigo wrote to him while he was in London. (11th August 1920).

"I am exceedingly sorry for the way in which you have been treated and the action of the Government is not likely to bring peace to Ireland. I have the greatest love for the Irish and my prayer is that God may always bless your people."

At the same time Bishop Amigo wrote to the Secretary of State at the

Vatican, Cardinal Gasparri explaining the circumstances in which the ship on which Archbishop Mannix was travelling had been forced to call in at Penzance to drop its distinguished passenger. The Bishop pointed out that even the Germans did not try such a manoeuvre against Cardinal Mercier during the war. The same letter contains an impassioned defence of the Irish against their oppressors.

" . . . Our Government unhappily does not seem to be able to understand the Irish. They are employing forces against a nation which resists this force, but they could so easily be more sympathetic. The influence of the clergy prevents great evils for the army and the police are exasperating the young men. They are trying to show that it is the Sinn Feiners who are killing policemen but the Sinn Feiners are good Catholics. It is some secret society which is responsible, possibly even enemies of Ireland. . . . Ireland has no more confidence in English politicians when it sees that they break their promises . . . when they speak of the necessity of helping small nations like Belgium, Poland, Yugoslavia and do not recognise the just demands of the Irish."

The Lord Mayor of Cork, Terence McSwiney, had been arrested and was imprisoned in Brixton Jail. He had started a hunger strike which would lead to his death. The Bishop gave him his full support from the start. On the 5th September he sent a telegram to the Prime Minister, Lloyd George:

"As Bishop of many Irish priests and people in the large Catholic Diocese of Southwark, I ask clemency for Cork's Lord Mayor who is dying in my Diocese. Resentment will be very bitter if he is allowed to die."

The Bishop left no stone unturned in the matter of appeals for clemency for McSwiney. He tried Sir Harmer Greenwood at the Irish Office, Sir Edward Troup at the Home Office and even Mr. Bonar Law who was in the Cabinet at the time. Mr Bonar Law had sided with Sir Edward Carson in Belfast in opposition to Home Rule and both of them had very nearly been imprisoned for their action then at the very start of the Great War. Bishop Amigo made use of this in his letter. (7th September 1920).

" . . . You have a splendid opportunity now of making up for the words and actions of your Party which brought upon you the warning of Mr. Asquith in the House on 31st July 1912. Even at a time when we were already engaged in a 'life and death' struggle, you yourself with Sir Edward Carson at Belfast on 28th September 1914 were speaking words which produce their unfortunate result today in Ireland. Cannot the clemency shown to you then, be now shown to the Lord Mayor?"

He wrote again a few days later to the Prime Minister:

"... The condition which you put upon him is an impossible one ... the dying man has no power whatever to stop the awful murders in Ireland while Irish people say that the outrages are being committed by soldiers and police which could be prevented by the Government. If the Lord Mayor dies in all probability the young people will keep quiet though greatly exasperated, but the good name of England will be much affected thenceforth through the whole world. Once more as a Catholic Bishop I ask for mercy and I beg you not to make it impossible to bring about a solution of the Irish difficulty."

These letters fell on very deaf ears. Other voices in England however were very worried at the Bishop's support for a hunger striker arguing that hunger strikes were a form of suicide. A certain Mr. W. Marchant of Hove wrote on 25th September to the Bishop asking for an objective answer as to the morality of hunger strikes. He complained that he had sought the advice of individual priests which were often in direct opposition one with another. While nearly everyone today would say that to prolong a hunger strike unto death is in effect suicide, matters were perhaps not so clear in 1920. The Bishop replied to Mr. Marchant, after a second letter from him.

" ... Till Rome speaks, opinions will differ amongst us, as they have done in the past in matters of faith and of morals before they were defined by the infallible Authority. At such a time as this, when so many other considerations enter, the Holy See is not likely to decide, but later on we may have a definite pronouncement for future guidance. Even if those who think that the Lord Mayor of Cork is committing suicide were actually right, most of them would acknowledge that he is in good faith. Just as no sincere Protestant should be disturbed by a priest on his death bed, so other well-meaning people must be left in their good faith. The Confessor judges the particular case and feels justified in giving the Sacraments as with the hunger

strikers at Wormwood Scrubbs a short time back. My own opinion is
that the Confessor is perfectly right in Mr. McSwiney's case, but I wait
till feelings do not run so high before answering your questions
whether hunger strikes are lawful when national interests are
concerned. I certainly would not condemn a besieged garrison for
dying of hunger rather than surrender an important post . . . ."

Miss McSwiney wrote on 26th September suggesting that the entire
English Hierarchy condemn the Government's action. In reply the
Bishop said he had been unable to contact Cardinal Bourne but he had
that very day delivered in person yet another strong appeal to Mr. Lloyd
George urging the release of her brother. For the first time there is a
reference to a possible funeral.

" . . . In regard to the funeral in case of death . . . in my own mind I
have no doubt that the body should be brought to the Cathedral. What
I fear is the demonstrations and perhaps counter-demonstrations
which are sure to take place. It would not be right for me to mix up in
these and besides it might become more difficult to take the body over
to Ireland. We need not however begin to arrange yet. It may be that
the miracle in which your sister believes may yet take place. Let us go
on praying."

On the 23rd October, two days before her brother's death, Miss Mary
McSwiney wrote to the Bishop to say she had been forbidden to visit
him on his death bed.

" . . . Could you even have imagined anything so utterly devilish as
excluding us from his death bed? I believe the real reason is that they
want to keep on feeding him forcibly and not let him return to
consciousness. Of course, when or if he does regain consciousness he
will begin the struggle all over again. His condition at present is such
that we can only pray God to take him quickly . . . "

The Bishop had previously informed the two sisters that they could
have a Requiem in the Cathedral provided that nothing was done which
could be regarded as a political demonstration and that there should be
no display of the Sinn Fein flag nor wearing of the Irish Volunteer
uniform inside the Cathedral. Before the final arrangements could be
made it was necessary to await the verdict of the Coroner's jury which
sat on Wednesday 27th October. The jury declared that the deceased
died from heart failure consequent upon his refusal to take food and this
was amplified by the Coroner into the formal verdict.

"Death was due to heart failure, due to exhaustion from prolonged refusal to take food."

Permission was given for the body to be removed to St. George's Cathedral where it arrived about 7 o'clock and from then until late evening people were allowed to file past the coffin. At one time it was estimated that more than ten thousand were gathered outside the Cathedral waiting their turn to pass through and it took a large force of police officers to keep order. At length the Cathedral was closed and behind the locked doors some members of the I.R.A., unknown to the Bishop re-opened the coffin and clothed the body in his uniform of Commandant I.R.A. The only real attempt to stop the funeral from the Government side was a personal phone call from the Home Secretary, Mr. Shortt.

At 11 o'clock the following morning, Dr. Cotter, the Bishop of Portsmouth, offered the Solemn Requiem in the presence of Bishop Amigo and also of Archbishop Mannix and Archbishop Kennealy of Simla. The Cathedral was packed to suffocation. One notable incident was the appearance of six men of the I.R.A. who stood as a guard of honour around the coffin. They had entered the Cathedral disguised in heavy overcoats which they threw off once inside to reveal the full uniform of the I.R.A. At the conclusion of the Mass, Bishop Amigo gave the Absolutions; and later in the afternoon before the cortege set out on its way to Euston en route for Cork, Archbishop Mannix read the final prayers and afterwards joined the procession in a closed car.

The '*Catholic Times*' described the procession thus: "Thousands of men and women, wearing the Republican colours and carrying aloft black-draped flags are marshalled outside the Church. At the first sounds of Chopin's Marche Funebre the cortege moves. An imposing array of police, foot and mounted, shepherded the mile-and-a-half long procession. Silence again and set, stern faces as the procession filters through the streets of Southwark. The skirl of the bagpipes playing a lament comes wailing in the breeze. Following the pipers walked a multitude of priests with the Emblem of the Redemption borne aloft. Followed the carriage containing the body, flanked by uniformed soldiers of the Republican Army and immediately behind walked the brown robed Caputchin, Father Dominic who had speeded the dead man's soul to Heaven. Archbishop Mannix in a closed carriage garbed in episcopal dress looked out at the masses of people lining the route. The attitude of the crowd was sympathetic and respectful to a degree. Women wept and prayed as the cortege passed and men stood bare headed in the biting cold wind until the last mourner had disappeared."

In view of the fact that the Bishop's wishes had been disregarded at the funeral, the Administrator of the Cathedral put out a statement in which he pointed out that the Bishop had expressed his wish that nothing be done that would savour of a political demonstration at the funeral.

The coffin also had an inscription in Gaelic which in translation read:

"Murdered by the Foreigner in Brixton Prison, London, England on October 25th 1920, the fourth year of the Republic."

Fr. O'Meara, the Administrator, made it clear that neither he nor the Bishop knew anything of this inscription until after the funeral.

The reference to Fr. Dominic is of interest. Fr. Dominic OFM. Cap. had been Terence McSwiney's Chaplain at Cork and was with him in prison when he died. During the war he had volunteered as a Chaplain and served with the 6th Munster Fusiliers and later with the 6th and 7th Dublin Fusiliers mainly in Macedonia. He resigned his commission in 1917 so as to be able to assist his people in their fight for freedom.

On his return to Ireland after the death of Terence McSwiney he was arrested and tortured by the Black and Tans and put on trial for treason by the British. They gave him five years penal servitude to be served at Parkhurst on the Isle of Wight. It was only due to the kindness of Bishop Amigo that he was allowed to say Mass there. The Bishop sent him the necessary vestments and offered to intercede with the Home Secretary on his behalf. He told Fr. Dominic that he had received information from a British official that prior to his arrest the British Government could not decide whether or not to put him on the Honours List for his services as an Army Chaplain or arrest him as a Sinn Feiner. Fr. Dominic refused the Bishop's offer of help as he would not take any favours from the British. He was released in the general amnesty of 1922 and received the freedom of the city of Cork for his assistance to Terence McSwiney. Later during the civil war in Ireland he acted as Chaplain to the Republicans though he would always give the last rites to any fighter in need. As a result of backing the wrong side he was ordered to leave Ireland and was posted to Oregon USA. He returned briefly for a Chapter of the Order in 1931 but was not permitted to stay when the Chapter had ended. He died in 1935 at Bend, Oregon.

There was plenty of criticism for the Bishop to face. In the next few days there were many letters complaining of the honour accorded to the late Lord Mayor. The archives at Southwark preserve about thirty. One letter attacked him however for not going in the procession after the Mass to Euston Station with Cardinal Mannix. To one Major James who protested not only about the funeral but also about McSwiney receiving the Sacraments the Bishop wrote. (29th October).

"I know what an excellent Catholic you are and I am very sorry to hurt your feelings in any way. There is too much excitement on both sides at present and people are prevented from looking on the question impartially. I as Bishop have been called upon to judge the particular case. After careful consideration I came to the conclusion that Mr. McSwiney did not intend to commit suicide but had every wish to live. This has been corroborated at the inquest. He exposed his life and has eventually lost it for what he considered a national cause; though we may not agree with him in this, I certainly could not refuse him the Sacraments as I did not consider him guilty of suicide and he has been a daily communicant for many years.

His relatives approached me about his body being brought here. Again I could not deny this request. He was an excellent Catholic and a Lord Mayor. He had every right to be treated with honour by the Church which while respecting nationality is the Church of all."

The most virulent criticism of the Bishop came from Lord Alfred Douglas in a magazine edited by him called *'Plain English'*. This journal was an extreme right wing paper very anti-semitic in tone. In the issue for 30th October 1920 the Editor notes that he had personally sent a telegram to the Holy Father on the day of McSwiney's death.

"In the name of all loyal and devoted Scottish, English and Irish Catholics, we humbly venture to implore your Holiness to intervene to prevent the fearful blow to the Catholic Church which is involved by action of Peter Amigo, Bishop of Southwark, placing the Cathedral of his Diocese at the disposal of the political allies of the late Mayor of Cork for the purpose of glorifying a suicide as a martyr."

In the text of his Editorial Lord Alfred Douglas added:

" ... When Peter Amigo Bishop of Southwark uses his power as a Bishop of the Catholic Church to place the Cathedral of his Diocese at the disposal of Irish politicians who are anxious to drag Catholicism in the mire in pursuit of their unscrupulous aims and when this Bishop endorses and upholds the wickedness of those who are attempting to give the honours of martyrdom to a man who has died by his own hand and in a state of determined and obstinate mortal sin it would be idle and ridiculous to blame 'English Catholicism' for this terrible state of affairs ... "

The noble Editor returned to the attack in a later edition of *'Plain English'* but it is fair to relate that he eventually made a full and complete apology to the Bishop for these unwarranted attacks.

Hove, Sussex. (21st November 1935).

"It has been on my conscience for a long time that I ought to write and ask your forgiveness for the attacks I made on you years ago when I was editor of 'Plain English' .... I feel I must write now and say how deeply I regret that I should have attacked you as I did. Please forgive me and pray for me."

On 3rd November 1920 the Bishop made a first attempt to persuade the Government to relax the ban on Archbishop Mannix entering Ireland. Arthur Henderson the Labour Party leader had attended the funeral and the Bishop asked him to use his influence with the Prime Minister. Henderson followed this up but on the 23rd November received a reply that the Government were unable to reconsider their policy with regard to the Archbishop.

Bishop Amigo also did his best to keep Rome informed. He sent a long letter to Cardinal Gasparri, Secretary of State on the 16th December 1920 in which he expressed himself very strongly indeed.

" ... The English Government is trying to force the people of Ireland in a more barbarous fashion than the Germans used against the Belgians during the war. There is a real persecution of our Catholics in Belfast where the workmen are losing their jobs solely on account of their religion .... The savages employed by the Government are men without discipline, even criminals sometimes who with the encouragement of their leaders terrorise the people, invade presbyteries and convents generally after midnight, burn down houses ... commit sacrileges in Churches."

The reference is to the notorious 'Black and Tans' used by the British to subdue Ireland in the months before partition. About this time Cardinal Logue the Primate of Ireland published a pastoral condemning the English actions in Ireland, and the Belgian Hierarchy in a letter backed their Irish colleagues in the struggle. These actions infuriated the ultra-conservative Catholic Union who felt impelled to rush into print to condemn both Hierarchies.

This action in turn caused Bishop Amigo to take up his pen yet again this time to the Editor of the '*Universe*'. In this instance he was backing up the Bishop of Northampton. In his own letter the Bishop of Southwark wrote:

" . . . It seems inconceivable that a body of English laymen should take upon themselves to criticize publicly the action taken by the Hierarchy of two other countries to whom the care of their flocks has been entrusted by God."

This letter drew forth one of the most sarcastic letters the Bishop ever received, from Bernard Trappes-Lomax. (26th December 1920).

"As a member of the Catholic Union and as an English Catholic I beg to make a few observations on your letter and matters to which it gives rise. I will begin by saying that I most cordially approve of Lord Walter Kerr's letter and trust that he will use every possible means to prevent meddlesome interference in the concerns of this country by any foreign potentate whether ecclesiastical or otherwise. The great crime seems to be that an English Gentleman should have dared to criticise the Hierarchy of Belgium and Ireland. I trust that there will always be found someone bold and disinterested enough to resist such a monstrous pretension. Bishops are neither infallible nor impeccable and here we have you rampant at the idea of anyone daring to criticise them. You go on to object to the Catholic Union of Great Britain as not being representative of Catholicity. I may venture to say in reply to this that it is at least as representative as yourself perhaps even more so. For the Catholic Union consists mainly of English Gentlemen while we all know your foreign origin. That a person of your extraction should by some unhappy accident or intrigue have been appointed to an English Bishopric is an insult to English Catholics while that you should set up as their representative or as a critic of their representatives is nothing but an impertinence."

Bernard Trappes-Lomax was a distinguished historian and expert in heraldry. Perhaps that accounts for the word 'rampant' in the above letter! The letter represents a kind of insular nationalism now almost forgotten.

82   *Amigo—Friend of the Poor*

Irish affairs crept into pastoral letters at this time. The Advent
Pastoral of Bishop Amigo for 1920 dealing with British so-called
reprisals says:

" . . . To tolerate, much more to condone such deplorable acts is to sap
the moral foundations of Government and it is the duty of Bishop
Priests and people to raise their voices in earnest protest against
them. We must not sin against the law of God . . . "

Bishop Amigo's views on Ireland were not shared by Cardinal
Bourne. On 13th February 1921 Cardinal Bourne had a message read out
in all the Churches of the Archdiocese of Westminster. The key wording
was:

" . . . I have grave reason to fear that some of my own flock impelled
by legitimate love of country and urgent longing for the realisation of
lawful aspirations are unwaveringly allowing themselves to become
implicated by active sympathy or even actual co-operation in societies
and organisations which are in opposition to the laws of God and of
the Catholic Church . . . .
. . . Parliament will meet again next week with the firm purpose it
is to be hoped of dealing justly and promptly with this tragedy of
Ireland."

To this message Cardinal Bourne attached the Pastoral Letter of
Cardinal Manning on Fenianism originally written in 1867 to be read
out after his own message. It must have caused several listeners to nod
off both when originally issued and when repeated in 1921 for it takes
over half an hour to read out! The Westminster Gazette however recalls
that there was a strong protest made at the Church of Corpus Christi
Maiden Lane when one gentleman shouted out "I protest as a Catholic
and an Irishman against an Englishman attacking us. It is disgraceful."
Considerable excitement followed in the Church and cries of 'Hear
Hear' came from all round the building.

The Cardinal's letter led a leading Irish MP Mr. Jeremiah McVeagh,
to write to the *'Times'* and castigate the Cardinal in no uncertain terms.

"If he has a shred of sympathy with the Irish people in the agonies
through which they are at present passing, he has succeeded in
keeping it under control; and I cannot recall that he uttered a word of
condemnation or extended a helping hand when his co-religionists
were being hunted from the factories, mills and workshops of Belfast

for no other crime than that they worship God at the same altar as himself . . . ." (Letter of 15th Feb 1921)

In fairness to Cardinal Bourne it must be pointed out that after it became clear that the Black and Tans were committing atrocities that no one could deny, then he in turn condemned there atrocities.

The Bishop had been in Rome in January 1921 briefing the Pope Benedict XV and the Secretary of State about Irish affairs amongst other business. There was some talk of a Papal pronouncement on the troubles. The Bishop sent a copy of Mr. McVeagh's letter to to Mgr. Cerotti, assistant at the Secretariat of State. He pointed out that it would be unwise of the Pope to speak while feelings were evidently running so high.

"It is my deep love for the Vicar of Christ which made me beg your Grace to put before His Holiness the difficulty of making any pronouncement on Irish affairs at present" (16th February 1921)

Cardinal Logue wrote to the Bishop on the 17th a letter describing in detail specific atrocities committed by the Black and Tans from the Gormanstown Garrison. This is the central part of what Cardinal Logue wrote:

"Things are becoming worse as days pass. It is a terrible thing to look on helplessly at the sacrifice of so many young lives and the destruction of so much valuable property.

With the assistance of the priests I have done my best to keep things quiet in this Diocese. Hitherto we have had comparative peace; but the forces of the Crown seem determined we shall suffer like the rest.

There is a camp of Black and Tans at Gormanstown on the borders of the Diocese; and while that camp remains we may give up all hopes of peace or safety. It seems to be a nest of bandits and homicides.

In the month of December they visited Ardee, a country town which was and is perfectly peaceful. As far as I could ascertain there was not a murder in that whole district for a hundred years. Those guardians of the peace invaded the house of the principal merchant, and carried away a quantity of goods to the amount of £150.

Their next visit to Ardee was made under their officers in lorries, some of the men having their faces blackened. They dragged two poor young men out of bed, in small hours of the morning and shot them dead. Others would have met the same fate, but fortunately took the alarm in time and were absent when sought for. Their last exploit in Ardee was to seize the whole stock in trade of two young people, a brother and sister, and load it on their lorries. These young people kept a drapers shop, and there was nothing left to them, hardly a reel of thread. Their loss amounted to £1,500 or £2,000 and now they are ruined.

The people about Drogheda and the surrounding country will soon be reduced to beggary. Their houses are raided day and night on pretext of a search, and money, valuables and anything that can be carried away seized at the point of the revolver. As an instance, one man who was raided and lost heavily some time since has just lost £400 in a second raid. Those who sell cattle or farm produce have not time to put the money in the bank for safety before it is seized upon. The poor people are afraid to complain lest their houses should be burned down.

Hitherto it was only robbery in the Drogheda district. Now bloodshed has commenced. A few nights since, two young men, fathers of families, were taken from their beds at dead of night, brought to a lonely place by armed men, and were found shot dead there next morning.

There is not even the excuse of reprisals for this action. There was no crime in Drogheda and the district, except the robberies to which I have referred. You may judge, my dear Lord, how vain it is to counsel peace or secure a spirit of peace and charity in such surroundings."

On the 21st February 1921, the Bishop made what may well have been his most decisive intervention. Cardinal Logue's letter had listed particular examples of the brutality of the Black and Tans. So in order to press home the point he arranged to send copies of this letter to several important figures in public life including the King, the Archbishop of Canterbury, and Sir Robert Cecil MP. The letter was carefully timed to be received before a big debate in both Houses of Parliament. Sir Robert Cecil obliged by actually reading the Cardinal's letter in the Commons. Randall Davidson, Archbishop of Canterbury, condemned the Black and Tans in the Lords. Lord Stanfordham, Secretary to King George V wrote back to Bishop Amigo on the 10th March.

"Please accept my apologies for the unavoidable delay in replying to your letter of 21st February in which you enclosed a letter to you from Cardinal Logue and which is returned herewith. Both letters were submitted to the King and by His Majesty's orders referred to the responsible authorities. The King is assured that in accordance with the invariable rule in dealing with all charges against the Troops, Constabulary or the so-called Black and Tans, the cases mentioned by the Cardinal have been carefully investigated but the concluding reports are not all yet to hand. His Majesty is deeply concerned at the deplorable condition of affairs still existing in Ireland."

The debate in Parliament at the end of February can be seen as a turning point. It became clear at long last that public opinion was running against Lloyd George's Government on the Irish question. The 'Times' had consistently opposed him. The Prime Minister shortly after, started negotiations. To start with Ulster was separated and King George V went over to inaugurate the new Parliament on 22nd June. His sympathy with the plight of the Irish could still be seen although he was bound by the conventions of his high office. As the editorial in the 'Times' put it on 23rd June ... "As is his wont, he rigidly observed the conditions of his high office; but in that very observance he showed how little they could restrict his sympathy, his foresight and his understanding."

In July 1921 Lloyd George at last started negotiations with De Valera. The Bishop attended the Royal Garden Party on 21st July and afterwards sent this letter to Lord Stamfordham.

"Though I had the honour of shaking hands with the King at the Garden Party on July 21st there was no opportunity of speaking to his Majesty when so many were anxious to see him. Will you kindly assure the King that many of those under my spiritual care here are deeply grateful for the sympathy which he has shown to Ireland. I hope that His Majesty's words at Belfast will bring about that peace between England and Ireland which all of us so earnestly desire."

When the Treaty was finally concluded the Bishop wrote again to Lord Stamfordham on 11th December 1921.

"... Since his gracious words at Belfast last June, I have always impressed upon my Irish friends that they have the real sympathy of King George. His Majesty has richly deserved this and when the truth is known he will certainly secure the deep gratitude of the Irish people by exercising his powerful personal influence in favour of peace ...."

Lord Stamfordham replied the following day.

"The King to whom I have communicated the contents of your letter of yesterday's date, greatly appreciates what you are good enough to say regarding the agreement come to on the Irish question; and your association of His Majesty's name with this important step towards the establishment of Peace in Ireland. The King is indeed thankful and all the more so in the thought that he may have assisted towards this happy achievement."

Bishop Amigo did not take any side or made any public statement over the troubles that beset the emerging Republic. He did however officiate at a solemn Requiem for Michael Collins and Arthur Griffith who were both killed during those turbulent months which followed independence. This act of kindness drew forth yet another abusive letter from Lord Alfred Douglas who claimed that the Bishop had incurred an excommunication for saying Mass for those who were themselves excommunicate!

In 1924 the Bishop was invited by the Catholic Truth Society of Ireland to give the concluding address at their Annual Conference in October of that year. The Bishop fell seriously ill at that time and could not attend and he received a personal letter of sympathy from President Cosgrave. The Bishop did in fact re-visit Ireland during 1927. In that same year he received a presentation portrait, painted by Sir John Lavery. The Irish people had wished for a public presentation but the Bishop stated that he wished only for a small private ceremony. The portrait had been commissioned by Mr. Charles Diamond who made the presentation in association with Mr. Francis Wellesley K.S.C.G. The latter said that the Bishop had chosen his line of action not when it was clear as to 'how the cat would jump', but when to take that line meant sacrifice and even calumny. The Bishop in reply said that the inscription on the portrait referred to courageous and statesmanlike action, but he desired to dissociate himself from that idea. He was not a Statesman nor a politician and what he had done was not a matter of Statesmanship or Politics at all, it was something he thought became him as a Bishop and he hoped that in the same circumstances he would do the same again. The wording on the portrait which hangs today in Archbishop's House Southwark reads as follows:

"Presented to the Right Rev. Dr. Amigo, Bishop of Southwark, by a number of his admirers in appreciation of his courageous and statesmanlike attitude on the Irish Question during a vital period in the History of that Country. September 1927."

Chapter 8

The Education Question

Throughout his life Bishop Amigo had a keen interest in the education of the young. Reading through his pastoral letters one cannot but be impressed by the zeal and determination he gave to the problem of securing Catholic Schools in the Diocese. As the Diocese continued to grow, many new parishes were erected and an effort was made wherever possible to provide a school as well as a Church for the locality. All this work was undertaken in spite of the near crippling debts that the Diocese had incurred at an earlier period. However this chapter would make very dull reading if it simply enumerated the schools built during his episcopate. What is more interesting for the general reader is to consider what part Bishop Amigo played in the national struggle for Catholic Schools.

When the Bishop took over the Diocese, education in this country was covered by the recently passed Balfour Act of 1902. This act marked the opening of a new chapter in education in this country. Financial relief was provided for Church Schools. The main difficulty to be overcome for the Government was to secure some public control of Church Schools as a condition for further state assistance without destroying their religious character. Under the Balfour Act the Church Schools became known as Non-Provided schools and on their governing body of six managers, four were to be appointed by the Church authorities and two by the local Education Authority. In return the cost of site and building of the school would fall entirely on the Church as would the cost of all external repairs. The Education Authority would pay all the running expenses of the school (salaries, books, furniture) *and* the cost of internal repairs.

Non-conformist bodies objected strongly to the new arrangements and the cry went up "Rome on the Rates." The Liberal Party supported the non-conformists and it boded ill for supporters of the Church Schools when the Liberals were returned to power in 1906.

Possibly as a response to the threat they saw coming the Hierarchy issued a statement in 1905 urging very strongly that all Catholic children be sent to Catholic Schools.

"We desire to call the earnest attention of all Catholics to the grave departure from Catholic teaching and tradition and to the very serious dangers to Catholic faith and spirit which are involved in the placing of Catholic children of whatever class in life, in non-Catholic schools. Owing to the usually proximate nature of these dangers, it is under ordinary circumstances a grievous sin on the part of parents to expose their children to such risks and this has been expressly declared in the Instructions of the Holy See and of the Bishops of the Province." (paragraph 1)

The third paragraph stated:

"No individual Priest or Confessor is entitled to decide where necessity of this nature exists, but the matter is one to be referred to the Ordinary of the Diocese for his counsel and judgement."

This declaration was repeated quite regularly over the next few years. The Southwark Archives possess about fifty letters asking for exemption and most of these letters date from 1906. It was really quite impossible to make it a general rule as there were not enough Catholic Schools to place all the pupils even at primary level.

In the first session of the New Parliament, Mr. Augustine Birrell, the new Minister Responsible for Education, introduced a Bill to secure full public control of Church Schools, which would include appointment of teachers without regard to religious belief. Despite intense Catholic agitation this Bill was passed by the House of Commons with a large majority. But the House of Lords for political as well as religious reasons altered the Bill fundamentally so that the Commons refused to accept it as amended and it was withdrawn.

There exists in our archives however an interesting memo drawn up I think by Father (later Bishop) Brown of Vauxhall, the Vicar General and expert on education matters. This memo indicates that the Irish Members of the House of Commons voted to reject the amendments of the House of Lords although these amendments were favourable to the Catholic cause. Thus according to Fr. Brown they had overthrown all the good work done by the Peers and it is said they had the backing of the

English Hierarchy for their actions. It must be understood that at this period Ireland sent members to Westminster and that these members led at that time by Mr. John Redmond, were in effect Liberals as the Liberals had promised Home Rule to Ireland. Possibly the Hierarchy did not want to force the Irish MP's to vote against the Government which might soon grant them Home Rule.

At the end of 1909 a grave constitution crisis had arisen over the power of the House of Lords and a General Election was scheduled to take place in 1910. It was decided that certain questions be put to all candidates standing for election as to whether they would support the Catholic Schools Policy of the Hierarchy. However a controversy arose as to what questions should be put and how many questions.

Two organisations then in existence to further the Catholic cause, the Catholic Federation and the Catholic League of South London, drew up a set of three questions, one about Catholic Education, one about inspection by Government Inspectors of Convents and one on the King's Accession Delcaration. In other Dioceses different questions were being proposed so to settle the disputes, the Hierarchy issued a Pastoral Letter for 26th December 1909. The relevant wording was:

"To help our Catholic voters to arrive at a true judgement on this grave issue, we order that the following question be proposed, in such manner as each Ordinary shall prescribe to all Parliamentary candidates:- 'Will you, if returned to Parliament, do all in your power to secure just treatment for Catholic Schools, so that, while preserving their Catholic character and management (including the appointment of teachers), for the maintenance of which they have been built at an enormous cost to the Catholics of this country, they shall receive from public sources the same financial assistance as that which is accorded to other publicly recognised schools, holding the same educational position?'

In order that this issue may not be obscured we desire that on this occasion no other question even though it affect the other Catholic disabilities be proposed to any candidate on behalf of Catholics. We beg the clergy to abstain from all allusion in Church to the political crisis except in so far as it may be necessary to do so in order to urge the Faithful to fervent prayer, or to make known the answers of the Parliamentary candidates."

Mr. M. J. Fitzgerald of the Southwark Catholic Federation made a speech at their next meeting in January which might just be construed as critical of this letter. He said:

> "As to whether that question is as good as our own, every individual Catholic must form his own opinion and every individual Catholic is simply bound by the moral law to vote according to his conscience and it is perfectly clear that the question is exceedingly easy for a candidate of either party to answer. I do not think that there is either intention or motive to slight in the slightest degree, the work done by this Federation."

However, as reported in the *'Universe'* it came over as rather more of an attack on the Bishops. Bishop Amigo was evidently furious. Although his own letter is not available, the reply of Mr. Fitzgerald is to hand. In fact four letters were exchanged before the Bishop accepted that the *'Universe'* had got it wrong. The matter was only cleared when Fitzgerald was able to produce a transcript of his speech and send it to the Bishop.

One of the great workers for Catholic education in London was Sir John Gilbert. On the 15th February 1909 Bishop Amigo wrote to him:

> "I most earnestly hope that the L.C.C. will continue to have you on its Education Committee. Your zeal and devotion have made you be appreciated on that committee, and your presence there as a Catholic educationalist has ensured their knowing the needs of the Catholic body. With the best intention in the world, justice cannot be fully done to us in this important matter of education, unless we have a Catholic like yourself to explain our position. We in London know your work on our own Education Committee and as manager of a large school. You are standing for a part of London very near to my heart, and I am sure that my old parishioners will do all they can to ensure your election. Wishing you every Grace and Blessing."

In two constituencies of the Diocese, Dulwich and Sidcup, there were serious problems. In each instance the local Irish League backed the Liberal candidate and opposed the Parish Priest who clearly supported the Conservative. The Dulwich case is the more interesting.

On the 13th January the Parish Priest, Fr. Francis Fulton O.S.B., wrote to the Conservative candidate, none other than the great Mr. Bonar Law as follows:

> "I write to say that I wish you every success on Monday next. Our

Catholic Bishops have urged us to make the Education question the one issue at this Election. On this point you and the Conservative party are sound while Mr. Asquith has made it perfectly plain that if his Party is returned to power he means to attack our schools again. I hope that every Catholic in Dulwich will record his Vote in your favour."

Mr. Bonar Law then used this letter as a 'handout' printed in red and headed "Roman Catholic Electors; Read This."

The United Irish League responded with a handout headed "To the Irish Electors of Dulwich." The key words in the handout were:

"This is the first time since 1892 that full Self-Government for Ireland has been made a leading issue at a General Election and on this occasion the Liberal Ministers are pledged not only to the policy of Home Rule but what is in our eyes of equal importance, they are pledged to the means necessary to carry that policy into effect; for they are solemnly pledged never again to accept office until they are furnished with powers to overcome the veto of the House of Lords. In these circumstances an Irish Nationalist Organisation can have no hesitation in directing all Irishmen to vote at the coming Election for the Liberal Candidate, Mr. Evan Cotton."

On the Sunday following the publication of the Liberal Handout the handbills were distributed at the Church by a young man. What happened next is best described in the protest letter sent by the local representatives of the Irish League to Bishop Amigo.

"On Sunday morning when some handbills (one of which I enclose) were being innocently and without any intentions distributed outside the Church by a youth, Fr. Fulton stopped the distribution and from the Altar said if it occurred again he would call down from the Altar the curse of God on the offender and on his family .... I deeply regret to have to complain but Irish Catholics cannot submit to have their feelings outraged in this way ...."

Bishop Amigo wrote at once to Fr. Fulton demanding to know what happened. The key parts of a lengthy reply run as follows:

"During the five years that I have been in Dulwich, a small but noisy faction of political Irish have persistently adopted a policy of trying to bring politics into this Church distributing their political leaflets at the Church doors. At the time of the last L.C.C. elections I had to forbid any political literature being so distributed ... forseeing what might occur (this time) and to guard against it, I put down in the Notices and had read out on Sunday last an order that no political literature was to be distributed at the Church doors, no matter to what political party they belong. I had refused permission to the Unionist Agent to allow my letter to Mr. Bonar Law to be so distributed ... (the letter goes on to describe how letters were distributed at the first Mass) ... At the two Masses that followed I told the flock how my orders had been disobeyed and I said I would denounce from the Altar anyone who in future attempted to bring politics into the Church and that I would call the curse of God upon them."

Even so I should imagine that the average reader would be astonished to hear that a Parish Priest even at that time could have acted in this way. Later on in his letter he indicated that he personally had dragged the issue into the school room by asking rhetorical questions of the children.

"Have your shools been attacked? Answer. Yes. By whom and since when? By the Liberal Government for the last four years."

The Parish Priest should never have let his name be used in a political handout of course. But the Irish side too were in the wrong for dragging in Home Rule when all they need have done was mention that Mr. Cotton too was entirely favourable to the Catholic side in the school issue!

Bishop Amigo dealt with the education problem in his Pastoral Letter of November 1909. This prompted Hilaire Belloc, who was standing for Parliament at that time, to reply:

"I am in receipt of your Lordship's Pastoral Letter which I have read with the greatest interest, and I am particularly anxious for a more detailed knowledge of the point upon which you touch upon page 4. I have the greatest dislike and contempt for Runciman. I do not trust him and I believe him to be an active enemy of the principles of toleration which he professes. Mr. Birrell I have always liked. He has a sincere and kindly mind and McKenna is simply null with no particular objects at the Education Office or anywhere else. But Runciman is dangerous.

If I am returned at this election and if there is a Liberal majority, I should like to take up the question of the secondary schools in some detail, but I do not understand it in the least as yet. I only know the broad fact that by differentiating financially between training schools which insist on a particular religious tone and those which do not, and by doing this by administrative order, the Board of Education is putting a handicap upon us. No parliamentary majority upon one issue like this can be conceived. The only thing that does good is for as many private members as possible to get the thing publicly known by questions, and the most valuable result is produced if one can convince the front bench that the Minister in question has by some blunder weakened the support of some proportion of the electorate.

I will not trouble your Lordship at the present moment. I only mention it as a subject which I desire to make myself familiar with if I am returned at the coming election.

Whether I will be so returned or no is a question more difficult to answer than a similar question with regard to any other Lancashire division. I am the only Catholic Member returned by Lancashire, and yet one quarter of that enormous population is Catholic! To be known as a Catholic Member and to have to specially defend Catholic questions in the House leads to any amount of cross-voting in one's constituency. But the general effect is prejudicial."

The education issue lay dormant during the war years until 1918 when the Education Minister was Mr. H. A. L. Fisher. He introduced and had passed an act by which a proportion of children at Elementary schools (we call them Primary schools today) would go on to Central or Secondary Schools at the age of 11. The problem for Catholics was that there were very few secondary schools available for Catholics at that time and they would usually have to go on to non-Catholic or State Schools. This act also provided for what were to be known as "Day continuation schools" whereby children who left school at 14 should continue their education on a part-time basis in the evenings for about eight hours a week. This part of the Bill was not fully implemented.

In 1920 he introduced another measure which would virtually have ended the dual system of education altogether. It was a time of great distress and shortage of funds following the war and expenditure had to be cut to a minimum. In outline the scheme provided that a grant be made to existing schools only for their alteration and enlargement to cover the raising of the school leaving age. It did not apply to the building of any new schools. The grant was only to be given on the condition that teachers pass under the control of the Education Authorities and that only a fixed number may be appointed to give religious instruction. These teachers were not to be appointed until and unless the managers were satisfied as to the teacher's willingness and competence to give religious instruction. Clearly this Bill was by no means intended as a full solution to Catholic problems but it found support among members of the Church of England. Bishop Amigo wrote to the Archbishop of Liverpool on 7th April 1920 and the letter hints at the degree of confusion which existed at that time in Catholic circles as to the best method of tackling the school problem. (This letter exists in draft form in the archives . . . hence strange expressions at times. HE means Cardinal Bourne. Mr. F. is Mr. Fisher):

"Again urge that we ought to have a meeting of the Bishops quam primum in regard to Mr. F's proposals. If . . . can conveniently come by all means let him do so but in the present state of his health we ought not to press him and the Bishops should meet even if he cannot be there. HE has been approached by Mr. F and your Grace acknowledges that he called a meeting of a few some two months ago, you being the only other member of the Hierarchy. Mr. F addresses himself to HE not as to a private person but as to the representative of the Catholic Church in this country. Mr. F does not know that there is such a constitution as the Episcopal Conference and that his Eminence is bound to hear all the Bishops in dealing with the Gov. It is for HE to state this clearly when consulted on such occasions. Secret diplomacy is objected to nowadays and rightly. If HE is free to consult experts a fortiori was he bound to ask the opinion of the Hierarchy. Mr. F does not mean this to be merely an academic question. The fact of his consulting Canterbury and the non-conformists as well as HE shows that he is in earnest about it. I know from Mgr. Brown that Cantab. has told him that the Church of England have agreed to accept the proposals and that the non-conformists with the exception of Dr. Clifford, have also been ready. Our Catholic papers and our people expect a lead and we ought to tell them what should be done. The matter brooks no delay and the Gov. should be told officially by the Bishops this time the Catholic Body means to take action while we must prepare our people before the proposals are formally put forward in a Bill. In 1906 the Gov. had a bigger majority when the Birrell Bill was before the country. We fought against the Bill and we won. The danger to our schools is greater because our position is weakened. We can save our schools now by the United action of the Bishops and we are bound in conscience to act. No Apb. except HE has the *right* to call us together but nobody can stop our meeting if we ourselves are willing to come together. If the Bishops realised the critical situation they would all wish to have concerted action. Your Grace has always been looked up to as the lover of the schools. Through the illness of the two Senior Archbishops, the saving of the schools depends chiefly upon you. It is not merely Lancashire, the whole of England has to be considered, as if we go under now in other parts, Lancs will also come under general system before very long however powerful the Catholics there may be. The Bp. of Notts has kindly sent me a copy of his correspondence with your Grace, and I have talked the matter over with the B of Northampton who is thoroughly with me."

The point was that the Archbishop of Liverpool was quite satisfied with the arrangements for Catholic schools and did not see the need for action. In the event the 1920 Fisher Bill was withdrawn.

In 1926 the important Hadow Report was published urging the raising of the school leaving age to 15 and the creation of secondary education for all by making a complete break at the age of 11. After that there would be secondary, senior (or grammar) and technical schools to suit ability.

At this point it is well to remind the reader that in 1918 the Government had passed the Education (Scotland) Act which settled once and for all the problem of Catholic Schools north of the border. Under this act the Churches agreed to sell or lease their buildings and the management of schools and provision of future schools was placed in the hands of the local Education Authorities, while staff appointments were to be in the hands of the Education Authority but in full collaboration with the Churches before the appointments were made. Mgr. Brown played a large part in negotiating this Act. In England we were never offered these terms but in 1931 the Labour Government of the day came very close as we shall see.

The 1920's were a time of continuing confusion among Catholic authorities. Cardinal Bourne produced a scheme whereby each pupil would have a voucher whereby the parents as it were "bought" education. This scheme was torn to pieces by Bishop Brown (he became Bishop of Pella, auxiliary to Bishop Amigo in 1924). It had not been thought through properly, particularly in its financial details. Meanwhile the Bishop of Shrewsbury came up with a complicated and inefficient scheme whereby the Education Authority would make a "payment for the use of the school" instead of the costs of maintenance. At the same time the Bishop of Hexham came up with a plan whereby the Board of Education would pay the extra 50% of maintenance at present covered by the managers. The funding would be arranged by creating a special sinking fund in each Diocese or province from which grants would be made to individual authorities controlling the schools in each area. This plan had the backing of the Hierarchy and the Catholic Education Council for a time.

Meanwhile individual authorities during the 1920's tended to try and take things into their own hands. One example which concerns our story is that the Kent Education Committee proposed a scheme in 1926 to effectively take over the Catholic Schools in its area. The Draft concordat they prepared allowed for two periods of religious instruction per week in the 'former' non-provided (voluntary) schools, while the rest of the teaching would be non-denominational. The ownership of these schools would be joint in that during school hours they would be controlled by the Education Authority while the rest of the time they would be in the hands of the Trustees who could use them for their own purposes out of school hours. Existing teachers would stay on in each school but no guarantee was given that when they moved they would be replaced by Catholics. The details of the concordat were sent out on the 17th May. One can only imagine what Bishop Amigo thought when he read of this scheme. He did not even bother to reply in person leaving that task to the Schools Secretary of the time, Fr. Alfred Wright:

"The Bishop of Southwark has carefully considered with his Advisers your draft 'concordat' inspired by the difficulties arising from dual control of elementary schools. He instructs me to say that the proposals are contrary to the principles and practice of the Catholic Church in England, and he cannot give his approval to them, either as a whole or in their several parts. No good or useful purpose, therefore, can be served by his appointing a representative to meet the special sub-committee on 21st June."

This letter was sent out on the 5th June 1926.

The following year the Kent Authority decided to open a secondary school for girls in Dartford to be followed by one for boys later. The Catholic Church objected to the scheme in that it would deprive their own elementary school of its top classes who would then receive no further Catholic education and the Authority seemed set on making sure that all pupils in junior schools would be transferred to their new secondary schools at all costs.

Before the election of 1929 Bishop Amigo arranged that in each constituency a deputation of electors both men and women should interview the candidates in each constituency submitting an enclosed question and to secure if possible a reply in writing. This at least was better than the arrangement proposed in 1910 and is similar to that obtaining today. In 1929 the question was put:

> "Do you agree to the principle that the same amount of public money should be expended on schools in which definite religious teaching is given as is expended on schools in which no such teaching is given? And in the case of Catholic Schools will you endeavour to persuade your party to introduce and will you support any measure which is framed so as to give effect to that principle which does not infringe the existing rights of Catholic managers and by whatsoever government it is introduced?"

In the event a Labour administration was formed under Ramsay McDonald and it proved itself to be very co-operative indeed about the Catholic claims. Indeed there appeared to be a real chance of something like justice for our schools when the financial crisis of 1931 intervened and brought about the creation of a National Government which had no cash to spare on education. The story however deserves to be told in a little more detail.

Before the election took place Labour Party Headquarters sent a copy of a memorandum to Sir John Gilbert who sent it on to Bishop Amigo. This memorandum was produced by Mr. Ramsay McDonald for all his candidates at the coming election in 1919. The letter to Gilbert was sent on 12th April. In this memorandum it is pointed out that the Scottish Act on Education is not really applicable in England because there are 5,000 single school areas in England and Wales controlled mainly by the Church of England. Also if the Labour Party met the claims of the Catholics in full it would re-open the old wounds of 1902 again. So their candidates will not give specific pledges but the whole question can be considered at a conference between local Education Authorities, the Board of Education and religious interests. The Labour Party would only act after an agreement had been reached.

On the 13th May Bishop Amigo wrote to Mr. McDonald asking that his candidates would draw attention to the calling of the conference in their election speeches. Mr. McDonald replied on 20th May 1929.

"Thank you so much for your note. I shall do what you suggest. I have
been very much surprised, however to find that the leading Catholic
newspapers seem to have treated the memorandum in a very hostile
spirit, and that has put up the backs of some of our people. However,
what is said in the memorandum will be done."

The Bishop was then drawn into a sharp controversy in the Liverpool Exchange Division. Both the Conservative and Labour candidates
were Catholics. The Labour candidate Mr. W. A. Robinson had communicated with Dr. Amigo about the memorandum sent out by Mr.
McDonald. At a public meeting on 27th May 1909 at St. Simon's
Schools, Russell Street, Mr. Robinson announced that the Bishop had
sent him a telegram to the effect that he was quite satisfied with the
statement from Mr. Ramsay McDonald in regard to Catholic Schools.

The meeting was reported in the *Liverpool Daily Post* next day and
this drew a furious response from a Mr. D. W. Clarke, a Liverpool
businessman. He sent the Bishop a cutting from the very same paper
describing a meeting of the Conservative candidate when certain
Labour supporters threw stink bombs at the platform. Here are some
extracts from his accompanying letter:

" . . . I also beg to enclose a cutting from the same paper reporting the
rowdyism of the supporters of the Labour candidate at the meeting of
Sir James Reynolds Bart, who is the most influential Catholic in
Liverpool and who was High Sheriff of Lancashire last year. I enclose
this cutting to give you an idea of the type of working people your
telegram lends support to and I feel reluctantly compelled to say it to
your Lordship, but I must say that it reads very much like that of your
being somewhat of a traitor in the camp in the present opportune
agitation for justice to Catholic schools . . . . I cannot see why a Bishop
at the other end of England should allow himself to be drawn into an
expression of opinion and by telegram with Liverpool . . . By your
action you have lent your name and high position to a particular
political party who will make the most of it. Your action . . . recalls to
my mind the action of certain Bishops at the time of the Reformation
in England and that of Dr. Dollinger in regard to the Vatican Council.
There always seems to be one who will queer the pitch . . . . To say the
least your telegram was a blazing indiscretion that one would hardly
expect to emanate from a Catholic Bishop . . . ."

One might well ask why indeed did the Bishop send such a telegram.

The answer is that His Lordship had already become well known as a champion of the poor and was well known also for his interest in the education problem. There was no particular secret either about his acceptance in good faith of the Labour Party Memorandum. In retrospect it was a serious mistake for the Catholic Press to make attacks on the Labour Party in that election. The Conservatives had done very little to help the cause since 1902. It must also be borne in mind that the Labour party in Liverpool at that time had opposed the Archbishop of Liverpool on certain issues, and that Bishop Amigo was about the only Bishop known publicly to accept the McDonald Memorandum.

When Labour was duly returned to power Sir Charles Trevelyan became the Minister responsible for Education. He tried three times to introduce Bills to raise the school leaving age. Each time the Bills were lost. Throughout the whole period of the Labour government negotiations were conducted with the Catholic authorities. In November 1929 matters had not proceeded very far. The Hierarchy produced a resolution on 14th November:

"The Bishops are of the opinion that any grant given to provided schools to enable them to meet the requirements of the Board of Education should in equity be given also to the non-provided schools."

At this stage the proposals of Sir John Trevelyan did not seem to include any special grant for voluntary schools at all. A conference on the question of aid to non-provided schools was finally held at the invitation of Sir Charles on the 13th and 14th January 1931. The Church of England, the Free Churches were represented. For the Catholics the representatives were Cardinal Bourne, the Archbishop of Cardiff, Mr. F. Blundell JP and Mr. John Scurr MP who played a large part in events around that time. The result of this conference was the publishing of Circular 3786 "Proposals for Aid to Non-Provided Schools." The main terms of this document were as follows:

"Associations of schools may be constituted in the area of any Local Education Authority, representative of the Managers of the schools of any particular Denomination and of its Church Authorities."

These Associations were empowered to make agreements with the local authority.

"Schools which come within an agreement shall be aided towards the necessary improvements or re-conditioning to the extent in the original agreement of not less than 50% and not more than 75% of the cost by the Local Education Authority.

The Local Authority shall have power to make future improvements and shall be able to pay THE WHOLE or such proportion of the cost as may be agreed in each case. The duty of the Managers to keep the Schoolhouse in repair remains unaffected."

"Teachers are to be in the employment of the Local Education Authority and are to be appointed and dismissed by them."

"The agreement shall lay down how many teachers shall be reserved as having religious qualifications . . . ."

Three different systems of appointing the reserved (i.e. Catholic) teachers were suggested, each allowing the managers of the school a say in regard to the teachers competence and religious suitability.

Now this arrangement although not a full solution for the Catholic School problem was intended as the basis for such a settlement. The proposals as set down in Circular 3786 were substantially those worked by Mr. John Scurr and Mr. Oldfield, the two leading Catholic MP's in the field of education.

On the 18th November preceding, Mr. Scurr had sent to Bishop Amigo his proposals (sent also to Sir John Trevelyan). Here he proposed a 50% absolute grant (for re-development) plus 50% as a loan from the Government. He also suggested the same three ways in which the reserved teachers might be appointed by the local authority. On the 3rd and 4th December Mr. Oldfield wrote letters to Bishop Amigo describing the speech made by Mr. Scurr to an amendment of Mr. Ramsbotham MP which asked that any extensions etc. to voluntary schools should be delayed until Bills were passed that arranged that Local Education Authorities should pay for the said changes. Oldfield added that conversations on this point were under way but formed only a partial settlement which might pave the way for a final solution. The conference of the 13th and 14th January which produced the White Paper had been agreed by all parties at the time, including Mr. Scurr. Now although the Rowbotham amendment was rejected in December, Mr. Scurr had spoken of introducing his own amendment, very similar to that of Rowbotham, if the negotiations due to take place (at the conference) failed. On 20th December (still before the conference) Scurr tabled his amendment for the report stage which was deferred till after Christmas. On 27th December Mr. Trevelyan announced the conference, and the report stage of the Bill was rescheduled to take place on 20th January and 21st January, that is, after the conference. Just before the conference the Catholic Bishops ordered exposition of the Blessed Sacrament to prepare for the conference by prayer.

When the report stage came up however, Mr. Scurr left his amendments in for discussion and they were passed. The effect of the Scurr amendment was to delay the passing of the act "until the (new) Act authorising expenditure out of public funds to meet costs incurred by the managers of non-provided schools in meeting the provisions of this act, was passed." Now the Scurr amendment was effectually a defeat for the Government as all the Catholic Labour MP's voted for the amendment against the Government wishes. This has been hailed by most writers on education matters up to now as a great triumph for the Catholics. I would question this attitude. It would have been far better to let the act go through as was the original intention and then introduce the new legislation. Scurr had said earlier that he would not press his amendment if the negotiations were successful. As all parties had agreed to the White Paper one may conclude that the negotiations *were* in fact successful. So why the amendments?

It appears that between the appearance of the White Paper and the report stage of the Bill, some Catholics had questioned whether the guarantees for the appointment of teachers were entirely satisfactory.

Another puzzle is why the Government then let their ruined Bill go on to the House of Lords before introducing the new act to help the Catholics. The Lords threw the Bill out with Lord Hailsham saying he thought the rejection of the Bill would assist Catholics more than accepting it. Trevelyan then resigned as Minister of Education. In the event this was nearest Catholics ever got to the 100% grant. If the limited relief could have been passed in 1931 it would have surely provided the basis for a more just settlement than that achieved in 1944.

It would seem then that the reluctance of the Catholic authorities to concede anything on the appointment of teachers to the local authorities sounded the death bell of the attempts of the Labour Government to bring about any settlement. Later in 1931 under the great emergency and financial crisis a national government was formed.

In 1936 a new Education Bill again provided that grants could be paid for the building or extension of Church Schools but only in connection with the raising of the school leaving age and only to proposals that were submitted before 1940. The grant would vary from 50% to 75% the costs being agreed between the managers and the local Education

Authorities. Such schools became known as "special agreement" schools. The appointment and dismissal of teachers was transferred to the local authority subject to rights of the managers to have religious instruction given by a number of reserved (Catholic) teachers, the number of such teachers to be agreed mutually between the managers and the local authority.

We come now to consider the Butler Education Act of 1944 which was to finally enforce the recommendations of the Hadow and later Spens (1938) Report on Secondary Education. Negotiations started in 1942 between Mr. Butler and the various interested parties. However the Catholic Church was about the last major organisation to be consulted in any way and by the time Mr. Butler got round to consulting them the main terms of the Bill were already clear. Bishop Amigo was actively involved in the negotiations as he was on a small committee set up to help in the negotiations. The key letter here is the one sent by Mr. Butler on 16th September 1942 to Bishop Amigo. The full text of this letter can be found in Appendix No. IV. The letter shows clearly that Mr. Butler had already worked out the entire scheme for fitting in Catholic schools at this point, although it would be two years before the Bill was passed through Parliament. In June 1942 Mr. Butler had already written to Sir Patrick Hannon, a leading Catholic MP that he was then about to consult the Church of England authorities. The Catholics were left to the end of the line! After Butler's letter was received, the Bishop replied on 16th November 1942:

> "I submitted your letter of the 16th Sept to the individual Bishops, and they met on Thursday October 29th to discuss your proposals. The first alternative was, as your anticipated, unacceptable to them; its provisions would, they consider, destroy the Catholic character of our schools.
>
> They gave long and careful consideration to the second alternative, although they recognised at once that the actual terms would leave us with a burden which it would be impossible for us to support. The Hierarchy recognised with gratitude that this proposal marked an unprecedented step forwards towards a sympathetic appreciation of our needs. They noted with pleasure that the Government was in favour of a continuation of the dual system and wished to enable us to persevere in our present contribution to the national system of education. But after the most careful considerations of future costs they determined that to leave us with the whole burden of providing new schools and only 50% contribution to the costs of necessary

repairs, alterations and improvements, would, in effect, nullify the offer as a practical basis of co-operation. Believing that the Government wishes to help us to overcome our very real difficulties, and sharing the common desire for improved conditions so that there should be equality of opportunity for all, we hope that you may find it possible so to amend your offer as to make it possible for us to complete the scheme of reorganisation and to bring all our schools up to that 'reasonably high standard' to which you refer in your letter. While not abating our claim to that full support which we consider to be our right we are eager to co-operate with the Government in any scheme which will help all the interests concerned, be acceptable to the country as a whole, and at the same time enable us to give our children the best possible education in that Catholic atmosphere which our conscientious conviction demands . . . Believe me, Yours sincerely, Peter Amigo."

Mr. Butler replied at once and asked to see the Bishop in person. This interview is described by Mr. Maloney, in "Westminster Whitehall and the Vatican", page 164. Mr. Butler received a frosty welcome in every sense of the word. This is the account from his own pen:

"My records state that 'after much sounding of the bell a sad looking, rather blue faced Chaplain let me in and we climbed a massive palace stair to the first floor where the Archbishop was sitting, fully robed, in a small room overlooking the ruins of Southwark Cathedral. His window was wide open on his left hand so that he could at once take in the tragic picture of the ruins and inhale the chilly morning air. The Archbishop asked immediately we had sat down what I had come to see him for. I obliged by informing him; but it was not an auspicious beginning. He said that a 50% grant was not sufficient and that he saw no chance of agreement with politicians. He said that if I had belonged to his community he would have suggested that we should pray. I said that I would be very ready to do so since I was also a churchman."

Butler added in his note; "This interview indicated the nature of the head-on collision with the Roman Catholic Church." He also observed, on learning that Amigo had been Cardinal Hinsley's Diocesan Bishop when the latter had been Parish Priest:

"This made me realise what a great age the man must be. He seemed to regard the 1902 Act as being passed in his comparative old age!"

After a further Committee Meeting on 7th January, Archbishop Amigo wrote again to Mr. Butler.

"On Thursday January 7th there was a meeting at Archbishop's House, Westminster, of the Committee appointed by Cardinal Hinsley and the Catholic Bishops of England for the Catholic Schools. The Archbishop of Liverpool presided and there were about sixteen representatives of both Houses of Parliaments, of the teachers of secondary and primary schools and of parents. I told them of our conversation on November 25th and they all decided that we cannot have any 'agreed syllabus on religion' and that we need the 100% of expenses if we are to secure equal opportunities for all children. We cannot let Catholic children be penalised on account of their religion. We must have Catholic teachers who know and practise their religion, and if this is properly guaranteed, we shall not object to Local Education Authorities having the appointment of teachers for our primary schools. The secondary schools will need special agreements. It would be well if the Committee were to be received at the Board of Education as they certainly wish to know what the Board would give, if we forego the appointment of teachers by our managers."

This letter marks the end of Archbishop Amigo's direct involvement in the negotiations. During the years of his episcopate he left much of the work in the fight for Catholic Schools to his Vicar General (later Auxiliary) Mgr. Brown.

On the Butler Act we can let Bishop Brown have the final word. He arranged a meeting with nun head teachers of the Diocese on the 16th October 1942. At this meeting he explained Mr. Butler's proposals. He told the sisters that he was sure that Mr. Butler and the Board had taken the line 'You would not relinquish appointments (of teachers); you cannot keep that and have *full* state aid; this is all you will get.' He went on to tell the assembly that the 1936 Act gave 75% (for redevelopment) and the Labour Government would have given 100% for everything.

Bishop Amigo retained his great interest in Catholic Schools right up to the end of his life. He was often to be seen visiting the local schools of South London and had a very easy way with children.

The Diocese had possessed Schools Inspectorate right from the start in 1851. The Diocesan Schools Commission was a separate entity first created in 1936 to implement the Education Act of that year. This lapsed at the start of the war and the present Commission was started by

His Grace again in 1943 to look into all the problems that would arise from the implementation of the 1944 Act, particularly over the building of new schools. The first Chairman was Canon Burt; Dr. Winham, then Schools Inspector was Vice-Chairman and Father Edward Mahoney the first Secretary. The first meeting of the revised Commission took place on 31st January 1944. The initial work was to plan the new Secondary Modern Schools throughout the Diocese and to match as many as possible with the 1936 Act proposals. In the event, twelve special agreement schools were opened, most with a 75% grant. The total grant received from these special agreements amounted to nearly £2.million. The Commission recommended the creation of a Diocesan Central Fund to finance the projects but His Grace replied that this should be left for his successor and the Diocesan Development Fund was started by Bishop Cowderoy in 1952.

Archbishop Kennealy of Simla, Bishop Amigo. Archbishop Mannix of Melbourne, and the Bishop of Cork at the funeral of Terence McSwiney. Oct. 1920.

The Archbishop with the Hop-pickers

The Archbishop in 1948 on the occasion of his Golden Jubilee

Chapter 9
Between the Two Wars

Besides the great events described in the earlier chapters it is time now to look at the Bishop's career in the inter-war years.

In 1918 the Bishop was closely involved in the problem of the application of the then new Code of Canon Law to England and Wales. As far as he was concerned the really important issue was the introduction of the decree known as "Ne Temere" to cover the marriages of Catholics. The original position in England and Wales was that a Catholic could contract a valid marriage outside of a Catholic Church while the "Ne Temere" decree insisted that for validity all Catholics must marry in a Catholic Church. This decree however was not made universal until the promulgation of the Code of Canon Law.

Bishop Amigo saw a problem arising in that many Catholics were marrying in registry offices either because they were lapsed, or even because they thought they could not afford a Church wedding. He estimated correctly that after the introduction of the Code, there would still be thousands of merely civil weddings amongst Catholics particularly if these were mixed marriages. He therefore requested without success that the Canons relating to the place of marriage should not be applied in Great Britain.

It is perhaps interesting to note that the new (1983) Code of Canon Law does allow for some exemptions from this rule when the Catholic party has in effect ceased to have any connection with the Church.

The Bishop returned again to the same point in 1936 when a certain amount of difficulty had arisen because priests had been validating civil marriages without checking the civil certificates first. The Director of Public Prosecution denounced thirty-eight priests including six from Southwark for performing marriages without a registrar when his presence was required by law. He informed the Bishop that in future any priest who broke this law would be guilty of a serious felony and be liable to imprisonment. This was particularly the case if the original marriage took place in a non-Catholic Church. The Bishop again appealed for a relaxation of the law and added at the end of his letter "Perhaps you would wish me to suffer imprisonment and see what would be the result." However again the appeal fell on deaf ears in Rome.

Bishop Amigo rarely took any direct interest in party politics as such, but in 1919 he was drawn into a dispute over whether Catholics could vote for the Labour Party on the grounds that it had recently published a manifesto which was profoundly socialist in tone. It seems that in February 1919 Sir Stuart Cott tried his best to get the Holy Father (Benedict XV) to condemn the party and stop Catholics from voting for it. In this work he was more or less openly assisted by T.P. Burns. Cardinal Gasparri at the Secretariat of State at the Vatican then asked Bishop Amigo in a letter dated 19th July, that the Holy Father wished to be informed if the Labour Party in Great Britain was a 'Socialist' party which might lead to its condemnation as far as Catholics were concerned. Without delay the Bishop consulted James Hope (later First Baron Rankeillour), Joe Devlin of the United Irish League and Hilaire Belloc. Some extracts of the replies are worth recording in the light of later history. Hilaire Belloc had spent five years as an MP and was totally disillusioned with politics. He wrote to the Bishop on 19th September.

"In practice what would be called the 'Labour Party' would simply be a caucus running candidates who would rely for their votes mainly upon the public disgust of the present Government in particular, and the breakdown of Parliament in general. It will have no theoretical socialist programme. The reforms which it will advocate will simply be going 'one better' than what the other caucus promise. Finally, when it comes to action in the House of Commons, even if there be a majority for this caucus which I doubt (though it is possible) the actual legislation will be almost exactly the same as it would have been under any other combination; we are in such a pass, especially financially, that anyone in power is pretty well bound to do the same thing. I trust my note will be of service, though it is a very easy task to undertake. It is highly probable that if any considerable space of time elapses before use can be made of these views something will have happened to modify them, for instance the present Prime Minister is working hard to get the leadership of the Labour movement, and he would certainly make the wildest promises if an early election were forced."

Mr. Devlin's reply stressed the strong links of the Irish with the British Labour Party. James Hope prepared a lengthy essay mainly on political theory. The sentiments expressed are broadly sympathetic to the Labour movement with certain provisos against extremism. He rightly pointed out that the old principle of "Every man for himself (Laissez Faire) and devil take the hindmost" was in essence unchristian and the Labour movement was a reaction to this. To the views of Mr Snowden (a prominent labourite) that taxation should be confiscatory, he pointed out that it was quite right that the rich should pay both absolutely and proportionately more than the poor, but if such taxes were introduced merely to impoverish the rich and not for the needs of that State then justice would be violated. He argued against the views of Mr. Ramsay McDonald that state rights should be exalted above the liberties of individuals because this would lead to the consolidation and centralisation of State machinery to the exclusion of private and local interests and could hit the Catholics in the field of education and eugenics.

The Bishop then sought the views of Archbishop Keating of Liverpool regarding someone to consult who was prominent in the Trade Union movement. The Archbishop recommended George Milligan of the National Union of Dock, Riverside and General Workers. In his letter to the Bishop he made it clear that his own sympathies were with T. P. Burns. He wrote:

"I suspect that it is they (Burns and his friends) who have been appealing to Rome for a definite judgement, and if they do, I should think that Rome would condemn those who join the Labour Party."

The Bishop of Salford, Louis Casartelli was giving active and open support to Mr. Burns. His Grace of Liverpool did not go quite so far but recommended a watchdog committee to report on how matters developed. In the event he did not bother but 'leaked' the news that such an investigation was under way, much to the embarrassment of their Lordships of Southwark and Northampton. Mr. Milligan's reply pointed out that there were a number of socialists in the party but that there was a strong element of non-socialist and Catholic opinion which had already by its persistence defeated the secular education aims of the socialist group:

"I certainly think the withdrawal of Catholics from the Labour movement would not only weaken the legitimate claims of Labour, but would create a new religious persecution that nobody wants. The harmful motions they sometimes carry are mostly verbal triumphs, sound and fury signifying nothing. There may come a time though I think not soon, when Catholics would be compelled to leave the Party. In my judgement that time is not yet . . . ."

One thing was common to all the replies, that there was no need for any ban from Rome. And so at the end of the consultation Bishop Amigo wrote to Cardinal Gasparri on the 25th November 1919:

" . . . . My own considered opinion after inquiry is that the Labour Party will probably be in power in a short time and that it is for us to try and work with them . . . . There is a small body of Catholics who have moved for the Pope to take action against the Labour Party on the grounds that it is socialist, but it would be a profound mistake if we were to condemn the Labour Party. Our own people consist mainly of working class, and mostly in favour of the Labour Party, and they look upon it simply as a political party willing and ready to help them with their difficulties, whereas the others have promised much and done little for them."

In the event, the wise counsels of the Bishop of Southwark prevailed at Rome and nothing further came of this attempt to discredit the Labour Party.

The Bishop's personal sympathies were always with the poor and later on he took a very different view on the General Strike of 1926 from that of Cardinal Bourne. The Cardinal went out of his way to condemn the strike. The Bishop made no public statement other than asking for prayers but his view can be seen in this letter to the Bishop of Salford (6th June 1926).

"We are going to hear a good deal for some time about the pronouncement of His Eminence on the Strike. Some of the poor people resent it very much and he himself is beginning a campaign defending the attitude taken.

In your Diocese you have many poor people and you will have the same difficulties as myself to face. We ought to study the question and get others to help us. The feeling in my working district is strong. The men say they could not break with their unions. They deny that they were going against lawfully constituted authority. They simply meant to defend those whom they thought to be badly treated. Their leaders now acknowledge that the General Strike was a big blunder, but even they maintain that it was no attack on the constitution. It certainly should have been avoided and only resorted to when every other means had failed of defending their brethren. I shall not be making any public pronouncement but shall simply urge my poor people to pray for God's guidance. I may however discuss the matter with His Eminence. I should like to know whether your poor are satisfied; the rich are certainly very pleased."

In 1924 Bishop Amigo at last received the help of an auxiliary Bishop. The appointment of an auxiliary had been mooted many years earlier but the appointment was delayed possibly because of the talk of dividing the Diocese. Bishop William Brown was consecrated titular Bishop of Pella and auxiliary in Southwark on 12th May 1924. As it happened it was hardly a day too soon. On the 29th August that year the Bishop was ordered to bed by his doctor suffering from a thrombosis in one leg. His condition deteriorated rapidly and by the 8th September he was unable to receive Holy Communion owing to sickness. Thrombosis was followed by congestion of the lungs and pleurisy and then a thrombosis in the other leg. The Bishop was given the last rites by Bishop Brown on 13th October and made his profession of faith before the Chapter. His life was in danger right up to 25th October. His diary records that he was unable to recite more than a fraction of his Divine Office and was often sleeping most of the day. By the 1st of November he was able to write a few letters from his bedside and was allowed up for the first time for just one hour on the 26th November. On the 8th December he was conveyed to L'Esperance Convent at Eastbourne to start his convalescence but was unable to say Mass until the 14th of that month. He returned to Bishop's House on Christmas Eve but did not feel well enough to say Mass in the Cathedral. On the 10th January he was taken to St. Mary's Worthing for two weeks and thence back to L'Esperance at Eastbourne. Here he built up his strength by taking long walks along the promenade with his sister who had taken over as housekeeper at Bishop's House. He remained at Eastbourne until the 22nd March and undertook no engagements during that time except that he was taken two or three times by car to the recently opened Junior Seminary at Mark Cross. His illness would have killed off many a lesser mortal but the Bishop was very robust. He had by then been Bishop for twenty-one years. Yet his episcopate was not even at the half-way mark!

The post-war years saw an increase in vocations and there was increasing pressure of space at the Wonersh Seminary which contained both the Juniors and the Seniors. At the start of 1924 the Holy Child Society decided to close down their school at Mark Cross, Sussex, which was owned by the Trustees of Louisa Catherine, late Duchess of Leeds. The Bishop was anxious that the property should remain in Catholic hands as it contained a fine chapel and was well situated, so he decided to buy it for the Diocese from the Trustees for the sum of £7,000. In addition to this sum it was necessary to spend £4,000 in renovating the buildings which were in a run down condition. His Lordship set up a special fund to cover the additional debt needed to cover this work.

The Juniors moved in on 7th November 1924 and the domestic arrangements were in the hands of the Sisters of the Sacred Heart of Jesus and Mary. The first Rector was the former Regent of the Juniors at Wonersh, Mgr. Ernest Corbishley, known affectionately as 'Corby' to one and all. The following year the Rector told the story of the early days in an article in the 'Southwark Record'. He recorded how the nuns arrived first on 24th October to find the whole area ankle deep in mud and the interior strewn with packing cases, beds, mattresses and other sundry articles. The new Reverend Mother was only 3ft 6ins tall and needed a pair of stilts to peer over the assembled stacks of furniture.

The necessary works included the conversion of some of the former nuns cells into rooms for the professors, the laying on of mains water and the installation of electric lighting. When the students arrived at 5.30pm on 7th November they had their first glimpse of their new Alma Mater by candle-light, as the new system was not ready. For the first three weeks each student had his own candle stick and candle to work by.

A Diocesan Travelling Mission was started in 1927. This served villages in the country areas which were some way from the nearest Church. Mass was said either in halls or in a large converted caravan towed by the Missioner's car.

In 1926 Bishop Amigo was asked to carry out an Apostolic Visitation in Gibraltar. The Bishop at the time, Henry Thompson, was a Benedictine Monk from Ramsgate who had been appointed in 1911. At the time of his appointment Bishop Amigo had suggested to Rome that Mgr. Bidwell of Westminster Diocese might be a good appointment as he spoke both Spanish and English. Bishop Thompson however spoke no Spanish and was reluctant to learn the language. The result was that he became distanced from his clergy and people. He was also unable to deal satisfactorily with a problem concerning some land used by the military which belonged to the Loreto Convent.

Bishop Amigo was able to sort out the land tenure problem and suggested to Bishop Thompson that he might consider retiring back to Ramsgate. The Bishop indeed complied with this suggestion and the following year was succeeded by Bishop Raymond Fitzgerald.

This was the last visit that the Bishop paid to his native territory. Indeed he seems to have visited the Rock only three times during his episcopate.

Between 1924 and 1933 James Hope (Baron Rankeillour) made a number of efforts to reform parish organisation by suggesting detailed schemes for the setting up of Parish Councils. In this work he was years ahead of his time. His first scheme proposed in 1924 was basically a council of temporal administration. However it would have fairly sweeping powers, the Parish Priest only having a casting vote on divisions. This council would only have had six members and would have controlled all financial expenditure in the Parish. Parish accounts would be properly audited and publicised each year in the particular Parish.

Charles Wellesley (who had helped the Bishop on the finance commission on Diocesan debts in 1908) sent a copy of the proposed 'Model scheme for a Parish Council' to the Bishop saying that he could give it no support of any kind and that he was in complete disagreement with the project.

By 1928 Hope had collected the signatures of eighty-seven supporters and sent a memorandum to all the Bishops outlining his plans. He tried to make it clear that he was offering help not intrusions. Article 11 of his memo was worded:

"It cannot be too strongly emphasised however that this suggestion is one for lay co-operation and assistance, not for lay intrusion into the spiritual sphere or for any derogation of ecclesiastical authority; one of the essential objects is to make the growing body of the laity—who have hitherto been only too loosely attached to their parishes and hardly conscious of their corporate responsibilities—mindful of their obligations and to encourage them to become more active participants in the common task."

In 1929 Mr. Hope notified the Bishop of his commission and its aims.

He suggested the formation of a committee of Bishops to look into the matter. Bishop Amigo replied on the 18th January 1929:

" . . . . The appointing of a commission will not depend on any one Bishop. I suppose that Cardinal Bourne will bring up the question in Low Week and ask the opinion of the Episcopal Bench. There are of course many imperfections in our present conditions, but some of them are being remedied by insistence on inventories, on the banking account being in three names, and on submitting plans for alterations.

I greatly fear that in the very places where temporal worries are greatest, the Clergy will still have to spend hours with the outdoor collectors on Saturdays and Sundays, and the priest will have no capable lay people to take the financial burdens from him."

Mr. Hope replied on the 20th January that he was very glad to know of the business checks already in force but they do not invoke a sense of corporate responsibility in a Parish. He expressed the wish that parishioners would take pride in their Parish if it were prosperous and feel ashamed if it were not and that this result could be attained in many places and in time everywhere.

Bishop Amigo was not averse to the existence of Parish Councils, and in fact St. Thomas of Canterbury at Wandsworth had possessed a fully operating council since 1901 with a set of rules remarkably like those that obtain today in most parishes throughout the land.

In 1931 the scheme was damned with faint praise by the Bishops' Conference which stated that "any Parish Priest is free to form a committee to assist him in the temporal concerns of his parish subject to the consent of the Bishop which, if wisely sought would not be refused."

In 1929 the Bishop celebrated twenty-five years as Bishop in Southwark. The celebrations were rather muted as the date fell during Holy Week, but unknown to the Bishop his Chapter had petitioned Rome in February that their Bishop should be appointed Assistant at the Papal Throne. This honour means that if the Bishop is present in Rome for a ceremony he will be a close assistant on the Sanctuary. In itself however it is considered a great honour. The Canons letter spoke of the esteem, affection and veneration in which their Bishop was held, the starting of the Junior Seminary, the building of many new Churches, his great devotion to the Blessed Sacrament marked by great processions at the feast of Corpus Christi with large numbers of men belonging to the Confraternity of the Blessed Sacrament taking part.

In his reply to the Holy Father the Bishop wrote: "What I appreciate most is that the Holy See places confidence in me, and that I have received the Blessing of the Vicar of Christ."

1929 was the centenary year of Catholic Emancipation. A series of events throughout the year culminated with a procession of Catholic men from St. George's to Westminster Cathedral on the afternoon of the 15th September. The march was led by the Bishop, supported by eleven other Bishops. About 24,000 people took part in this march and it was particularly fitting that they assembled at St. George's for it was almost on the same spot that the Lord George Gordon had assembled his riotous assembly to march to Westminster in 1780 to protest about the relief being given to Catholics.

In the same year the Bishop opened the new John Fisher School to give secondary education to boys living in the Croydon and Sutton areas. This was a time when there were very few Catholic Secondary Schools and the area south of Croydon was developing fast. The school was opened first in 1929 at Duppas Hill Road in Croydon but within two years moved to its present site in Purley. The Bishop arranged that it would be run by secular priests and hoped (correctly as it proved) that many vocations would flow from the new venture.

The Bishop's foreign travels were almost entirely restricted to annual visits to Rome and to Lourdes. He was an enthusiastic supporter of the Diocesan Pilgrimage. After 1926 he did not return at all to his native Gibraltar. His two remaining unmarried sisters who lived in Gibraltar came often to see him. Margarita had married an Englishman, Mr. Heywood, and they lived nearby. Leonore became his housekeeper until the Sisters took over in 1947. His brother Joseph died in 1931 and the Bishop arranged that his wife Katie should come over from Cairo and live with Sisters at the Convent at Staplehurst in Kent. The other brother, Fernando, had settled in Mexico.

However in 1933 the Bishop was invited by the Catholic Association to lead a pilgrimage to the Holy Land. This was quite an adventure in those days before air travel became commonplace. The pilgrimage lasted six weeks and travelled overland and then by steamer. The visit included Istanbul, Cyprus, Athens, Smyrna, Syria and Palestine. There was danger too for the party. There was much unrest then as now in the Holy Land. Serious rioting had been reported amongst the Arabs. Whilst the party were travelling by car from the Syrian (now Lebanese) town of Tripoli to Damascus, two priests in the party, Fr. Gerald O'Boyle OP and his brother Canon O'Boyle of the Diocese of Down and Connor, were seriously injured when the car in which they were travelling hit a large stone in the road and overturned. Fr. Gerald nearly bled to death before assistance arrived. There was a strong rumour that the stone had been placed in the road by Arabs who knew the party was coming, but no firm evidence was produced to that effect.

When the party arrived at Jerusalem further Arab disturbances made it impossible for the party to visit the Temple Area.

An interesting travel note in the diary reveals that the party travelled from Jerusalem to Suez in one day by rail. This line along the Mediterranean coast has long been closed.

Cardinal Bourne died on 1st January 1935. He had been ill for some years and the old controversy over division of the Diocese died with him.

Did the Bishop have a role in the appointment of Bishop Hinsley to Westminster? We cannot be certain. It is well known that this was a personal appointment of Pope Pius XI who was a great friend of the future Cardinal and played cards with him. To most people in Great Britain his appointment was a complete surprise and Hinsley himself thought he would live out his days in quiet retirement in Rome. For Bishop Amigo however the appointment came as no surprise at all. He wrote to congratulate the new Archbishop the very day the appointment was made almost before anyone else could have known. Bishop Amigo had been in Rome in January 1935 in connection with the Canonisation of Sts. John Fisher and Thomas More and his diary lists among the subjects discussed between himself and the Holy Father 'The succession to Westminster'. Bishop Amigo had welcomed the young priest to Southwark in 1905 and he taught at Wonersh besides being Parish Priest both at Sutton Park and Sydenham before his transfer to the English College as Rector. Certainly it is possible that the Bishop may have whispered the name 'Hinsley' in the Papal ear in that January interview.

The Bishop always thought he had been hard done by over the reception of Papal Legates. In 1911 he had been told by the Duke of Norfolk that he was not the right person to receive the Papal envoy at Dover in spite of being Bishop of the Diocese where Dover is situated. The same problem recurred in 1937 when a Papal Envoy was sent over to represent the Holy Father at the coronation of King George VI. This time the Bishop wrote first to the Duke of Norfolk, who contacted Lord

Granard, Comptroller of the Royal Household. Granard wrote on 1st
May 1937:

"There will be no objection to your being on the Pier at Dover to
receive the Papal Envoy, but you will quite understand that you must
not take precedence of the Officer attached to the Papal Suite, who
will go down to meet the Envoy at Dover. I shall go if I can, but if not
Captain Legge will be there. He is as you know a Papal Chamberlain . . . ."

The Bishop replied to this little snub:

"Very many thanks for your letter. Under the circumstances it it
better for me not to be at Dover next Sunday when the Papal Envoy
arrives but I shall ask Fr. Leake, the Parish Priest, to represent me. I
realise why the late Duke of Norfolk stopped my going to welcome
the Papal Envoy in 1911. As Bishop of the Diocese, I ought to receive
a representative of the Pope, but I cannot be there as an onlooking
spectator."

Perhaps this apparent brush-off affected the Bishop's thinking on
Papal representatives for in 1938 he was active in trying to present the
appointment of an Apostolic Delegate to Great Britain. This matter is
treated of by Moloney in his Chapter "The Coming of the Apostolic
Delegate." Up to 1938 Bishop Amigo had always been in favour of the
appointment of a Delegate because he understood that this would be a
help in trying to prevent the takeover of Southwark by Westminster.
He was now about to do a complete volte-face. As his relationship with
Cardinal Hinsley was excellent he no longer saw the need for a Delegate
in quite the same light. The Bishops prepared a belated protest to send
to Cardinal Pacelli after their October meeting in 1938 but Archbishop
Amigo had put in his own oar in July. He wrote a very long letter to
Cardinal Pacelli listing various examples of anti-Catholic prejudice in
recent years which he indicated would be rekindled by the appointment
of a Delegate. He ended his letter as follows:

" . . . . Four centuries of separation from the See of Rome have
strengthened the objection to what is not English, and with many the
difficulty in becoming Catholic is that they look upon us as foreign.
There is unfortunately a very strong dislike of foreigners, and an
Apostolic Delegate would have to be Italian. In these days we are able
to communicate with the Holy See easily, both by letter and by

journeys. We are delighted to write to Rome and to pay our homage to the Vicar of Christ. We have a Cardinal at Westminster who not only is deeply attached to the Holy Father and to all that breathes of Rome, but who at the same time is becoming daily more and more influential with Government officials. He is thoroughly English and esteemed as such, while his loyalty to the Vicar of Christ can never be called in question. He can help the Holy See better than an Apostolic Delegate could do. He has the whole Hierarchy with him and he is gaining ground continually with all.

I therefore strongly feel that the interests of the Holy See in England are perfectly secured at present without the danger of rousing prejudice by appointing an Apostolic Delegate. It is of course for the Vicar of Christ to decide this matter, and we shall all most humbly and loyally abide by his ruling, but as a Bishop of long experience in this Protestant land, I have felt it to be my duty to express my opinion. With the example of our great Martyrs St. John Fisher and St. Thomas More, we shall always be true and devoted to the Vicar of Christ.

Kissing the Sacred Purple, Believe me, My Lord Cardinal, Yours Devotedly in Christ."

In the event the letter of all the Bishops prepared in October was never sent. Archbishop Godfrey was appointed in November 1938 so Archbishop Amigo's fears about an Italian appointment were false.

In 1938 the Bishop celebrated his Sacerdotal Golden Jubilee and was rewarded by Pope Pius XI with the personal title of Archbishop. This is a very rare award for the title Archbishop is normally reserved for Bishops who are metropolitans and the Diocese of Southwark did not have that status at the time. The Jubilee Mass was celebrated at St. George's Cathedral which was crammed to capacity with many left outside in the freezing cold. The Bishops of Brentwood and Nottingham and the two auxiliary Bishops of Westminster, together with three hundred clergy, filled the front rows of the Cathedral. Near the sanctuary stood a massive candle bearing the inscription 'Presented to Archbishop Amigo by His Holiness the Pope on the occasion of his Sacerdotal Jubilee, February 25th 1938'. At the end of the Mass, Bishop Brown read the following message from the Holy Father:

"Pope Pius XI. To our venerable Brother, Peter Emmanuel Amigo, Archbishop-Bishop of Southwark, Assistant at Our Throne. Venerable Brother, health and apostolic benediction.

The joyful celebration of the Golden Jubilee of your ordination to the Priesthood affords Us the happy opportunity of offering you a public mark of Our fatherly esteem and love. For We know well the zeal and diligence with which you have carried out your pastoral duties over so long a period, and the eagerness and enthusiasm with which you devote yourself to the good of the faithful.

We congratulate you therefore, Venerable Brother, with all Our heart, on this sacred and blessed anniversary that brings joy to all your people and We earnestly pray that God may grant you the fullest enjoyment of this day and of your sacred ministry, and also the happiness of seeing the daily increase of the flock committed to your care.

In order that Our share in this day's celebration may be more manifest, We are pleased to confer upon you who have deserved so well of the Church and Civil Society the dignity of Archbishop so that endowed with this sacred honour and dignity, you may by the help of God's grace in the exercise of your pastoral office earn more fully the fruits of salvation.

Furthermore, We gladly grant you the faculty of imparting in Our Name and by Our authority to those present at the Pontifical Mass, Our Blessing and a plenary indulgence in the customary form of the Church. As a pledge of heavenly gifts and as a mark of Our special affection Venerable Brother, We lovingly grant to you, to your clergy and to the faithful committed to your care, the Apostolic Blessing."

The Archbishop-Bishop had refused to take any personal gift on the occasion of the Jubilee, but a committee which had planned the celebrations had issued an appeal pointing out that there was an opportunity now to present to the Bishop a sum adequate to fund the building of a hall to be named after him as a reminder in the years to come of his great work for God at St. George's. On the 25th March that year, the anniversary of his consecration in 1904, His Grace was presented with a cheque for £7,092. Work started on the new Hall in 1939 and the Hall was blessed and opened by the Archbishop on 3rd February 1940. It was to prove an even greater asset to St. George's than could ever have been imagined at the start. Soon it would be acting as a Pro-Cathedral.

A serious allegation against Archbishop Amigo is made by Evelyn Waugh in his biography of Ronald Knox. (The Life of the Rt. Rev. Ronald Knox, Chapman and Hall, 1959). It is stated that Archbishop

Amigo was opposed to the translations both of the Manual of Prayers and the Holy Bible prepared by Mgr. Knox between 1939 and 1944. On page 256 Mr. Waugh wrote of the draft proofs of the Manual:

"Some resistance was expected from Archbishop Amigo who constitutionally resented change of any kind."

When the draft of the translation of St. Matthew's Gospel was circulated to the Hierarchy and was allegedly 'rejected' by Archbishop Amigo, Cardinal Hinsley wrote a strong letter to the Archbishop which led him to apologise to Mgr. Knox. However on page 290 it is implied that the apology was reluctant and Mr. Waugh added:

"He bided his time and had not long to wait for his retaliation."

The supposed retaliation is taken to be the fact that in May 1943 just after the death of Cardinal Hinsley, the Hierarchy withdrew the Manual from publication.

The Archives of the Archdiocese present a very different picture of these events. First we can take the case of the translation of the Manual of Prayers.

The proofs of the Manual were sent round to the Bishops early in 1939 for their criticisms to be prepared. Archbishop Amigo entrusted this work to his Censor Deputatus, Canon Fennessy. The good Canon was totally out of sympathy with the work. Here is his introduction:

"The Manual of Prayers is intended for Congregational use. The style therefore, while it should be dignified, should avoid all obscurity or anything that is far fetched. Moreover since most of these prayers are already familiar to our people, they ought not to be changed without a good reason. It would seem that many of the changes in the proposed edition are being made without any reason save for the sake of change. Our people have recited or heard recited these prayers for many years. Why should these new fangled versions be thrust upon them when the original prayers are adequate, dignified and hallowed by the tradition of many years? One would not assert that the former (present) edition is faultless. But if changes are to be made, let them be in the direction of greater simplicity. Most of our Catholics are simple people who would be puzzled by the diction of the new edition. The translation of some of the Latin hymns is deplorable, bearing hardly any relation to the original."

An indication of Canon Fennessy's opinions of Mgr. Knox can be seen in the following extract from a letter sent to Archbishop Amigo on 28th April 1939.

"A man was telling me the other day that Mgr. Knox as an Anglican was eccentric in speaking and writing. In the pulpit he would say 'Hirosolima' and 'Ahbrahahm'. It isn't fair to set one man to do a job such as that on his own. There should be others—with just ordinary literary knowledge—to check the tendency to express individual eccentricities."

On or about the 20th April the Archbishop sent Mgr. Knox a copy of Canon Fennessy's criticism with a covering letter which is not to hand in draft form. Mgr. Knox wrote from the Old Palace, Oxford on 24th April in reply.

"Thank you for your letter. An extremely kind turn of phrase at the end of it gives me grounds for the hope that you have either not yet fully explored or not yet adopted without reservation, the criticisms which you enclose. It is in that hope that I offer this explanation of the principles which underly the Draft revision of the Manual. It was not intended in the minds of those who suggested it to consist of a few stray corrections here and there; it was to go much deeper. But of course I do not imply that the Bishop of Shrewsbury for example would associate himself with the view I am here urging. It is purely my own.

We are not, it seems to me converting England. It does not seem to be the experience of priests who are in touch with movements outside the Church that we are making any real headway. Obviously no one cause is responsible for this situation, and no one remedy would be expected to meet it. But among the barriers which divide us from our fellow countrymen, and make it difficult for men to understand us, there is one which has a certain (though limited) importance and has always forced itself on my attention. In our vernacular devotions we do not use the same idiom as Christians outside the Church. And this is the more serious in that the prayers used by the Church of England are, by general admission, models of dignity and faultless prose rythm. No convert, I think, has ever failed to experience a sense of loss over this difference. The convert however may reasonably be expected to put up with such a minor deprivation, in return for all the treasures of grace which God's mercy has opened to him. What is more unfortunate is the effect produced by this same contrast on those who attend our churches before they have received the gift of faith; Protestants who have married or intend to marry Catholics, Protestants who are beginning to feel the weakness of their own position etc. It is a pity if these go away with a sense that our prayer-idiom is something much inferior to their own and that our priests rattle off the service as if conscious that it had not beauty of language to recommend it . . . . When it was a question of translation from Latin or Italian I tried to go back to the spirit of the original, re-translating it with due attention to the claims of pure English and of rhythmical effect. All this was a considerable labour . . . . I hope your Grace will make allowances for the vanity of authorship when I say that I do not find it easy to rest content with the communicated criticisms of an anonymous priest who plainly misunderstood the scope of the proposed alterations. . . . ."

Most of this letter is quoted also by Evelyn Waugh on page 254 of his biography but he wrongly dates it as "some years later." A few days later Knox wrote also to Bishop Brown (1st May).

"Thank you awfully for your letter. I quite agree of course that literary appeal or lack of appeal in our vernacular devotions only affects Norwood (a middle class area), not Bermondsey (working class area). I only doubt whether Bermondsey very much minds what our official devotions are like. It always seems to me to say its rosary pretty continuously and what better occupation could it have? I find it hard to believe that poor people have a consuming passion for the existing version of the prayer to St. Joseph as the Bishop of Hexham and Newcastle seems to imply. As you say I don't suppose the Manual is ever destined to be more than an official source. I had never heard of it till I was asked to revise it. And I don't feel certain that the Archbishop will allow it even to be that! What worries me about his attitude is that he has taken the opinion of only one priest who dislikes each and every change as such, giving a long string of criticisms but admitting that they are only specimens of his general dislike. And I don't see that it can be much use the Committee considering in detail criticisms of that sort, only to be told at the end that the book won't be used in Southwark anyhow."

At the beginning of May the Archbishop replied to Mr. Knox.

"The Bishops in Low Week were told to let you have their criticisms of the Manual of Prayers as we had no time to deal with them during our meeting. In sending you those of my censor, I never thought that you were responsible for any of the faults which he had pointed out. I should certainly have hesitated to send them to you as I have the greatest confidence in you. I fully agree with you that we ought to have the very best for our services. I think however that the poor English of our prayers and hymns is not so much the cause of the lack of conversions as our neglect of prayer and mortification. There are many reasons against our making progress, but the chief reason is that we do not sufficiently realise that the Truth comes from God and that we must ask His blessing upon our work in England.

I have never had the opportunity of a conversation with you. I am delighted that you are undertaking the translation of the New Testament and I hope also of the whole Bible."

There is no indication in the archives that Archbishop Amigo made any further intervention over the Manual of Prayers either then or in 1943. There still remains though the problem of the translation of St. Matthew's Gospel.

In 1941 the proofs of the translation were made available and once again Archbishop Amigo sent a copy to Canon Fennessy who not surprisingly slated the work in no uncertain terms. He concludes his review:

"I am more than conscious of the fact that I may be utterly in the wrong. All I can say is that to me this version is horrible, illbalanced and unpleasing."

This time though the Archbishop also sent the proofs to Canon Rory Fletcher who was far more sympathetic. He wrote on 21st July:

"You say you disagree with such a translation; whether you mean any modern translation or this particular one I am not sure. I am not enamoured of it because I am prejudiced in favour of the old diction in the Authorised or Rheims editions having been fed on them for over 70 years .... As a 20th century English Edition I think it is excellent and has the advantage of being concise without losing clarity, a great advantage in a document for public use, both for remembrance and in the bulk of the printed testament."

On the 26th August the Archbishop wrote to Mgr. Knox.

"I have read your translation of St. Matthew's Gospel with great interest, but it has given me something of a shock. When Archbishop

Williams told the Bishops in October 1938 that you had received a
request from the United States to produce a translation of the Bible in
English that could be used on both sides of the Atlantic, we agreed
that you should be commissioned to make a translation of the N.T. in
English. Knowing your wonderful gifts I felt justified in giving my
vote, especially as you were to have a Committee of your own choice
for consultation. Since then the American Catholics to my surprise
have brought out a translation which will considerably affect the sale
of ours. The reason why I say that on reading St. Matthew I had a
shock, is that at my age, after being familiar with our version, I did not
expect such a wholesale change. I am afraid that I shall not be able to
adopt it as it stands, although I regret very much that your labours
may be in vain as far as my diocese is concerned. I think it only fair to
you to let you know straightforwardly what my attitude is, before you
carry your work to completion."

Mgr. Knox was evidently very upset indeed at this letter for he wrote
back saying he was writing to the Bishop of Lancaster to say he was
discontinuing his work of translation. (This letter is printed by Mr.
Waugh in his biography page 289).

Knox however also communicated with Cardinal Hinsley and the
result was that the Cardinal wrote to Archbishop Amigo on the 6th
September.

"I am very sorry you wrote to Mgr. Knox that stiff letter. It was not
fair to him; it was not fair to his committee. It was not fair to the
Bishops. You have a right to speak for your diocese, but though all
important, your diocese is only one of 18 dioceses. We ought to act
together and if you cannot agree, your disagreement should be made
in a general question like this *conciliariter*. I fear there will be another
of our frequent rumpuses, which are not edifying to the Catholic
people. How matters will go now after Mgr. Knox's reply is hard to
say. He is evidently completely upset, and my fear is he is going to be
bombarded by Bishop after Bishop; he does not deserve such
treatment, for he has done his best. I am sorry to write of my strong
regret for your letter . . . ."

(The rest of this letter deals with other matters).

The receipt of this letter prompted Archbishop Amigo to write again
to Monsignor Knox. (8th September).

"I am exceedingly sorry to know that my letter has upset you so much that you are seriously thinking of giving up your work on the translation of the Bible. I never for a moment dreamt that it would lead to such a disaster. I wrote simply on my own and not in any way as representing the Hierarchy. I hope that you will reconsider your decision. You have been appointed by all the Bishops and you should not take the opinion of one as sufficient reason to withdraw from what you are doing to the full satisfaction of all the rest. My difficulty is not about the excellence of your translation but about substituting it in public worship when it is such a complete change from what we have been used to so long. I most gladly contributed to your expenses and I should not think of taking any money back or of ceasing to contribute. I feel sure that if we meet we could soon put an end to this unfortunate misunderstanding. Wishing you every grace and Blessing."

Monsignor Knox evidently showed this reply to Cardinal Hinsley for the Cardinal wrote to the Archbishop on the 18th September.

"Your letter (to Knox) has made me ashamed of having lectured you. I felt deeply for Mgr. Knox because I could tell from his answer to you how keenly he was disappointed. It is hard for a writer after spending days and nights over some work to have all his efforts torn to pieces. We can perhaps comfort the stifled feelings. It is unfortunate that the Americans got out their translation. I do not suppose it would find favour here and certainly not with you. One Scripture expert, a reliable Jesuit, has pointed out a very queer American translation in the new version. At the marriage feast of Cana Our Lord is made to say 'Lady, what can I do for you?' . . . ."

After some other business the Cardinal concluded this letter:

"Will you add the enclosed to my contribution? You know how much I feel for you about the Cathedral, and how your disaster makes me hate still more the Nazis and all they stand for. Yet I pray for the conversion of Hitler, Goebels, Himmler and the rest of the crew— renegade Catholics."

The final letter in the file is a reply from Mgr. Knox on 11th September. The letter mainly concerns an attempt to fix a meeting between them but the salient sentences are as follows:

"I needn't say how glad I was or how grateful I am for your most kind letter. As long as I can feel that I am continuing the translation with your Grace's approval in general, the particular question of its use in public worship whether in Southwark or elsewhere is not for me to trouble about since the decision lies in other hands than my own . . . . I have never supposed that the Hierarchy would decide on this point without considerable searchings of heart. With renewed thanks . . . ."

There is no evidence at Southwark that the Archbishop took any further active part against Monsignor Knox. The reader may well feel that the version put over by Mr. Waugh does less than justice to the Archbishop.

Chapter 10
The Canonisation of
Sts John Fisher and Thomas More

Perhaps the real "high point" of Bishop Amigo's episcopate was the canonisation of Sts John Fisher and Thomas More in 1935.

Fisher and More had been beatified along with fifty-two other English martyrs on 29th December 1886. This group of martyrs were beatified 'Equipollently,' that it is to say on the basis of an immemorial cultus based on the existence of the famous paintings of the martyrs on the walls of the Chapel of the English College in Rome and the veneration continuously paid since. In effect the equipollent beatification is a confirmation by the Holy Father of the existing cult. No miracles are required provided the cultus can be firmly demonstrated.

For many years after it was decided not to press for canonisation until the causes of almost six hundred other martyrs had been considered and then the whole group could be canonised together.

In 1923 the causes of two hundred and thirty-four further martyrs were taken up in Rome leading eventually to the beatification of one hundred and thrity-six of this group in 1929. In 1926 the English Hierarchy at their Low Week meeting agreed that the time was ripe to press for the canonisation of Blessed Thomas More and John Fisher on the grounds that they were pre-eminent among the English Martyrs and that it would be a great boost to the English Catholics if they were canonised. Bishop Amigo was entrusted with the task of taking up the matter with the authorities in Rome on account of the fact that John Fisher as Bishop of Rochester had an intimate connection with the Southwark Diocese. His London house was only one hundred yards from the present Archbishop's House Southwark. Also Cardinal Bourne felt he could not personally supervise the cause and relations between the two Bishops were now greatly improved.

Bishop Amigo went to Rome in November to plead with the Holy Father for the re-opening of the cause and the Southwark Archives preserve the original memorandum which he presented to the Pope.

"The English Bishops at their Low Week meeting in 1926 invited the Bishop of Southwark to take up with the permission of the Holy See the cause of the canonisation of Blessed John Fisher and Blessed Thomas More. Cardinal Bourne found himself unable to undertake this task. Southwark has a 'locus standi' as Blessed John Fisher was Bishop of Rochester part of Southwark, for more than 30 years. Blessed Thomas More lived in Sevenoaks for a time and his head is at Canterbury; both these places are in Southwark Diocese.

The English Martyrs were beatified in 1886. No miracles have been performed by them so far as we know. The above two martyrs stand out prominently among the Beati. Fisher was the only Bishop who withstood Henry VIII and was rewarded by Paul III with the Cardinal's Hat. More as Lord Chancellor of England was known for his learning throughout Europe. Their canonisation should strengthen our bonds with the Holy See. Both were executed for the Supremacy of the Holy See and no other cause.

Contemporaries had no doubt about their martyrdom. This doctrine for which such prominent men died brings out that England before the Reformation was distinctly Roman Catholic.

It is a doctrine which Protestants in England continually attack. Some of our Catholics were exceedingly weak at the end of the 17th century and the beginning of the 18th on this doctrine. It is important to strengthen our present day Catholics in their allegiance to Rome.

The canonisation of these two will have great influence in England even outside the true Church. Oxford and Cambridge Universities are proud of these two and will greatly rejoice. We hope that it will lead to many submitting to the authority of the Holy See. It would be a most fitting commemoration of the centenary of Catholic Emancipation in 1929 if they could be canonised in that year. I ask most strongly for authority to start this work in England. The Venerable English College founded to keep up the faith in England would be a centre in Rome for information and I suggest the Rector, Mgr. Hinsley for the Postulator of the Cause."

The Holy Father showed himself to be enthusiastic about the cause of Blessed John Fisher and Thomas More and the Congregation of Rites willingly gave permission for Mgr. Hinsley to become the Postulator.

But within a year Mgr. Hinsley was posted to Africa as Apostolic Visitor and it became clear that he could not continue to do the necessary work in Rome. There was a two-year delay in Rome. Meanwhile back in England Mgr. Philip Hallett, rector of Wonersh was appointed as Vice-Postulator with the task of raising the interest of British Catholics in the cause. This work he performed most ably over all the years leading to the canonisation and it is perhaps fitting that the actual 'Bull' of the Canonisation is now preserved at Wonersh in his memory.

Mgr. Hallett gave lectures on the martyrs, wrote pamphlets about them and organised petitions to Rome for their canonisation. He arranged to collect evidence of miracles worked by their intercession and in 1929 organised a grand exhibition in London of all the known relics, books and portraits of the two martyrs. He produced a prayer leaflet which was widely distributed.

It was not possible to have the martyrs canonised in 1929 at the time of the beatification of the one hundred and thirty-six martyrs for although work was under way, the official resumption of the cause was not yet signed. However the priest in Rome who was looking after the cause of the main batch of martyrs suggested to Bishop Amigo that he might employ Fra Agostino dell Vergine, a Basque Trinitarian who was well known at the Congregation of Rites and well versed in the necessary procedures. Matters then started to move again. The official resumption of the cause was agreed to by the Congregation of Rites on 18th June 1930. But even now there were some hiccups. When the Congregation met on the 17th June to agree to the resumption, this move was opposed by Cardinal Laurenti because he considered that their causes should be taken together with all the other martyrs. We learn this from a letter of Fra Agostino to Bishop Amigo (in Spanish) dated 27th June. A certain Mgr. Salotti of the Congregation of Rites replied to Cardinal Laurenti giving good reasons for the resumption of the cause without waiting for the rest of the martyrs. In spite of his pleading, the resolution was 'deferred' on that day. Mgr. Salotti promptly referred the proceedings to Pope Pius XI who set aside this 'deferrment' and ordained that the decree of the Resumption of the cause should be granted in conformity with the desires of the authors. Fra Agostino wrote that he saw the hand of Cardinal Bourne in this delaying tactic and indeed just at that time there had been another deterioration in the relations between the two prelates. Cardinal Bourne insisted that the official statements should all be headed 'Westminster' and he seems to have raised also some objections to the possible miracles that were being investigated on the grounds that they did not take place in the right diocese. As late as March 1931 Bishop Amigo was still worried about the attitude of Cardinal Bourne and Fr. Agostino wrote to tell him his fears were groundless.

During the course of the next four years Fra Agostino wrote many times to Bishop Amigo describing the progress of the cause but one factor kept on coming up in this correspondence; money. Every letter was in fact a begging letter. For instance on 9th December 1934 he wrote to Bishop Amigo (translation from Spanish):

> "Today I wrote to Mgr. Hallett saying I need more money, much more money because the ceremonies in Rome are very costly and at least 250,000 lires if not more, £5,000 at least, because 'sin pecunia no se hace nade.' (Without money you can do nothing)."

Indeed the costs of the canonisation process are an ever recurring theme in the canonisation correspondence. Eventually the total cost including the ceremony came to over £12,000 (about £250,000 in today's terms). Much of this money was raised by national collections but one can but imagine the worry this must have caused Bishop Amigo troubled as he was by the large debts still owing in Southwark. The Holy Father himself understood this problem and in 1930 offered to pay the expenses of those who would visit the many libraries of Europe to find out what contemporaries thought of our two martyrs. He knew that in the Ambrosiana at Milan where he had been librarian for years, material existed which would show their martyrdom. The Historical section of the Congregation of Rites were deputed by the Holy Father to study the question of martyrdom.

Meanwhile in England both Mgr. Hallett and Bishop Amigo did their utmost to promote the cause. The Bishop constantly referred to the martyrs on his Parish visitations while Mgr. Hallett continued to give lectures and collect evidence of favours. Although hundreds of letters were received by him about favours granted he reported "It is doubtful, however whether any of them would bear the rigorous investigation of an ecclesiastical court and be declared certainly miraculous."

In July 1934 Bishop Amigo received a letter from the Cardinal Prefect of the Congregation of Rites written at the express desire of His Holiness which informed him that Cardinal Manning had many years previously sent to Rome exact copies of what the English State Papers contained regarding our martyrs and that the Historical Section had been ordered to make a special study of the circumstances surrounding their deaths. Then their report would be submitted to the Cardinals of the Congregation in the hope of a favourable decision being arrived at so that the Pope could proceed to the canonisation without waiting for miracles. In his reply to the Holy Father, the Bishop wrote (23rd July):

" . . . It would be a glorious commemoration of the 400th anniversary of their martyrdom for the Vicar of Christ if next year Your Holiness were to place them in the catalogue of the Saints . . . though many petitions to these Martyrs have been favourably answered, no miracle has been wrought through their intercession which could stand the severe test of a canonical process . . . . Catholics and non-Catholics in England are proud of these two outstanding Englishmen. Nobody would think of them as traitors to King or Country . . . . I am sure that these Martyrs are praying for the conversion of England and their canonisation will not only give the greatest pleasure in this country but will help to bring many to recognise the Apostolic Authority for which they laid down their lives."

On the 20th November the Historical Section finished its report and it was circulated to the Cardinals of the Congregation of Rites so that they might give their opinions at a meeting fixed for the 29th January 1935.

Again there was a slight hiccup at this point. There had been no miracles proved so the question arose as to whether the two martyrs would be simply canonised equipollently, which in effect would be done by a simple decree from the Holy Father, or by full process of canonisation with the requirement for miracles dispensed. In the case of full canonisation there would be the customary ceremonial in St. Peter's. Father Richard Smith on the staff of the English College had been helping Fra. Agostino prepare his work. He wrote to Bishop Amigo describing this small problem and speaking of the many letters received from England pleading for the full canonisation. (17th December 1934).

" . . . The Holy Father has now decided it is canonisation tout court, and so we go ahead again. The Congregation to be held on January 29th is to be a plenary one including not only the Cardinals but also all the Consultors, and in the presence of the Pope himself. Which means, surely that the answer is going to be favourable . . . . I have been fiercely busy these last ten days, working for Fra Agostino over the Postulatoriae Litterae, and for Father Grisar SJ. with his historical introduction to the Postulator's Processus. It was impossible to print more than a fraction of the letters received. The Pope read every one; he has even made marks on some. We have copied out over 200 these last few days, so that they could be printed and give an idea of what the Holy Father calls 'questo vero plebsicito dell'Inghilterra.' He is immensely impressed, and when Cardinal Rossi went the other night on Consistorial business he couldn't get on at all; the Pope talked about nothing else but these letters he had been reading. The Historical Section of the Rites has of course reported favourably, but their printed work is jejune; a few documents, a whole booklet taken straight from Constant's clear but rather superficial work on the Reformation, and then just a few obvious comments of Quentin's. So the introduction of Grisar for whom I have devilled, helped greatly by Monsignor Hallett's prompt answer to a windy telegram, will be of added importance. I didn't get to bed all week before midnight but it was well worth it. And I'm glad the old Venerabile has had a hand in the canonisation after all."

At the meeting on the 29th January, Dom Quentin's report was presented together with many other documents including the dissertation just referred to prepared by Fr. Grisar SJ. On this occasion the Promoter of the Faith often nicknamed the 'Devil's Advocate', belied his popular name, for far from objecting to the proposed canonisation he advanced most powerful arguments in favour. He held that the way was open for equipollent canonisation and for formal canonisation with a dispensation from the miracles as the fact of martyrdom was incontestable. He admitted that there had never been before an instance of the kind but he argued that it was quite in accordance with the spirit and even the letter of the law. His argument was accepted by the Holy Father.

Bishop Amigo was already in Rome as Fr. Smith had indicated that his presence at this time would be useful and he could read the official request for canonisation which would have to follow the decision of the Congregation of Rites.

The Bishop had an audience with the Holy Father on 4th February. Again there was a slight delay at this point. The Bishop wrote to Bishop Brown that evening:

"The Audience was today, due at 12.15 but I did not get in till 1.15 as the Pope was delayed. The Abbott Primate came unexpectedly to announce to the Pope that Abbott Quentin had been found dead in bed and Cardinal Bisleti had been prevented from coming earlier and called at the Vatican at 12.45. I had twenty to twenty-five minutes and presented the *Times* History and the medallions with which His Holiness was delighted; arranged about next Sunday's function at which I am to read the little speech in English and he told me that May 19th will be the date for the canonisation. As this date is to be fixed strictly speaking in Consistory later, it would be better for us not to publish it too much. Fr. Agostino thinks that the Bishops can be told and the agencies for travelling like the Catholic Association. If the Papers mention it, they had better say that it will be settled in Consistory but that May 19th is most likely. Next Sunday the decree is to be read at the Vatican in the presence of the Pope and his court and a good gathering of people. I am then to read my little speech which the Pope has to have a copy of beforehand, and he will reply in Italian . . . ."

On the 10th February, the decree was read out by Mgr. Carinci the Secretary of the Congregation of Rites in the presence of the Holy Father and Bishop Amigo then made the following speech in English:

"MOST HOLY FATHER,

We have long been praying for this decree, and there was Exposition of the Blessed Sacrament in every diocese of England and Wales on Sunday, January 27th, in all the churches and convents where it was possible. The hearts of the Catholics of England and Wales are full of gratitude today for the great honour which your Holiness has given to our two martyrs, John Fisher and Thomas More; and we come to your feet, now, on behalf of the bishops, of the clergy, of the religious and of the laity of our country to thank you most heartily for this gracious proof of your fatherly good will towards the English people. We are especially grateful for your choosing the fourth centenary of their glorious death to give this solemn witness to their martyrdom and, as we fervently hope, ultimately to bestow upon these two martyrs the supreme honour of canonisation.

Our Catholics in England and Wales are proud of the many martyrs who shed their blood for the Faith in the XVIth and XVIIth centuries; but these two stand out prominent among them all for their devotion to the See of Peter. They could not take the oath of succession because that oath implied that the Pope was wrong in deciding the validity of the marriage of Henry VIII with Catherine of Aragon, and they knew that what God has joined together no man may put asunder. They refused, too, to acknowledge the King as supreme head on earth of the Church in England, because Christ, the Son of God, appointed Saint Peter and his successors to feed the lambs and the sheep of His flock. When so many bishops and priests miserably yielded to the tyrant's will and separated from the See of Rome, these two heroes stood firm, suffering a long imprisonment and a cruel death for the Vicar of Jesus Christ. Like Phineas of old, they stood up in the shameful fall of the people; in the goodness and readiness of their souls, they appeased God for Israel. (Eccli: XLV.29).

Both these illustrious men stir up in our hearts greater and greater love for the divine authority of the Catholic Church. John Fisher, the holy, zealous and devoted bishop, inspires bishops and other pastors of souls in their work for the Church of the living God, the pillar and ground of the truth. Thomas More, the model husband and father, makes the laity realise the importance of the sacrament of matrimony in sanctifying the christian home. Not only England but the whole world will gain by the canonisation of John Fisher and Thomas More.

We wish to be always filled with the affectionate loyalty to the successor of Saint Peter which prompted our martyrs to be faithful even unto death. We tried during the Holy Year to overcome many difficulties and to come in large numbers to Rome to pay our humble homage to the Vicar of Christ. If our coming rejoiced the heart of our Common Father, we can assure your Holiness that all of us went away full of gratitude for your paternal kindness, and feeling more strongly and more firmly bound to the See of Rome. It was Pope Saint Gregory the Great who sent Saint Augustine and his companions to preach the gospel to the Anglo-Saxons, and England was united to Rome for well nigh a thousand years. We venerate those brave men and women who remained true to Rome in the evil days which came, and especially these two great figures, John Fisher and Thomas More. And we pray earnestly that, following in their footsteps, the Catholics of England and Wales may ever be loyal to the successors of Saint Peter, and that our separated brethren may, by God's grace, recognise that divine authority for which John Fisher and Thomas More laid down their lives.

In the humble hope and petition that today's decree may be a happy augury of a yet more solemn one in the near future, and thanking you once again, most Holy Father, we implore the Apostolic blessing for ourselves and for our country."

The next few months were a busy time in England preparing for the pilgrimage to Rome for the canonisation. There was a problem about official representation from England. On 12th April Archbishop Pizzardo wrote from the Secretariat of State:

"It has been suggested to the Holy Father that it would be opportune to invite to the solemn function of the Canonisation of Blessed John Fisher and Thomas More the Speaker of the House of Commons, the Chancellors of Oxford and Cambridge and possibly also the Chancellor of the Exchequer. In view of the fact that Your Lordship is the Promoter of the Cause, the Holy Father commits it to you to issue these invitations. Availing myself of this occasion to renew to Your Lordship, the assurance of my esteem and of my religious devotion."

Unfortunately none of these esteemed dignatories made the journey. At St. Edmund's House, Cambridge, Fr. John Petit, the Master wrote on 27th April:

"I received the following from the Vice-Chancellor today. 'My dear Rector, In accordance with my promise to you I raised again the question of the representation of the University in Rome at the canonisation of the Blessed John Fisher. The Council, however, still wish to take no action in the matter.' So that's that. The Master of Corpus, one of the biggest forces in the University and probably the biggest wire-puller we have was set against the motion and the Vice-Chancellor consulted him. I tried to get him to change his point of view but he said he had nothing useful to add to the discussion. I hope Oxford is more inclined to our wishes but I have my doubts. It would serve Cambridge right if Oxford sent a representation."

Oxford however did not deign to send a representative and in the event Fr. Petit attended the canonisation as a semi-official representative of the University.

The Bishop tried to use the influence of Lord Rankeillour to approach the Chancellors of the Universities but this move failed. On 5th May 1935 he wrote to the Bishop:

"I am sorry but I cannot get Halifax to do anything. I fancy it is partly the influence of the Vice-Chancellor and partly the suspicion that rests upon him owing to his own views. I much regret it but there it is.

I have not heard from Baldwin but I am sure he would not differ from Halifax in this matter."

The Bishop wrote to the leading Catholic member of the Judiciary, Lord Russell of Killowen, to sound out the Lord Chancellor. The Chancellor's reply is not to hand but Lord Russell replied on the 10th April:

"It is as I expected. The concluding part of the Lord Chancellor's letter makes it quite impossible for me to attend even in an unrepresentative capacity . . . . I cannot but think however that the world will wonder how it comes about that the English Judiciary is absent and unrepresented when the most signal honour is being paid to the greatest man it ever produced."

There were problems also about the seating for the pilgrims at the actual ceremony. Lineal descendants of Blessed Thomas More, including George Eyston of East Hendred, found that they could obtain no special favours in the way of seats at the ceremony. However Fr. Smith in Rome did his best to see that the English in general had good positions in the Tribune and that they were all seated rather than standing. While the canonisation was not exactly welcomed with open arms by the establishment in Great Britain, there was little active hostility except from the Protestant Truth Society whose Secretary, J. A. Kensit, wrote to the Congregation of Rites after the canonisation was announced to say that there was evidence that John Fisher was in favour of a Spanish invasion of Great Britain and that there was a document to prove this to be found in Vienna. The Congregation of Rites gave him short shrift and told him merely to look up the State Papers again. Nothing further was heard from Kensit.

The official pilgrimage from Great Britain left London on 15th May by rail. Contemporary accounts say that it poured with rain all the way but brightened up in Rome. On the 17th the pilgrims gathered in St. Peter's for a solemn High Mass sung by Archbishop Hinsley. Then for two days the pilgrims were shown the sights of Rome, often led by students from the English College.

The great day, 19th May, was a Sunday. St. Peter's interior was illuminated by a myriad of candles in the Dome. These illuminations used to be an optional extra at canonisations. However not only was the cost extremely dear, but the fire risk was high and the practice has since been discontinued.

The entry procession was highly spectacular. The "Ordo Servandus" is a four-page document listing the order of the procession. All those taking part carried lighted candles. First came the members of religious orders. They were followed in by the Secular Priests who in turn were followed by the members of the Sacred Congregation of Rites according to their rank.

Next came the standards (Vexilla) of the two Beati. Each standard was preceded and followed by six priests with more elaborate twisted candles, while the standards were carried by six members of the Sodality of the Archconfraternity of the Holy Sacrament from St. Michael's Church in Burgo. Each standard had four long silken tassels which were carried by a further four priests. Then came the members of the Papal household and in the centre of this group were found the Sistine Choir singing the hymn "Ave Maris Stella." At the end of this section came the Penitentiaries of the Vatican Basilica dressed in red soutanes surrounding two clerics bearing two large bowls of flowers.

Next in line came the mitred abbots, Bishops and Archbishops the Patriarchs, the Cardinal Deacons, Cardinal Priests and Cardinal Bishops, the Papal Master of Ceremonies and then at last the Holy Father with the Masters of the Papal orders of Knighthood and certain other members of the "Custodia Pontificis" surrounding the "Sedia Gestatoria." The Pope carried a lighted candle in his left hand leaving the right hand free to administer his blessings to the assembled throng in the Basilica.

Behind the Holy Father came a few more members of the Papal Household and the Protonatory Apostolics (a Rank of Monsignor). Near the rear came a further eight members of the choir also singing "Ave Maris Stella."

On arrival at the high altar the "Te Deum" was sung and the Bishop, together with Archbishop Mostyn, leader of the English Pilgrimage, stood in' front of the Pope as he proclaimed the solemn decree of canonisation. The Holy Father then sang the first Mass of the two new Saints and the bells of Rome rang out in their honour. Shortly after one o'clock that day the Holy Father was duly borne out of St. Peter's, somewhat fatigued but evidently very happy.

There was some disappointment however over the seating for pilgrims. Although the English Pilgrimage arrived in good time for the ceremonies and were directed to their various sectors, they found that the best places in these sectors were already occupied by hordes of Italians and Germans.

On Monday evening the pilgrims were received in audience by the Holy Father and that day the pilgrims had a Mass of thanksgiving celebrated by Archbishop Mostyn at St. Paul's outside the Walls. And so the great event passed, but not unfortunately the monetary problems. For some reason Bishop Amigo believed that the total costs would be under £7,000 and he was somewhat surprised when he was asked to pay more and more after the ceremony was over. Faced with a demand for £2,500 he sent only £1,000 and Fr. Smith at the English College had to point out that the British were being attacked for their miserly attitude.

In a letter of the 28th June he writes to Bishop Amigo:

"We are cutting a very sorry figure in Rome. Last year, quite small religious institutes paid on the nail, borrowing where necessary. For a whole nation to be so slow in paying is producing a very bad impression. I have already explained to Your Lordship that there is no long term system of credit in Italy. Fr. Agostino insists on this and I must admit that our experience here at the Venerabile amply confirms his statement. Many of the payments have been reduced from the estimate . . . . Therefore in Agostino's name, I beseech you to send the money at once or arrange for it to be sent. England's good name is at stake. Agostino and I hardly dare appear in public, we are instantly besieged—and the things which are said do not make pleasant reading. It is terribly hot here, 97 degrees in the shade yesterday and today is going to be worse. I am perspiring just writing to Your Lordship—not for fear, I thank God, as St. John Fisher might have said—but by reason of this great heat that God hath sent."

The debts were finally paid off by the end of the year by means of a further collection in many dioceses. In spite of all the trials and tribulations, the delays and the money problems, it must surely be judged that this canonisation was for the Bishop the greatest achievement of his episcopate.

Chapter 11
The Fascist Regimes of the 1930's

The charge was laid against Bishop Amigo during the 1930's that he was Pro-Fascist. There is a certain amount of truth in this allegation. First of all he did not seem aware of the problems arising in Nazi Germany until 1938. Back in 1933 certain Jewish organisations in London were making efforts to interest the British in the plight of the Jews in Germany. In April of that year there was a proposal to hold a symposium on the Jewish question and in June there was a large protest meeting at the Queen's Hall headed by Viscount Buckmaster. However in reply to a letter asking for his support Bishop Amigo wrote (17th April 1933):

> "I am very sorry for anyone who is being persecuted but at the same time I am pained that those who are making such an outcry and seeking sympathy now, never had a word of sympathy for the Catholic Church when her priests and faithful were being martyred in Mexico and she was being persecuted in Mexico and latterly in Spain."

Throughout the 1930's the Bishop was rightly convinced that Communism was a real evil added to the atheism that was spreading through Europe. In 1938 he joined in the "Silent March against Atheism" which was held on Sunday 18th September, from Southwark Cathedral to Westminster Cathedral. The aim of this silent march was to pray for Divine Protection against infiltration of materialistic atheism and Public reparation to Almighty God for the public insults offered to him. In particular this silent march was an organised Catholic reaction to an anti-God congress being held at the time. The *'Tablet'* reported that 45,000 men joined the march, some coming down from as far away as Newcastle. There were four separate Benediction services given at the end of the march. Archbishop Amigo presided from a balcony overlooking Ashley Place. The Daily press barely mentioned the march, giving more prominence to a flotilla of 78 canoes en route from Kew to Wapping. The BBC did not mention the march at all. The Holy Father sent a message to the assembled crowds.

"The Holy Father greets from the depths of his heart, the Apostolic Benediction sought on the occasion of the silent procession of men from the three Dioceses of Southwark, Brentwood and Westminster ardently trusting that these fervent prayers of reparation will obtain from the Sacred Heart universal peace and the reign of Christ in the hearts of men throughout the whole of our society."

It should not be overlooked also that this march took place at a time when war seemed imminent because of what became known as the Munich crisis.

It is quite clear that the Bishop had a great personal regard for Mussolini right up to the outbreak of war. His approval of Mussolini was voiced on more than one occasion in public. In 1929 on the signing of the Vatican Treaty which restored normal relations between the Church and Italy, he spoke out with vigour in praise of the Italian Duce. So much so that it prompted one of the strangest incidents of his episcopate, a forged letter to the Clergy.

This letter was sent on the Eve of Corpus Christi 1929 to all Priests of the Diocese. It is a sustained attack on fascism and an encouragement to Italians living in this country to join anti-fascist organisations. The whole document is worth reading and it is re-printed as an appendix at the end of the book. The Bishop took steps at once to correct the damage with the Italian Government. He wrote to the Consul General in London.

"My Vicar General, Mgr. Banfi, has told me of the letter which purports to have been sent round by me to my Clergy. You already know from him that I have not written such a letter but you will be glad to get a disclaimer from me also. The Holy Father has not sent any letter to the Catholic Episcopate about Signor Mussolini. I certainly have not seen one. I have not written or spoken against one who has evidently done so much good to your country. The letter is a very scandalous forgery, and I shall be delighted if the author is severely punished."

In fact the author of this astonishing forgery was never disclosed;

presumably it was a priest of Italian descent who felt that the Bishop's stand was intolerable for Italians living in England.

In 1936 the Italians invaded Abyssinia much to the disgust of the League of Nations and the majority of people living in England. The Bishop however welcomed the event and stated in public in February his full confidence in the Duce. The newspapers of the day condemned this attitude but the Bishop defended the position he had taken up for some months to come. On the 18th February 1936 he wrote to one of his critics by way of his secretary.

"Dear Miss Dance,

His Lordship the Bishop of Southwark thanks you for your letter and directs me to point out that in his words last Sunday, he was referring to the possible danger to religion in Italy, if the present government there were to be overthrown. He remarked that the policy of the League of Nations was calculated to bring about a revolution in Italy. It has never been the practice of the Catholic Church to be silent through fear of persecution, nor is there any reason why we should not express our opinion in a country that boasts of its freedom of speech."

Looking back after fifty years it is quite clear that Bishop Amigo had made a very bad error of judgement over Mussolini. What evidence he had that there was any real threat to Il Duce in Italy at that time is not at all clear. Most Italians welcomed the military victories. On the 8th May 1936, Fr. Benedict Williamson, a Southwark Priest who acted as a Chaplain to a Hospital in Rome wrote to the Bishop on news of the great Italian 'conquest.'

"I heard the sirens sounding in the distance, then the nearer ones, the great bell of the Capitol and finally the Church bells. Workmen rushed from the factories, shops closed like lightning and the whole city was in motion towards the Piazza Venezia .... Rome has never been so strilled since the signing of the Treaty of Lateran. During these months the people have been united to an extent that exceeds anything in history, as they have constantly said 'we have one heart, one soul, one will'."

It was Spain however that provided the main drama on the European scene in 1936. The Republicans had gained strength since the end of the first world war. They had been leading forces in Spain against Germany at a time when many Spaniards were pro-German. Fanning the flames of the anti-clericals and anti-monarchists they forced King Alfonso to leave Spain in 1931. By 1936 they appeared to be firmly in power and the regime began to appear increasingly atheistic and hostile to religion. Support for the monarchy and the faith had always been strong in military circles and the outbreak of civil war came as no real surpise. The bitterness of the fighting and the many atrocities committed have been well documented by Huw Thomas in his majestic study of the Civil War. I am not here concerned with the events of the war but rather with the Bishop's attitude and reactions to the events.

Officially the policy of the British Government and also of the English and Welsh Hierarchy was to stand aside—the policy described as 'non-intervention.' It is quite clear that Bishop Amigo did not adhere to this policy. He made it evident from the start that he was fully behind General Franco. Most of the press and the majority of British people were backing the Republicans and the Bishop once again came under attack for his forthright views. He regarded the fight as between religion on the one side and communism and atheism on the other. Thus when the Germans sent help to Franco we find no trace of any complaint from the Bishop.

His Lordship's active involvement in the Civil War started in August 1936. On the 4th August he wrote to John Walter, Proprietor of the 'Times'.

"In my opinion the present Government has been too weak and the Communists have gained the upper hand. The military in their love for order, seeing their country going completely 'red' have determined to seize power. They may fail, but the state of Spain then will be worse than anything which we have heard about Russia. The Soviets certainly wish the so-called 'Rebels' to be beaten, but if they succeed in Spain they will stir up more trouble elsewhere. I am ordering special prayers for peace in my Diocese . . . . I shall have Exposition of the Blessed Sacrament in all the churches under my care on Sunday August 16th making that day a special day of intercession. We cannot side with the Communists in Spain . . . ."

The *South London Press* reported the events of the 16th August.

"There were over 1,000 Catholics in St. George's Cathedral, Southwark on Sunday when Bishop P. Amigo gave a vigorous pulpit criticism concerning the Spanish Civil War. He began by advising the congregation to ignore most newspaper reports. 'The people who are fighting the Spanish Government are described as rebels' indignantly remarked the Bishop. 'If they are rebels, then thank God, I am one' vehemently added the Bishop.... The people in Spain who were attacking the Government were not rebels, they are fighting for the Church of God."

The *Catholic Herald* on the other hand attacked the attitude taken by the Catholic Church in Spain. In the issue of 21st August 1936, in a review of the newsheet 'The *Catholic Worker*' the Editor Charles Diamond wrote:

"It should be remembered that the Communists who are now sacking churches are baptised Catholics who received their first Communion in the churches they are now desecrating. But the church failed them. It seemed to them unjust and unChristian and unless Christians in other countries realise that the Church has a social teaching and unless they strive to put it into practice, they will have to pay the same price. Christ was a worker, and according to Bossuet, it is the poor who now reflect the image of Christ. Thus they should be treated with extra special respect."

Looking back with hindsight one can probably agree that the Catholic Church lost the working classes because of a too close identification with the upper classes, but that hardly excuses the appalling atrocities of the Republicans in Spain. However I doubt if the Bishop agreed with the sentiments of a certain Ernest Lashmar of Storrington (who signed himself with a cross like a Bishop, following the example of Augustus Welby Pugin who alleged that this indicated the mark of a Christian gentleman not merely a Bishop). Lashmar wrote to the Bishop sending him the cutting from the *Catholic Herald* and adding in a postscript.

"The statement also that Christ was a worker is pure nonsense. He was a pure fascist. Workers and Socialists work only for class war. Christ like fascists works only for class union."

Meanwhile the Bishop's sermon in St. George's caused a furore locally at least. The local Labour MP, T. E. Naylor (East Southwark) wrote to the *South London Press* on 21st August.

"The recent pronouncements of Bishop Amigo in regard to the Italo-Abyssinian war and later on the Spanish Rebellion are very sad reading and make one despair of our Churches as leaders of mankind. It is almost incredible that a respected dignitary of the Catholic

Church should uphold Italy's crime in using all the resources of modern armaments against an almost defenceless and nominally Christian nation in a wanton unjustifiable war of conquest and defend the action of the military elements in Spain, employing Moors and Foreign Legionaries from Africa in a revolutionary war against a constitutionally elected Government. I trust he has been misreported. Perhaps he will explain."

To this attack the Bishop issued a special statement for the *South London Press*.

"His Lordship takes no side in Politics. His public announcements are concerned only with good order and justice. At no time has he spoken in defence of the invasion of Abyssinia or of the use of Moors and foreign legionaries in Spain.... In the Bishop's reference to Spain he said the Spanish government was too weak to put down disorder and that priests were being murdered, churches burnt and religion attacked. Therefore there was urgent need for prayer that Spain might have peace, good government and religious toleration.... As a matter of principle any nation may rise against a government that is guilty of grave injustice and unable to maintain public order. The evidence of such injustice and weakness is so overwhelming in the case of Spain, one wonders at the blindness of those who deny it."

This announcement did nothing to quell the trouble. The following week Miss Monica Whately, a Catholic and President of the Clapham Labour Party, had a leaflet printed giving the republican side of the picture with reference to Barcelona, which also indirectly attacked the Bishop. This leaflet was handed to parishioners at the door of St. Mary's Clapham Park much to the annoyance of most of them it seems. The *South London Press* printed a grossly misleading feature headed "Catholics may be forbidden to vote Socialist." It was alleged that the Bishop had said "Catholics must scuttle their politics when their religion is attacked." Even if the Bishop had uttered these words they referred to Spain and not to Britain. Personally as already noted, the Bishop was very sympathetic to the British Labour Party.

In view of the mounting attacks on him the Bishop then issued an official press release to the national dailies which was printed in the '*Times*' and '*Manchester Guardian*.' (5th September 1936).

"It is difficult for many in this country to realise the present situation in Spain. Ever since the Republic was started, there has been a movement against religion which need not have been. It was shown in the attack on religious education. Violence broke out in Madrid in 1931 and in Asturias in October 1933. The Election of February 1936 brought about a still greater change. A weak government took charge but churches were burnt and people were murdered, yet few or none were punished. The communists and anarchists became the masters and government was powerless. Last July after the awful murder of Carlos Sotelo, which was attributed to officials, the military under Generals Franco, Mola and Cabanellas rose up to prevent what they considered the total destruction of their country. There may be exaggerations now, as there were in our own case during the Great War, but undoubtably many churches have been burnt in Madrid, Barcelona, and elsewhere; bishops, priests and nuns have been cruelly murdered; sailors in the service of a weak government have killed their officers. Those who are called here rebels and insurgents are fighting for God and their Country."

The very day this letter was published, the Bishop addressed a large meeting of the Knights of St. Columba in Brighton in which he made a strong attack on Republican atrocities. The *Brighton Evening Argus* reported (6th August):

"Dr. Amigo said a woman married to an English Protestant who had just come from Carthagena told him how 346 naval officers were put to death. 'Do you call it a government that cannot put down that sort of thing?' he asked. 'A government that allows churches to be burned down and priests and nuns to be slaughtered cannot be called democratic. It is too weak to govern."

This drew forth a virulent attack on the Bishop and the Catholic Church in general from Cdr. R. Dickens of Brighton. (7th September).

"... I venture to express that your friends the fascists did revolt against a legal non-red and non anti-Church government like the majority of Bolsheviks did in Tsarist Russia, you didn't sympathise with them over that fact I guess, though you mentioned that elections were a farce—they generally are when the opponents are lucky. Queer is it not, how the R. C. Church upholds Christ in these upheavals and then spurns him in the normal times. However he did have the courage of his convictions added to great simplicity, he did not resort to murder, lies, etc etc to make this a better world, not even castor oil and Spanish R.C. Inquisitions. You apparently think that murder and lust and oppression is a good foundation for the Christian (?) religion and for curing the Evils of this world. Maybe for safe cushy jobs for the Higher Clergy, I venture to say that Religionists are more atheist than the atheist himself, so far we have had about 1903 years of Christianity issuing from Rome, and I think we are lower than the beasts of the jungle for all that because we sin with such finesse and subtlety, the veneer of civilisation and religion.

Overleaf I mentioned your friends, the Fascists—Fascism—the political weapon for oppressing the humble and meek, and lauding material (not spiritual) wealth, for Robbery, murder, rape, sodomy etc. ... We English ought to be very proud of Henry VIII, I admire him, for not wanting to be bossed by an Arch-hypocrite, I raise my hat to him also to Lenin, though I am not communistic and not particularly anti-God .... You know it may be intuition but when I have been among strangers, I have generally spotted out R.C.'s not all, by their countenance, exuding hatred. Is it their religious tyranny that causes it, or is it communism or Anglicanism, which is my professed faith?"

This letter is given as an example of the anti-Catholic feeling that was still common in this country during the 1930's.

The Bishop was then prompted to write a further letter to the *'Times'* on 22nd September 1936. As this letter clearly states the Bishop's position, it is given in full.

"Sir,

The letters on Spain, which have been appearing recently in your columns, prove how easy it is to get away from principles and argue on side-issues. My attitude in championing the anti-reds in Spain could cause a crisis among Catholic Socialists only by a complete misunderstanding of the issue. My remarks have been prompted solely by the consideration that the Government in Spain was communistic, and that Communism is the greatest danger to Church and State and to the dignity of man. To make clear what I mean, allow me to enumerate some of the doctrines of Communism.

1. There is no God and no such thing as an immortal soul.
2. There is no future life.
3. The individual man or woman, as such, is of no importance: only the community matters.

4. No individual has "rights" against or apart from the community.
5. No individual can claim any liberty, nor has he any "right" to indissoluble marriage, to the control or education of his children, to worship publicly, to spread his religion or to express his opinion on the policy of his rulers.

Such doctrines involve the destruction of all personal and public liberty, and reduce man to the level of a mere cog in a machine. The Catholic Church has ever upheld the dignity of man, his liberty and his right to possess, and can never come to terms with Communism, which destroys whatever is noble in life.

The Spanish people have as noble a concept of the dignity of man as the people of England, and when they saw their cherished institutions being systematically destroyed, they rose against an iniquitous Government. That is the real issue in Spain. Can anyone condemn a people for fighting in defence of their God, their liberty, both political and personal, and their homes?"

The Civil War produced at least two special organisations in Great Britain acting mainly on behalf of the nationalist cause. The first was the 'Bishops Committee for the Relief of Spanish Distress.' This was formed to assist sick, wounded, refugees and children. Funds were sent into Nationalist Spain and were often used for the purchase of medical supplies for the wounded and the prisoners of the nationalists. A specifically nationalist organisation was entitled 'The Friends of National Spain' under the Chairmanship of the Rt. Hon. Lord Phillimore MC. The purpose of the organisation was to put the Spanish Nationalist cause before the people. After the war ended it was transformed into the 'Friends of Spain' with the purpose of interpreting the new Spain to the British public and preventing misunderstandings of Spanish affairs in future. Archbishop Amigo was involved in both organisations and became a Vice-President of the latter.

During 1937 a certain Councillor Eugene Egan organised public meetings at various venues in South London to promote the nationalist cause. The Bishop gave his support. In March 1937 he wrote to Mr. Egan:

"I am very sorry I cannot be with you tomorrow night. I hope you will have a most successful meeting and that the excellent speakers will show the audience how the Catholics are suffering in Spain. Most of our daily papers unfortunately seem blind to the truth.

Franco and his followers are not Fascists nor are they rebels. They are opposed to a Government which was not properly elected by the people, and which was powerless to prevent outrages of every kind which had been committed before last July. If Franco had not courageously come forward, Spain would be a complete ruin by now. The enemies of religion, chiefly from Russia have been undermining Catholic Spain for years . . . . The nationalists hope to put an end to this awful state of things, and there is peace for the Church and happiness for the people where Franco rules. We wish him a speedy and complete victory over the enemies of God and of religion. Christ our Lord will triumph."

In April 1937 there took place the notorious incident of the German bombing of Guernica. The '*Times*' published a merciless attack on the nationalists for allowing this atrocity. This prompted the Bishop to write to his old friend John Walter (4th May 1937):

" . . . You will be able to use your influence with the Times on behalf of the Nationalists in Spain. You know that country and you realise how Russia has been undermining it for years past. It was high time after so many murders and sacrileges that something should be done to save the religion of the nation. There was a merciless attack on the Nationalists in the *Times* when the news came about Guernica, now that today the nationalist Communique is published. The Reds are capable of doing any amount of harm. My fear is that if they were successful in Spain we should have trouble in England. I am sure you will do your best to make our people see the truth."

At the start of 1938 the Archbishop sent a goodwill message and congratulations to General Franco. In St. George's Cathedral he said:

"General Franco is a good Catholic beloved by the Spanish soldiers. Those in high places who say the struggle in Spain is between Franco and democracy are wrong. It is a question of God versus the Devil. The so-called government of Spain has been repeatedly warned against the burning of Churches and the murder of Priests. These misdeeds continue despite protests and Franco continues in his duty to strike."

It was perhaps rather badly timed for just about then the bombs were dropping on Barcelona in quantity and it was widely reported that it was entirely women and children that died.

The report of the Bishop's sermon roused a few letters of protest. The Bishop replied to Percy Hills of Eltham (via his secretary). 2nd February 1938.

"While the Bishop is by no means indifferent to the terrible suffering inflicted on all of either side, he does not wish to disguise that he considers the appalling atrocities and sacrileges which took place before the beginning of the war, in which the Government elected thanks to shameless manipulation of the voting, at least connived, justified General Franco and his followers in their rising, and that the establishment of the General's power over all Spain would ensure the peace and tranquility of public order. His Lordship has no concern with politics as such nor has he any quarrel with any political system whether inclined to the right or the left as long as the liberties of the people including their liberty to Worship God, are respected . . . ."

None the less, one must admit that his original statement was very badly timed and as with the bombing of Guernica, one might have expected some kind of expression of genuine regret. We have to bear in mind when judging the Archbishop's remarks that the atrocities committed against priests and nuns by the republicans including over six thousand secular priests killed, were never properly recorded by the English press while the nationalist atrocities received the banner headline treatment.

In 1938 the main concern turned towards Nazi Germany. The British people in general at last came to realise the true nature of that terrible regime. In April that year the Germans took over Austria (Anschluss) and refugees started arriving in quantity in this country. The work of caring for these refugees was put into the hands of the Lord Baldwin Fund for Refugees. The Christian Council for Refugees and Council for German Jewry were parent bodies of this organisation. The Catholic Committee for Refugees from Germany was a constituent part of the Christian Council for Refugees. The President was Cardinal Hinsley and the four Catholic Archbishops including Archbishop Amigo were nominated as Vice-Presidents. The main force in the organisation as far as Catholics were concerned was Father Joseph Geraerts DCL.

Many of the early Catholic refugees from Austria were either Jewish converts or married to Jews. Despite an appeal from all the Bishops of England and Wales made after the Low Week meeting of 1938, funds did not flow in well up to the end of the year. The Archbishop of Birmingham was forced to send out a letter asking his priests to press upon the laity the need to be generous, and pointed out how generous they had been in response to an appeal from the Archbishop of Cardiff for relief to the poor in the mining communities. (Ad Clerum 13 December 1938).

Priests came over to minister to the refugees. Fr. E. Reichenberger was a refugee himself. He had been leader of the Sudenten German opposition to the Nazis. The Nazis stole his property, money, books and clothes when they marched into Sudetenland (Czechoslovakia) after the Munich Agreement.

The Archbishop was rather chary at first about refugee children. In 1937, many Basque children came to England and were used as political pawns in the Spanish Civil War. When Dr. Calnan of Surbiton wrote in December 1938 about appealing for funds for German refugee children in his area, the Archbishop's secretary replied.

"I asked His Grace the Archbishop this morning what was his attitude towards the refugee children from Germany and he replied very firmly that he would have nothing to do with them. When I pointed out that there might be Catholics among them he said that of course we should have to do all we could for Catholic children . . . . I doubt if there will be much support coming from our religious societies some of which were badly bitten over the Basque children nor is there any likelihood of large scale relief. If I may venture a word of advice, you would be wise to commit yourself to nothing as you will certainly be left holding the baby (probably several). But I infer from your letter that you already realise this danger. The trouble as I see it is that charity soon grows cold and unless help is forthcoming from public funds, it is impossible for us to undertake any responsibility for the relief of refugees."

Not everything went smoothly in the care of the refugees. On 28th May, the Vicar General, Mgr. Banfi, wrote to the Chief Refugee Chaplain in Southwark, a Father E.J. Eisenberger DEM at Maidstone that he had received a complaint that no spiritual ministrations were made to the Catholics at Richborough Camp near Sandwich. Fr. Eisenberger replied that he would go at once but he had been to the camp a few weeks previously to be told by the Camp Director that the camp only had Jewish refugees and no Catholics. He went on in his letter to say that he was trying to convert forty Sudeten German refugees who were communists now living in Maidstone. "They of course are very hard nuts to crack and they have no idea of the real point of any religious life."

In another letter he mentions another group of thirty Sudeten Catholic refugees living miles from any Church at West Hoathly, Sussex and requests permission to say Mass for them in the house they are living in.

The Archbishop was asked to be a patron of another organisation, the Austrian Centre (for Refugees). He wrote to Fr. Geraerts to find out about the Centre and received the reply that there might be a slight tendency to leftish political activity, but nothing of real consequence. Fr. Geraerts went on to say that the organisation was too small to merit the patronage of the Archbishop and suggested a lay patron instead. The Archbishop replied that while he welcomed all efforts to better the condition of the refugees and assist them in any way he could, he could not depart from his rule only to give his patronage to general societies and not to any particular branch of a society.

After the outbreak of the Second World War the Refugees Organisation was transformed into a new body dealing with all refugees. 'The Catholic War Refugees Spiritual Welfare Committee.'

In the months leading up to the outbreak of war the *'Catholic Herald'* spearheaded a grand peace appeal. The headlines on 14th April 1939 ran: "Appeal to 300 million Catholics, Ask Your Bishops to press Their governments for a Peace Conference. A Petition that Christian teaching on War and Peace may be observed."

It is quite amazing looking back to consider the naivety of the editor who could say of the situation:

"There is a patent artificiality about everything that has led to the present deadlock. As though it had taken place in a world of make-believe. At most there is moral indignation on one side at the unilateral attempts already largely successful of the other to expand its domination at the expense, so far, of smaller nations in no position to resist.

There is no less moral indignation on the other side at the virtual domination by two or three great Powers of the richest territories and markets of the globe, a domination which in their view, was legalised by an enforced peace treaty and considered ever afterwards as morally sacrosanct."

The Bishop made no response at all to a personal appeal from the Editor as far as I can discover.

Two other organisations which arose at this time did meet with Episcopal approbation. 'The League of God' strove to bring all men to the knowledge and love of God, and they took the line that the evils besetting the world were caused by man's selfishness and greed and by his disregard of God's laws. When the war broke out the League produced reading material for the troops with the aim of ensuring that they did not turn against God for supposedly causing the misery now afflicting mankind.

Another organisation was the 'United Christian Petition Movement' which sought to prevent poverty and remove the economic causes of war and to establish a Christian Social Order. The Archbishop replied to their request for support.

"There will always be inequalities among men, but it is a reproach that in the civilisation in which we live with its as yet little explored resources, and the wide opportunities it affords for a decent living for all, there should be so much poverty and destitution.

The Catholic Church, while striving by spiritual means to help the poor to bear their burden, often almost insupportable, has never been indifferent to their temporal prosperity.

The Popes, faithful to the great traditions of their Sacred Office, have stood forth as champions of the poor, asserting their right to work for a living wage, sufficient to support them in frugal comfort and provide for their old age and the necessities of a normal family. Without entering upon any political controversies I welcome your efforts to bring these truly Christian principles before our people and trust that you may be able to awaken the public conscience to the enormity of waste and luxury at a time when many are in want for the barest necessities of life."

Chapter 12
The Second World War

Archbishop Amigo was seventy-five years old at the outbreak of war in 1939. Today all Bishops have to tender their resignation at this age but for the Archbishop the next six years were to be as busy as ever, if not more so. The regular visitations were kept up with as little interruption as possible. Whenever a Church or school was damaged or destroyed the Archbishop would hurry along at once to console the local residents. The Diocese was to suffer terribly during the war and for the Archbishop there was the fearful blow of the loss of St. George's Cathedral to an incendiary bomb.

Yet in addition to all the additional burdens the Archbishop had other responsibilities. Cardinal Hinsley could not undertake all the burden of negotiations with the Government and his health was not good, so the Archbishop was called in to assist.

To return to 1939, on the very day that war was declared he wrote to Neville Chamberlain, the Prime Minister.

"You have my heartfelt sympathy. You certainly have done your utmost to prevent war; I heartily congratulate you on your splendid effort and I am sorry that you have not had the success which you richly deserved. I will do my best to help you with my prayers and those of my people."

Chamberlain is usually portrayed as a weak Prime Minister, particularly with regard to his dealing with Hitler in 1938 at Munich. Amigo evidently thought better of him than many for he wrote again in October 1940 following his resignation from the Government. The letter is now lost but Anne Chamberlain replied on 9th August 1941.

"I have wished before this to write to tell you how much my beloved husband appreciated the letter which you wrote him last October in connection with his resignation from the Government . . . . He had no opportunity of writing to you before he died just three weeks later. He read your letter to me and reading it again now I see how truly you understood what he was striving for, amid—as you said, so many difficulties and with so great a devotion and courage. Those qualities remained with him to the end accompanied by the knowledge that we should go on unflinchingly—and by the faith that right would ultimately prevail . . . ."

The first major negotiations undertaken by the Archbishop concerned the exemption of Church students from military service. The Military Service Act of 1938 had made no provision for the exemption of Church students and with the agreement of Cardinal Hinsley the Archbishop first visited Sir Herbert Creedy at the War Office, on 1st June 1939. Sir Herbert agreed to contact General Weymes who evidently made a few small concessions but nowhere near enough to satisfy the Catholics. He wrote on the 9th June again to Sir Herbert making the following argument:

" . . . . If soldiers need to be trained, the training of a priest is longer and more necessary. You will not have Chaplains unless they are trained. The Act will upset the training at a most critical age. We lost many students owing to conscription in the Great War and others suffered through the interruption of their spiritual training . . . . Bishop Dey (The Military Bishop) is rightly asking for more Territorial Chaplains. If war comes we wish to be able to help the soldiers. How shall we be able to do it if you do not give us the chance of training future chaplains? You have plenty of young men available without taking away those who can be prepared to serve the Nation in a very special way hereafter and who should therefore be exempt from the Military Training Act. If any student gives up the idea of being a priest, it will be the duty of his Bishop to report him to the Military Authorities and he can then be taught to shoot and fight as a soldier."

Strangely perhaps, Bishop Dey was opposed to the Archbishop's actions. He wrote to him on 8th July and made the following points in favour of military service for students:

"Among the advantages are . . . 1, compulsory physical training which should benefit their bodily health. 2, the opportunity of mixing with other youths with its possibilities for Catholic Action. (I would suggest a 3 months course of Apologetics for every student before beginning his military training). 3, the especial emphasis shewn in military life on prompt obedience to an order and the complete and careful fulfilment of a duty. From my recent experience as Rector of a Seminary I am disposed to think that the modern church student is too easily satisfied with an indifferent fulfilment of any task and thereafter, too ready with specious excuses for his failure. A good Sergeant-Major will rapidly destroy all his illusions about the amount of perfection necessary before one can consider a duty really well done and the specious 'slacker' will be rather rudely stripped of his complacency . . . ."

The Archbishop's reply to this letter is not to hand but Bishop Dey was to have occasion to write several letters of complaint later to the Archbishop about the lower number of Southwark Chaplains.

Sir Herbert replied on 13th June that he was afraid that there was no chance of any exception being made in the case of his students though he fully appreciated the Bishop's natural interest in them.

The Archbishop was not deterred by this apparent brush off. He decided to contact the Ministry of Labour instead. On the 21st July he secured an interview with Ernest Brown, the Minister, and persuaded Brown to re-open the case with the War Ministry by contacting the Secretary of State, Mr. Hore-Belisha directly. The Archbishop had used a rather subtle ploy. In his letter to Hore-Belisha, Ernest Brown wrote (22nd July 1939):

" . . . . His Grace explained that in general priests commence their training at the age of 14 years. The training takes 12 years in all and that if their training were interrupted for a period of military training, it would have a serious effect on their spiritual training. He accordingly pressed that when they were called up the men should not undergo military training but should be trained as chaplains."

Of course the Archbishop realised that not every priest would in fact be called upon to be a Chaplain so he backed up the letter of Brown with a lengthy memorandum which stressed the usefulness of the Priest in time of war. He pointed out for instance that as priests they would not merely give spiritual succour to their people in times of stress but also be a powerful means of preserving morale. To this argument he added that the wish of the Holy See that those destined for Holy Orders should not bear arms and that Catholics might with reason regard compulsion in this matter as an infringement of their religious rights.

It took until September for the required concessions to be granted. A deputation headed by the Archbishop called on the Minister of Labour in late September, and the Minister finally gave way. The Minister wrote to Cardinal Hinsley:

"I propose that the matter should be dealt with by the addition of the following entry in the Schedule of Reserved Occupations:- Theological students; a man who was before September 1939 established in his course as a student at an institution recognised by any religious denomination as a training institution for Holy Orders or for regular Ministers of that denomination, while he continues as such a student and intends to qualify for Holy Orders or for appointment as a regular Minister."

It only remained for the Bishop to ensure that those students who had already been called up should be released and enabled to return to their seminaries. He wrote to that effect to Sir Victor Warrender at the War Office on 25th September, and within a few weeks all the remaining students were demobbed and returned to their seminaries.

The next major matter to attend to was the evacuation of children from London to country areas to avoid bombing. The Archbishop was particularly concerned that every effort be made to safeguard the faith of these children while away from home.

The L.C.C. had agreed that in general Catholic parties of children would only be sent to places where there was a Catholic Church within walking distance. The general plan was to try and keep entire school parties from Catholic schools together. The Archbishop rejected any idea of merging Catholic parties with non-Catholic schools. In many instances the entire evacuated school was able to function as a complete unit. In the Archbishop's letter on Evacuation addressed to all his priests he wrote (13th May 1940):

"In view of the willingness of Officials to facilitate these special arrangements for Catholic children, the work of all concerned will be much simplified if the children can be readily identified as Catholics e.g. by wearing a badge of the "I am a Catholic" type. When parents are in future signing forms asking them for the evacuation of their children, special care should be taken to get them to write the word 'Catholic' in large letters at the head of the form."

A later memorandum (undated) reveals that not everything went according to plan. The main problems concerned those children sent to country and rural areas where the villages were far apart. The school at Tooting was completely merged with the local state school at Compton while the poor children from the Cathedral Parish found themselves scattered over a wide area of Dorset around Sherbourne. The memo records the confusion:

"(4) The L.C.C. was responsible for the evacuation of the children from London, and the local billeting officers were to see to the billeting of the children. It would seem that these billeting officers did not know what children were coming or where they were coming from. The L.C.C. kept the destinations secret because at the last moment, destinations might have to be changed owing to the destruction of railways and roads by enemy action."

This was a case of a stupid administrative blunder. The evacuations for the most part were completed before the bombs came and the supposed risks did not exist at all.

Where the children were scattered around, the Bishop arranged that one priest from the London Parish should accompany the children and say Mass for them, returning during the week to his own Parish.

The advent of war meant that there was an immediate need for a large number of full-time Chaplains. Archbishop Amigo provided nine Chaplains initially. Dozens of priests wrote to him offering their services but most were turned down. Most dioceses gave about ten per cent of their priests for active service as Chaplains. If Southwark had followed the same pattern there should have been thirty-four full-time Chaplains from South of the Thames. Bishop Dey kept on writing to Archbishop Amigo for more Chaplains and every time was turned down. He considered that his priests would be better employed looking after their flocks at home during the bombing.

Many priests have alleged that the Archbishop was in practice against Forces Chaplains. There is some truth in this. In the first world war he had difficulties with the Chaplains returning after the war. who found it difficult to settle back into civilian life. There were seemingly endless problems over chaplaincies to the army and navy establishments in the Diocese. In 1916 the Bishop had taken up the cause of appointing a full-time Bishop for the forces mainly because he wished to see a diminution in the powers accorded to Cardinal Bourne. Although on friendly terms with William Keatinge the first forces

Bishop, they did not see eye to eye on military chaplaincies even in peace time. In June 1930 Bishop Keatinge had asked Bishop Amigo for an interview regarding the possibility of one of the Southwark priests becoming a Naval Chaplain. He wrote on the 10th June 1930:

> " . . . it seems incredible that you could not see me for a few minutes in the last three weeks, or even in the near future, even granting you were busy. I don't think any other Bishop would test a brother Bishop like that. However my Lord, you can rest assured of one thing, and that is, I shall not trouble you again for an interview."

Eventually in 1942 Bishop Dey lost all patience with Archbishop Amigo and wrote a very stiff 'Open Letter' a copy of which was sent to all the Bishops of the country and to Rome. This letter is dated 5th August 1942. Bishop Dey first relates an account of their meeting on 14th July of that year. The Bishop had pointed out that the Diocese was well stocked with priests while many of the parishes had become depopulated owing to the war. Surely he could spare a few priests as Chaplains. According to the Bishop, the Archbishop then said not only could he not send any more priests as Chaplains but *would not* and that was his last word on the matter. The Open Letter continues:

> " . . . . This attitude in an English Bishop at this time seems to me to be so outrageous that I am led to wonder whether Your Grace realises all that it implies. By refusing to allow Southwark clergy to minister to Southwark men and women in the forces, 1) you place under a virtual interdict all Catholic men and women who are your subjects and who are loyally risking their lives in defence of their religion, their country and their freedom 2) You throw an unfair burden on all your brother bishops, whose priests will have to undertake the care of your unjustly forsaken people in addition to their own proper responsibilities. Your failure to fulfil your just obligations will make an undue call on their Christian charity in order that your shortcomings shall be made good. 3) You stultify the action of the Holy See, which as a result of the sad experience in the last war, established the appointment of an Episcopus Castrensis precisely to secure for Catholic soldiers what you are now deliberately taking away from them i.e. a ready access to the Sacraments . . . "

The Archbishop seems not to have replied directly to this letter but attempted to defend his position to Cardinal Hinsley. In the draft letter (undated) to the Cardinal he writes:

" . . . Priests are also wanted at home. They can make people pray for our Forces; they have to administer sacraments to civilians; they have to keep up the morale of the Nation. In my diocese I have 344 priests of my own on active work, and Bishop Dey makes his quotas without taking into account what these men have to do. My directory shows that we have 194 churches registered for marriages. That means churches where at least two Masses have to be said every Sunday. In addition there are what the Catholic Directory calls 'other public churches' with public Mass on Sundays which number 82. The chapels in communities, institutions, Asylums and Prisons are 152. I have had to borrow priests from Ireland and there are 41 here at present but they are liable to be recalled. We lost nine last year. My aim in my long episcopate has been to give facilities for Mass and Sacraments to my scattered flocks and hence the increase in public churches from 92 in 1904.

It is true that we have 216 regulars but they only supply 32 churches as the Carthusians and the teaching Orders have their own special work to do . . . . My priests have been wonderful and I cannot speak too highly of them. They are in the front line of battle and they have had a big share of suffering. South London and the coast towns have had continual attacks but even inland places like Petworth have had enemy visits. Two of my priests have been killed in raids and in several cases priests' nerves have been terribly shattered. In some places I have sent priests with the evacuated children to safer parts of England, in others through the destruction of our large churches the Masses in the halls were so crowded that we even had to have more Masses on Sundays as the accommodation was much less. I have to point out that in Southwark we have now thousands of soldiers on account of our proximity to France, and more than fifty of our priests are employed as officiating chaplains . . . ."

A few more priests were eventually sent out near the end of the war. One of the Southwark Chaplains, Fr. Cyril Scarborough was taken prisoner at Dunkirk in 1940 and spent the rest of the war in prisoner of war camps including a spell at the famous Colditz Castle where he witnessed the arrival of the Allied troops who captured the fortress near the end of the war.

Towards the end of 1940 London was heavily bombed and many churches were destroyed or badly damaged. The Government introduced a Bill to cover war damage repairs. On 20th December 1940 Cardinal

Hinsley wrote to all the Bishops suggesting the setting-up of a small committee of Bishops plus others to deal with the problems throughout the country and to enter into negotiations not only with the Government but also with other churches.

About this time the body known as the Churches Main Committee was set up to deal with the problem and Bishop Brown was the Catholic representative on this body. Archbishop Amigo was chosen as the Chairman of the Bishops' Committee. Their work was to deal with the specific problems of the Catholic community and to liaise with the Churches' Main Committee. In the House of Commons Sir Patrick Hannon represented their interests while the real work of the committee was in the very able hands of Fr. William Anderson MA, the Parish Priest of St. Mary's, Cadogan Gardens.

The Government was most anxious that the Bill should include the interests of all religious bodies and that a common policy be adopted by all of them. One of the early problems was the question of whether churches should pay contributions (virtually insurance contributions) towards the costs after the war. Another problem concerned the amount to be paid out on buildings which were total losses. Would the amount be based on an estimated value of the original building, or on the cost of the work involved in re-building? The general drift of the Bill with regard to churches and schools which were totally destroyed was to provide in their place buildings of a simple nature which would accommodate the same number of people as the original buildings. The question of total re-building was to provide a problem later on after St. George's Cathedral was bombed. Already at the start of 1941 the Diocese had seen serious damage or total destruction of twelve Churches and twenty-five Churches with lesser damage, while three presbyteries had been destroyed, two schools seriously damaged and the Girls Home at Rotherhithe (together with its Church) destroyed by fire. Worse was to follow as the war progressed.

Before looking at the total losses sustained by the Diocese I should like to cover other aspects of the Archbishop's work in relation to wartime conditions.

At the start of the war a 'Black Out' was imposed and the Archbishop complained bitterly to Sir John Anderson the Home Secretary on 20th October 1939.

" . . . I am pleading against the present regulations of the Black Out. It is doubtful whether it is a real protection against enemy air raids as the Germans are ready to come even in broad daylight, and they have actually done so. It is certainly the cause of innumerable accidents, many of them fatal. You have the returns from London and from the whole country. It is most damaging to shopkeepers as their business has to close just when in poor districts most of it would be done. No end of people are greatly inconvenienced by the darkness. The cinemas and other places of amusement have again been opened in order to prevent many being down-hearted, but the return home is made exceedingly difficult. ... As the days become shorter in November and December we shall be in darkness each day, except for about seven hours. Why make people more miserable? If the Government is determined on continuing the black out why not confine it from 10pm to 6am? Need it be as severe as it is at present?"

Sir John Anderson sent a courteous reply (25th October 1939).

"The whole policy of the Black Out has recently been under review by a Committee of responsible Ministers, and I can readily assure you that full weight was given by that Committee to all the considerations to which you refer in your letter. No Minister of the Crown would be anxious to maintain conditions fraught with the disadvantages to which you refer, unless overriding considerations of national security made it essential to do so. After considering both sides of this difficult question, the Government have come to the conclusion that it is necessary in the national interests to maintain the present policy; and while I fully recognise the force of the arguments used in your letter, I must ask you to recognise that the Ministers of the Crown are in the best position to assess the value of the strategical considerations which led the Government to decide that the present lighting restrictions must continue in force."

In July 1940 the Archbishop was writing to Sir John Anderson again, this time to complain about the internment of Italians resident in this country following Italy's declaration of war.

The problem of Italian internees had been made worse by the Government decision to ship off a large number of them to America on board a liner, the 'Arandora Star.' This liner was torpedoed with great loss of life. The Archbishop said in his letter:

"Italian men have all been interned and matters were made worse by suddenly shipping off a large number to America. No adequate protection for their safety was taken. At a time when we specially need the blessing of God, we commit what other Nations will call a terrible crime. When we should be making friends instead of increasing our enemies we unfortunately send excellent men to an undeserved death . . . . I beg of you to use all your powerful influence to obtain that those Italians who have borne a good character in England for some years be allowed to remain with their families and to go on earning their living instead of being interned. The wholesale internment of foreigners will be a huge burden for the Nation and will unnecessarily irritate those who could assist us in these very critical days. I have been in contact with many Italians among my flock and I know that the greater part are thoroughly reliable and worthy of esteem. We shall never regret showing mercy to those who through no fault of their own belong to a Nation dragged into war with us."

In November 1941 the Archbishop attempted to obtain exemption for priests from compulsory Civil Defence Duties. He wrote directly to the Home Secretary, Herbert Morrison, who told him that there could be no exemptions because of the wide resentment that would be caused if such exemptions were granted. However he was prepared to concede that the duties allocated to Ministers of Religion should be so arranged as to cause the minimum of interference with their spiritual functions and in general that they should be assigned fire prevention duties at their own churches or in the immediate vicinity.

In 1942 the Archbishop took up the matter of Sunday Bus Services with the Minister of Transport, Lord Leathers. In November of that year there had been an order that no buses should operate until 1.00pm in most areas. This of course caused hardship to congregations in rural districts.

Lord Leathers replied that he understood the problem but it was necessary to conserve supplies of motor fuel and rubber and also to relieve the strain of war conditions on the attenuated staffs of road transport undertakings. The elimination of services of a Sunday morning would enable one shift of drivers to have a rest and also to allow overhauls to take place in daylight.

The Bishop made two broadcasts on BBC foreign services during the war, the first to Latin America on 3rd April 1941 on the attitude of the Church to the war, and the second to Spain and Portugal on Christmas Day 1942.

In order to illustrate the Archbishop's own feelings on the war I have given the text of an article he wrote for the '*Evening Standard*' on 14th May 1941. This is given in the Appendices. The Archbishop said much the same thing in his war time pastorals and on visitations at this time.

The most serious event of the war for the Diocese of Southwark was the loss by fire of St. George's Cathedral. The building designed by the great Augustus Welby Pugin had been solemnly opened in 1848 before the restoration of the Hierarchy in 1850. Even before disaster struck there had been minor alarms. In November 1939 the boiler at Archbishop's House burst and flooded the lower regions of the house. The same boiler burst twice more during the course of the same month. However it seems that it was not enemy action but a lazy stoker who was responsible for the trouble.

The cathedral escaped the first bombing onslaught on London in the Autumn of 1940 but on the 16th April 1941 the enemy struck. On that night German planes showered down on London thousands of incendiary bombs starting fires all over town which it soon became impossible to control through lack of water. The water mains had been put out of action by heavy bombs and the Thames was a low ebb. The London Fire Service were compelled to stand helpless by their engines. Shortly after midnight one small incendiary bomb struck the roof of the Cathedral. Fr. Cowderoy from Archbishop's House was quickly on the scene with a stirrup pump but could do little to halt the advance of the flames and within a few minutes the hundred-year-old timber was ablaze from end to end. In a very short time nothing was left of St. George's but a smouldering ruin. Luckily the fire did not spread to Archbishop's House or Cathedral Clergy House. The Archbishop was down at the Junior Seminary, Mark Cross, at the time and it was left to the Rector, Mgr. Corbishley to break the news to His Grace, who left at once to see the damage.

The loss of the Cathedral was an enormous blow to him. He was already an old man but this one event aged him even more. To some extent one could say he never recovered from the loss of his beloved Cathedral even though he lived a further eight years. That is not to say he was any the less busy after the disaster but it is clear that it was always on his mind thereafter. His study window looked out over the Cathedral and he usually kept the window open even on the coldest days while looking out over the ruin.

To replace the Cathedral the Amigo Hall, opened just before the war, was used as a pro-Cathedral and when this in turn was required for school rooms when the children returned from evacuation, the Sisters of Notre Dame offered the use of their Hall as a pro-Cathedral. At the end of the war the Amigo Hall was once again used as a pro-Cathedral until the opening of the re-built St. George's in 1959.

By the end of the war the Diocese could count up the toll. Seven Churches as well as the cathedral were totally destroyed. Nearly every other Church and presbytery in the London area suffered some damage, even if not directly hit. Several schools were destroyed also. Five Diocesan Priests were killed by enemy action. In 1940 Fr. Edward Dockery was killed when German raiders machine-gunned his car in broad daylight and Fr. Richard Barry, the Assistant Secretary to the Southwark Rescue Society, was killed by a bomb which struck the Boys Home at Clapham in South London. Then when the war was nearly at an end a terrible tragedy befell Holy Trinity Dockhead. The Church there had already been practically destroyed earlier in the war but the presbytery remained. On the 2nd March 1945 a V2 rocket fell and three of the four priests were killed outright; the Parish Priest, Fr. Michael O'Riordan and two of the curates Fr. Stephen Spillane and Fr. Finbar McCarthy. The other curate, Fr. Edmund Arbuthnott, was pulled from the wreckage very seriously injured. He made a good recovery thanks to the devoted care of surgeons and later became the Priest in charge of the Young Christian Workers organisation. His story was also featured in the 1960's in the well-known programme 'This is Your Life.'

At the very end of the war, the Queen and Princess Elizabeth visited Southwark. The date was the 19th May 1945. Canon Bogan in his book on Southwark Cathedral 'The Great Link' tells us that the Queen accompanied by the Mayor of Southwark and Princess Elizabeth was met outside the door by His Grace and the Cathedral Clergy. As Her Majesty passed through the cheering crowds of parishioners and other Catholics on her way into the Cathedral ruin she stopped to speak several times taking special notice of the children. Both she and the Princess were most sympathetic at the destruction of the Cathedral and asked many questions about it. As they were leaving, the National Anthem was sung with tremendous enthusiasm and the Archbishop assured the Queen of his deep appreciation of her kindness. Her Majesty was obviously pleased at her reception and said she admired the bravery of the people of Southwark and hoped the Cathedral would soon be re-built.

Two further matters deserve a closer examination. Firstly the plight of the Gibraltar Refugees and secondly the Archbishop's connection with the 'Sword of the Spirit' movement.

In August 1940, about 12,000 Gibraltarians, mainly women and children, came to this country. Gibraltar occupies a strategic position in wartime as a key base controlling entry to the Mediterranean. Only those men required for the operation of the bases were left while the garrison was heavily reinforced. Early in 1940 the Government had come to hear of a German plan to invade the town known as 'Operation Felix.' First of all the citizens were moved across the sea to Casablanca but after the fall of France they were sent to England. The British Government wanted them to move to the West Indies and about one thousand of them sailed directly to Jamaica. Archbishop Amigo took an active interest in their welfare. As they were fellow countrymen he considered it his duty to do everything he could to help them as they received very shabby treatment indeed from the British Government. We should remember that they were not refugees in the ordinary sense of that word but had been compulsorily removed to make way for an enlarged garrison and for their own supposed safety. Most of them were housed in empty flats and hotels but not in the way their former residents would have appreciated. Cases were reported of twenty-five persons occupying flats designed for five, inadequate washing and toilet facilities and terrible food. They were not allowed ration books because food was provided by Government catering services. Stale meat pies were the staple diet it seems! The last meal was served at 6.00pm and if the menfolk had not arrived by that hour, it was just too bad.

To start with the Government looked like insisting that all the Gibraltarians moved on to the West Indies but Archbishop Amigo intervened on their behalf. He went in person to see Mr. Malcolm McDonald who had charge of their affairs, on 4th September 1940. McDonald pressed home his argument that the Gibraltarians would be better off in the West Indies because the climate was closer to that of their own land, and they might die off in the cold London winters. Amigo pointed out to him the dangers of a sea voyage. Some Italian migrants had already been lost when their ship was torpedoed. He wrote on 18th October to Mr. McDonald:

".... Remember the scandal will be much greater if these poor people are torpedoed in the Atlantic. The Government has already stopped sending children overseas on account of the danger, and it seems strange that the refugees from Gibraltar should have to cross the ocean especially as they are dreading the sea voyage. They are loyal British subjects and should not be forced to go to the West

Indies. I hope that you will see your way to let them remain in
England, but their present conditions are not satisfactory. You know I
feel very strongly on the subject."

By January 1941 the threat of virtual deportation to the West Indies had
ended but the Archbishop was now concerned about the education of
the children. Some could not get in to local Catholic Schools and were
attending non-Catholic schools while some spoke only Spanish and no
special arrangements were being made to help them. The Archbishop
had hoped they might be transferred to Ireland, to which land the
Christian Brothers and Sisters of Loreto from Gibraltar had returned.
However the Irish were not willing to take any further Gibraltarians.

The Archbishop had appointed Fr. Smith OFM. from Peckham as his
representative on a Committee looking after Gibraltarian refugees but
he maintained an active personal interest and would frequently visit the
various centres where they lived and the schools they attended. His
protests about the lack of educational facilities led to special temporary
schools being set up, including one inside the Victoria and Albert
Museum.

In 1944 there was an outcry in the *'Times'* about the poor treatment
accorded to the Gibraltarians. After receiving a series of letters including one from the Archbishop, the *'Times'* devoted an article to their
plight. About this time flying bombs started falling on London and the
Gibraltarians like many other British citizens had to take refuge in
underground stations at night.

The reaction of the British Government was that the only way to ease
the situation was to send most of them to Northern Ireland. However
they were no better off there and many of them could not find work.
Lady O'Neill wrote to the *'Times'* on 4th December 1944:

" .... There are 1600 of them living in Nissen huts in four camps in
this valley and about 3,500 in other camps in Ulster. They came in
July and rightly or wrongly were convinced they were only to be here
a short time on their way home. These camps are quite unsuitable for
people used to a warm climate. At present there are seas of mud,
there is no electric light and the sanitation is of the most primitive
kind. The evacuees' clothes and shoes are most inadequate and many
of them have not the means to purchase more .... Theoretically the
Gibraltarians are at liberty to leave the camps but as residence
permits are needed for strangers living in Northern Ireland and are
not granted to the Gibraltarians and travel permits to Great Britain

are almost unobtainable, these people are to all intents and purposes in concentration camps . . . ."

The Archbishop backed up Lady O'Neill in his own letter to the 'Times' on 4th December 1944:

" . . . . It seems little short of tragedy that these people should return to Gibraltar with the feeling that they have suffered a great injustice. They are the most loyal British subjects and they have been very badly treated. I know it from my visits to them in London. I earnestly hope that something will be done to remedy their circumstances and that they may soon return to the Rock. It is most important."

Most of the refugees did not have long to wait. Repatriation started in 1945 but some unlucky ones did not see their home territory until early 1947.

One of the best known movements to arise during the Second World War was the 'Sword of the Spirit.' Originally merely an anti-fascist organisation, under the leadership of Cardinal Hinsley the whole emphasis was quickly altered. The purpose of the revised organisation can be seen in a circular letter to the clergy prepared by the Secretary, Barbara Ward, dated 21st September 1940.

"The purpose of the organisation is briefly to try to bring home to our fellow-Catholics and to as many non-Catholics as we can reach the important Christian issues at stake in the present war, and also to insist that no post-war settlement or reconstruction whether social or international, can hope to last unless it be founded upon a truly Christian basis . . . . The 'Sword of the Spirit' as its name implies, lays great emphasis upon the spiritual aspect of this campaign and recognises that the measure of its influence with others must, in the last resort be that of its members' practical appreciation and living of a full Catholic life . . . ."

By 1941, the movement had acquired an ecumenical dimension with the active support and blessing of Bishop George Bell of Chichester. Archbishop Amigo had indeed refused to let Barbara Ward circulate the clergy with her prepared letter, but had not stopped groups forming in the Southwark Diocese. However His Grace could hardly be said to be noted for his ecumenical enthusiasm at any time. In November 1941 Cardinal Hinsley had circulated all the Bishops about the future of the movement, particularly over the vexed question of whether any public act or joint prayer could be allowed at 'Sword' meetings. Archbishop Amigo replied:

> "We welcome the reception which has been given to it by non-Catholics but there is always the fear and danger that we should appear to recognise any other than the one True Church.
> Let us keep the Sword of the Spirit as a Catholic campaign under your guidance. Let non-Catholics make any use they like of it for the future restoration when the war is over. Avoid joint meetings if possible but in any case let there by no prayer in common."

In January 1942 the movement effectively split into two, the Catholic side remaining the 'Sword' while the other churches founded the 'Religion of Life' movement. In May they pledged themselves to work 'through parallel action in the religious field and joint action in the social and international field.'

Bishop Bell however did make one last attempt to involve the Catholics in Brighton more directly. He wrote to Archbishop Amigo on 6th July 1942 asking for the co-operation of Catholics in a 'Week of Christian Witness' in the social and international field to be held in Brighton in October. The week was devoted to such subjects as 'Religion in the Home,' 'Religion and School,' 'Religion and Industry' etc. Bishop Bell wrote:

> "Naturally the more the Roman Catholics felt able to do in co-operation with the Church of England and the Free Churches during the week, the happier we should be. But it would be a great satisfaction to us if they could take part at any rate in some of the public meetings, whether or not making their own arrangements for other meetings specially organised by Roman Catholics . . . . I need not say that it would be a very great joy to me personally if your Grace were able to allow it on this occasion . . . . If it were possible for your Grace to come and preside yourself over one of the meetings or to speak, it would give very great pleasure to us all. I should personally welcome it with whole-hearted satisfaction . . . ."

The reply of the Archbishop is not available but evidently he did not dismiss the idea entirely at that stage. Bishop Bell had to write again on the 4th August asking for a definite decision. The Archbishop then decided to call a meeting of the clergy in Brighton to ascertain their views on possible co-operation.

This meeting took place on 11th August. The main speaker was Fr. McGillivray, a convert clergyman who was violently opposed to any co-operation. He spoke of 'cheats liars and humbugs' to be found in the other local churches. This stringent line upset Fr. Arthur Flanagan, then Parish Priest of St. John the Baptist's, Brighton who wrote the following day making several telling points.

"There is already collaboration. The Holy Father at least countenances it; the Cardinal is up to the neck in it; many Bishops have adopted the principle, and as the letters you read show, with good results. If then we stand out, we only make for disunity and a House divided against itself . . . will fall.

You ask us in our own pulpits to preach on these fundamental social principles. Then we must have the capacity. If we are bound to exercise that teaching authority in the case of any individual coming to us—even Chichester himself—surely we ought to be prepared to carry that teaching to the hungry multitudes outside the Church . . . . Are we quite sure that our hesitation does not arise from mental laziness or from pure 'funk'?"

After having considered all the points raised, Archbishop Amigo wrote again to the Bishop of Chichester on 17th August.

"I have now carefully considered your invitation to join in the 'Week of Christian Witness.' Catholics of course have always been intensely interested in the matters which you propose to discuss as is shown by the Encyclicals "Rerum Novarum" and "Quadragesimo Anno" and many others. We are doing all we can to influence the Nation to adopt a Christian attitude towards them, and we are very glad to know that you are making similar efforts.

As you know however we believe that the Catholic Church alone has divine authority to define what Christian principles are, and I fear that in a joint gathering opinions would probably be expressed with which we could not agree, but which by our presence we should appear to countenance. Moreover the Catholic Church cannot consent to be grouped with other bodies as 'one of the Churches.'

I have decided therefore that it is better for us to act separately, and I am arranging for a series of lectures by Catholics to be given in Brighton the following week, chiefly on the lines of the Bishops Joint Pastoral Letter of last June. I hope to sing Mass and to preach in the Church of St. John the Baptist on Sunday October 25th."

This decision not to participate caused much resentment in the town. The Catholic Mayor of Brighton who would normally have been re-elected to serve a second term was not asked to stand again and was replaced by a staunch Protestant. In the end the Archbishop issued a carefully worded statement which was read in every Church in Brighton on Sunday 11th October.

"Our separated brethren are holding a special 'Week of Christian Witness' in Brighton beginning on October 17th. Our best contribution is prayer. The dangers of the present and of the future challenge all men and women of good will to work unceasingly for Christian regeneration and reconstruction. We admire the earnestness with which our friends take their share in this task, and we appreciate the generous motives which inspire them. Christ the King is 'Chief Corner Stone' on which man and society can find stability and salvation. To Him, therefore, we must wholeheartedly turn. If the world is to be made better, God must be known and loved by all. With us Religion means the Catholic Faith and we earnestly ask that all men should recognise God's authority in the Catholic Church. Following our Divine Master, we love our neighbour for his sake. We rejoice when we see that our friends wish to have religion in the home, in the school, in industry, and in the Nation and we have every sympathy with their desire to turn the whole nation to God. We therefore ask every Catholic in Brighton, Hove and district to receive Holy Communion on the last Sunday of this Conference, the Feast of Christ the King and we must pray that God may richly bless the endeavours of all who have the welfare of the Nation and the Empire at heart. The God of Peace be with you all."

To end this Chapter I give in full the text of the special message sent by Pope Pius XII to the Archbishop and the Diocese in 1944.

August 15th 1944

"We are very happy to take advantage of an extraordinary opportunity to send you a message of fatherly affection. Our greetings and good wishes go first of all to Our venerable Brother, your reverend Archbishop, whose long years of zealous service have earned for him your love and gratitude; and then they reach out to you all, beloved Children. You are among those, we know it, who have been put to a hard trial under the horrors of air warfare, and your sufferings are again being renewed intensely today. Mindful of your afflictions what can We do but repeat the deeply earnest words of our Easter message of 1941 which we have pronounced more than once since that day when speaking of air-attacks that have struck at residential districts: 'O that the belligerents—for they, too, have human hearts formed in the womb of mothers—that they might be stirred by charity for the sufferings of the civil populations for the women and helpless children, for the sick and old, who are often exposed to more immediate and greater dangers of war than the men in arms at the front!' All on both sides of the battle line, who share your lot, come within the embrace of Our very special fatherly care and affection. You are in Our thoughts and in our prayers, that Almighty God in His mercy may transform your present sufferings into graces and blessings for you and your dear dead.

What we have heard of your life inspired by religion and devotion to the Church. has been a source of great consolation to Us and leads Us to address to you the words of the Apocalypse (2.19) to the Church of Thyatira; 'I know thy works and thy faith, and thy charity and thy ministry and thy patience.' The more you may perhaps be witness to the shifting uncertainties that presage a weakening and break up of religion, so much the more look steadfastly for security and protection to the rock of Catholic truth, which is Christ and in Christ, Peter and his successors, and so much the more surely make your faith the measure of all your conduct. Be assured that in this way you will be helping thousands of your fellow-citizens, who are seeking God, to find the way of Truth and Salvation . . . ."

The Archbishop replied on 8th September 1944:

"Most Holy Father,
We are all deeply grateful for the kind letter which your Holiness has deigned to send to the clergy and faithful of this Diocese of Southwark through the Archbishop of Westminster. I ordered it to be read in all our churches on Sunday September 3rd, so that all my people might know the sympathy which our Common Father has shown to us in our terrible trials. . . . (The letter then lists the sufferings of the diocese).

. . . It is heart rending for me to see my Cathedral in ruins since April 1941 and not to be able to have the pontifical functions which I dearly loved. We were cut off from Rome and could not tell our Common Father the cruel sorrows which we were experiencing so long.

The gracious letter which your Holiness has addressed to us, has given us all the greatest consolation. We feel honoured and happy to have the sympathy of our Common Father in our affliction. We thank you, Holy Father, with all our hearts. We renew our loyalty and homage to the Vicar of Christ. We humbly beg the Apostolic Benediction on all the devoted clergy, the religious and laity of the Diocese of Southwark."

Chapter 13
Personal Characteristics and Selected Anecdotes

The Archbishop's life was based on constant hard work backed by constant prayer. At the start of his Episcopate he took as his motto 'Age pro Viribus' (Work with all your might) and indeed he was able to keep working up to within two days of his death. His life was marked by great personal austerity, he never smoked or drank alcohol and his own apartments were sparsely furnished. This spirit of austerity he may well have learnt from the saintly Rector of the Hammersmith Seminary, Bishop Weathers who in his day was well known for his austerity and holiness.

He told the London 'Evening News' in 1945 that he liked no recreation as much as hard work. Up to that year he never owned a car but preferred to travel by public transport whenever possible. Again he told the 'Evening News': "If my people have only buses and trams then who am I to ride about in luxury?"

Matched against this austerity was a great love of the priests and people of his Diocese. This was especially marked when it came to the poor and the children. He visited his Diocese parish by parish every three years, but the poor parishes near Southwark saw him more frequently. Indeed he visited Holy Trinity Parish Dockhead no less than forty-five times. Perhaps this parish reminded him most of his early days at Commercial Road. He used to refer in his Pastoral Letters to the heroic lives lived by London's poor and told the rich they too had to work hard. At the same time he would warn the poor against criticising the rich or being jealous of them. "It is urgent that among Catholics at least, all classes should try really to know and respect each other in unity and friendship, not in envy and strife." Right at the start of his episcopate he had established a special mission to the hop-pickers in Kent. He knew from his days in East London that many of London's poor went to the Kent hop-fields in September for up to three weeks at a time with no opportunity for Sunday Mass. He charged the Franciscans with the pastoral care of the hop-pickers and through their ministrations many lapsed Catholics were discovered and restored to their faith. Every year the Bishop himself came down on a Sunday and said Mass at one site and preached at two others.

The Bishop's first consideration was always for people and to this end he trained his memory to remember names, dates and faces connected with those he met. At the age of 80 he still remembered up to one thousand birthdays. After a gap of fifty years he would still remember people he knew at Brook Green or Commercial Road and would remind them often of their first meeting. One husband who came to see him about a problem with his marriage was astonished when the Bishop told him that he had taken their marriage service about forty years previously. The Bishop asked him if he remembered the day and when the poor man replied "No" the Bishop replied "Your wife certainly does because she has had to put up with you all this time!"

He kept meticulous notes of each visitation and always reminded the parishioners to pray for their deceased pastors whom he invariably named. He would also never fail to find an opportunity to ask them to increase their generosity, be it towards reducing their parish debt, or assisting the missions or the Southwark Children's Society.

The Bishop loved children and there are many photographs remaining showing him surrounded by youngsters. He knew the value of Catholic Education and always tried to establish a Parish School in each new parish that was founded. He wrote often on Catholic Education in his pastorals.

> "Our chief concern is the children . . . if we expect a better state of things after the war religion must be taught in schools by teachers who believe in its importance and care for the souls of the little ones of Christ."

He made a point of visiting the schools on his visitations and once stated he would far rather go around talking to the children than listening to an entertainment laid on by them on his behalf. He would often go round on foot to the schools in the neighbourhood of the Cathedral to meet the children, both at work and play.

He was always conscious of the fact that poverty led to lapsation and spoke out many times in his pastorals on social justice for the poor. Nor would he lose the opportunity of trying to bring back the lapsed. At times he would be seen in the local hospitals visiting the sick, even on Christmas Day, and was known to seek out the lapsed and drive them back to the Sacraments.

His relationship with his clergy was in general excellent. Yet this state of affairs was not reached easily. When he came to the Diocese he was a virtual stranger to most of the priests and to make things worse he was regarded as the nominee of their last Bishop, Bishop Bourne. It needed much tact and diplomacy to win over the clergy who thought he would merely be a carbon copy of his predecessor. Some priests remained rather too loyal to Archbishop Bourne after the differences between the two men had developed, but that did not stop the Bishop from knowing where to find true merit, for instance in his appointment of Fr. Philip Hallett as Rector of St. John's Seminary Wonersh. With priests the Bishop used to try and regard each of them as a friend. He was very approachable and up to the Second War he would make himself available on a Friday morning to any priest or layperson who wished to see him without prior appointment.

He insisted in his synods and the frequent clergy retreats he gave personally, on the need for a true spiritual life among his priests. This should be based on the Holy Mass, daily meditation, careful recitation of the Divine Office and daily rosary. He would stress also the need for parish visiting and getting to know one's flock and their problems. He was always concerned about the supply of priests to serve his ever-growing Diocese and to this end started recruiting on a large scale in Ireland both for priests to serve on short term loan and also to become full priests of the Diocese. With regard to the pastoral work of the Diocese he was particularly anxious to encourage missions and retreats in the parishes. There were several 'General Missions' when the whole Diocese had a mission going at around the same time. Another special interest was the formation of guilds, particularly men's guilds like the Guild of the Blessed Sacrament. Up to three thousand men would walk in the annual procession of the Blessed Sacrament at St. George's Cathedral. Devotion to Our Lady was fostered also, with an annual pilgrimage to the shrine at West Grinstead in Sussex.

His sole interests lay in his love of his people and defending the rights of the Church. Beyond these confines he had few outside interests. Fr. Peter Mason recorded that he took no interest in beautiful scenery and when they were crossing the Alps by rail he did not look up once from his breviary to admire the view. Later on passing through Ashford where Fr. Mason was then stationed he called his Bishop's attention to the pleasant surroundings to which the only reply was "I prefer London."

Yet with all his Diocesan concerns the Bishop found time to involve himself with national and international affairs. Fr. Mason again recalls that these interventions were not the result of pride but simply of his great concern for the Church in the areas affected, notably in Spain and Ireland. He learnt early on at Commercial Road how to deal with public authorities, never to take 'no' for an answer if at all possible and the value of direct and frank interviews with the most senior persons to obtain whatever benefit he wanted, be it building controls lifted, more facilities in hospitals, or more schools for his beloved children.

Bishop Amigo was always anxious to see Converts coming into the Church. He was particularly glad to welcome convert Anglican parsons. In 1910 an entire congregation of Anglicans at Brighton became Catholics and two of their ministers became Catholic Priests. The Bishop's views on our separated brethren are well expressed in this extract from one of his pastoral letters:

> "We love and respect our separated brethren and long to do them service. But our love and our service must not involve any compromise with regard to the deposit of faith entrusted to us for true charity is based on justice and truth."

The Bishop refused the co-operation of Catholics in joint prayer when this was proposed at a 'Sword of the Spirit' meeting in Brighton and only agreed to let Catholic children assist in a Shakesperian pageant at Southwark Anglican Cathedral in 1945 on the condition that no prayers were said.

One of his convert parsons who became a priest was Fr. Arthur Stevenson, for many years Parish Priest of Tunbridge Wells in Kent. Mr. Stevenson as an Anglican was an assistant at a small parish near Lambeth. One day he met the Bishop walking towards Lambeth Palace, the official residence of the Archbishop of Canterbury. Mr. Stevenson said to him: "Surely you are going in the wrong direction?" "No Sir!" replied Bishop Amigo, "It is *you* who are going in the wrong direction, you ought to be a Catholic and a priest too!" Within a few weeks Mr. Stevenson left the Church of England to become a Catholic and shortly afterwards became a priest. However this kind of approach did not always work. Another Anglican Vicar working near Southwark was told that he too should be a priest. On this occasion the reply was a curt "No thank you."

Archbishop Amigo was not without his faults. He readily admitted to being quite blunt and abrupt at times. In his early days as Bishop he was a great stickler for correct ceremonial and many priests and servers were rebuked sharply if things went wrong. The Archbishop loved the great ceremonies of the Church, not from a sense of pride in his own position but because he regarded the Mass as an actual approach to the Divine Person.

He saw in the rich ceremonial action a means whereby the mind and hearts of the people were elevated towards God. Thus each ceremonial action had to be correctly performed to give greater glory to God.

The Archbishop had a waspish sense of humour which was certainly not to everyone's liking. He tended to apply nicknames of his own to certain priests, much to their discomfiture at times. Fr. Hickey had tried his vocation as a Jesuit before going to Wonersh Seminary to join Southwark Diocese. The Bishop, who used to visit the Seminary several times a year and chat to the students at recreation, had the habit of calling him 'The Jesuit' in the presence of the other students. Father Wilson, a former Vice-Rector of the English College in Rome, had been at Caterham Barracks and the Bishop called him 'The Grenadier' in later life.

Slightly more serious was his inability to realise the traumatic experience that befell the Catholic Chaplains during the First World War. When they arrived home the Bishop expected them to take up duties as if nothing had happened. Researches have shown that all of them had difficulties as a result and three of them left the priesthood shortly after the end of the war. The Bishop never really liked service chaplains in full time commission. He used to say that they looked proud and arrogant strutting around in their uniforms. In the Second World War he refused to release more than a few priests as full-time chaplains although this was in part due to the needs at home.

Archbishop Amigo was one of those figures sometimes described as larger than life. Such personalities often give rise to stories both true and false and certainly the Archbishop was the subject of many a tale. Here I have taken only those stories which have an authentic ring about them. I have already mentioned the Archbishop's love of correct ceremonial. When things went wrong he would call out instructions in Latin. For instance if he wanted the lights put on he would call out "Fiat Lux." The unsuspecting server would often reply "Et Cum Spiritu Tuo" at which the episcopal finger would point upwards to the ceiling, nothing further being said until illumination was provided. The most amusing story in this regard concerns a High Mass on the feast of St. Joseph at St. Joseph's Mark Cross, the Junior Seminary. The Rector, Mgr. Ernest Corbishley, arose at the end of Mass to read the indulgence. However he arose far too early and the servers and students were astonished when the Bishop appeared to call out to the Rector "Silly Ass." In fact the fatal word was "Sileas," the Latin for 'be silent.' It is said that the Rector spent a whole week in bed suffering from shock as a result of this rebuke!

There are many stories about the Bishops and various Missions and retreats. He tried to call in (always unannounced) at Missions and address the congregation for a few moments. He took careful note of the attendance and would draw the attention of the Parish Priest if he thought there should have been more people present. Once at the Church at Melior Street, close by London Bridge Station, he entered and found a half empty church for the mission sermon. In his own few words he said that if that was the level of their devotion they did not need three priests to serve the mission and promptly withdrew one of the curates.

Fr. Mason related that when a Mission was being given at Streatham, the Bishop walked down the aisle while the missioner was lecturing on Confession. He was nearing the end of his discourse on the words used by the priest. As he was about to say "Go in Peace . . . ." the Bishop strode down the aisle and the preacher, petrified, stopped dead. The Bishop said his customary few words and walked out again up the aisle and through the folding doors at the end. Imagining that the Bishop was out of earshot the preacher continued "Go in Peace, your sins are forgiven you." The Bishop of course heard and in mock rage re-entered the Church and said "Thank you very much" and walked out again!

Fr. Mason himself was on the receiving end of the Bishop's wry sense of humour when giving the students retreat at Wonersh. This was while he was Parish Priest at Ashford. At the end of one talk on the duty of obedience to the Bishop, he ended up by telling them that obedience to the Bishop was absolute like our Lady's obedience when she said "Fiat Voluntas Tua" to the Angel Gabriel. (Thy will be done). The Bishop stopped him at the entrance to the sacristy and said "Yes, very good, and now Fiat Voluntas Mea (My will be done). I'm moving you to Croydon, go there next week."

As can be imagined the Bishop knew a vast number of priests and laity and nearly all could be counted as his friends. When however the friendship was not quite so close the strange sense of humour became apparent. Fr. Wilson, former Vice-Rector of the English College relates how Bishop Amigo was the only Bishop who could make Pope Benedict XV laugh. The Pope could not understand the differences that had arisen between the Bishop and Cardinal Bourne and asked the Bishop his view on the matter. The Bishop replied: "Your Holiness, the Cardinal is a man very keen on always doing the will of God. But unfortunately for me the Holy Ghost always seems to be north of the River."

Cardinal Lepicier who in earlier times had conducted an Apostolic Visitation on Westminster and Southwark, later became Cardinal Protector of the English College. The Cardinal was none too popular it seems and Bishop Amigo was asked by a student how long Lepicier would remain Protector. The reply given by the Bishop was quite subtle "He is a very good man, a very holy man, a very clever man, and if you know what he means when he is speaking to you, you will be a very clever man too!" This Cardinal had an irritating habit of stroking a person's hand after shaking hands. When Bishop Amigo received this treatment he exclaimed: "My pulse is all right thank you!"

The Bishop had clear and some might say old-fashioned ideas about the role of women in society. In his early pastorals he suggested that the normal role of women from the families of the poor was to enter domestic service before marriage. He found no time for the idea that they should work in factories or do labouring jobs. During the Second World War he heard the voice of a woman announcer at Waterloo Station and he said to his secretary: "She should be at home cooking the evening meal for the family." He was quite appalled at the modern low-cut dresses that were becoming popular in the last few years of his life and was known to call out to ladies from taxis and cars that they should be properly dressed.

Although of average height the Bishop was an imposing figure as he went around the streets of South London wearing his wide-brimmed clerical hat. When travelling by rail however he chose to wear a black cap which gave him a somewhat sinister appearance. On the pilgrimage trains to Lourdes he would go up and down the corridors talking to the pilgrims but rebuking priests who had fallen asleep over their breviaries, or reciting office in a desultory and casual fashion.

Not only did the Bishop have a great concern over his priests but he made certain he knew all of them well even when they were students.

This he achieved by going down almost every month to Wonersh and Mark Cross to meet the students at recreation. Fr. Charles Tritschler has given me an account of the Bishop's kindness to him personally as a student. In 1930 after studying for six years in the juniors and the two years of philosophy, he applied for the tonsure and the Rector, Mgr. Hallett told him he would have to leave as his education was not up to standard. At that time an edict had come forth from Rome that students must have a higher standard of education. However it had been already arranged that he should return to the Seminary to act as Sacristan for the Priests retreat. He told the Head Sacristan, none other than Cyril Cowderoy, that he could not come back as he had been kicked out, but Cyril replied that it was too late to obtain a replacement. When the retreat came round the young Charles went up to vest his Bishop. The Bishop seemed annoyed. "What are you doing here? I thought you had been kicked out." During the retreat however he spoke with the Head Sacristan who must have given a good report for a few weeks later the Bishop called him up to Bishop's House. First he suggested that Charles should be a lay brother since he was good with his hands. But Mr. Tritschler was determined to be a priest so he arranged for him to have more training including a spell at Walworth, the House of Studies for late vocations and then on to Osterly. After this the Bishop sent him to Lisbon for theology studies. The Bishop wrote regularly to him encouraging him in his studies. When he received the subdiaconate he wrote:

"I congratulate you very heartily on your subdiaconate. You have had many difficulties before taking this important step, but I hope that they have strengthened your determination to give yourself whole heartedly to God's service. You are now a sacred minister and you will remain one for the rest of your life. Realise your weakness in study and make up your mind to overcome this by hard application. God will bless his minister. You must throw your heart and soul into your work and keep up your studies always. You may take the diaconate but I should like to give you the priesthood myself. Wishing you every grace and blessing."

In a similar way Canon Edward Mitchinson relates how Bishop Amigo wrote regularly to him at the Proganda Fide College in Rome where he was studying as the English College was full. He wrote also to his mother who was widowed and sent her a free ticket for a Rome Pilgrimage so that she could visit him at a time when holiday visits home were unknown. Canon Mitchinson also relates that when in Rome he had asked to be realeased from the diocese to take the missionary oath. Peter replied fiercely: "You are going to be one of MY priests," and that was the end of it.

Later on Canon Mitchinson was appointed the first 'Youth Chaplain of the Diocese.' The Archbishop became greatly interested in youth work at the end of his life. The importance of working with youth was in part in response to the Hitler 'Jugend,' but the Archbishop's interest was with the J.C.W. movement. When Fr. Mitchinson was explaining its working to the Archbishop, he suddenly asked if it was the same movement he had observed among the crowds of French and Belgian youth at Lourdes. When told that it was indeed the same movement he replied: "If you can produce a youth movement like that then God bless you."

About this time a dialogue Mass was introduced and Fr. Mitchinson soon introduced this in his Masses for the semi-lapsed youth at the centres he worked at. He went further and arranged that good readers would read in English the parts he said quietly in Latin except the words of Consecration. He told the Archbishop, who merely asked: "Is it for the good of souls?" However after one Mass like this at a Convent, he received a letter of reproof from the Chancellor, Mgr. Cowderoy who knew nothing of the earlier agreement. So Fr. Mitchinson asked for an appointment with the Archbishop and went over the matter again and obtained permission to carry on as before. Finally he asked: "Would you put that in writing" but the Archbishop replied quietly: "No, go away go away" but still gave him his blessing! Time and again later on he would tease Fr. Mitchinson with that strange rather perverse sense of humour already noted: "Are you still saying Mass in English?" knowing very well that in those days he could not do so and did not do so.

His Grace had little time for ordinary reading. He kept up with world news through the '*Times*' and was on friendly terms with the Proprietor, John Walter. According to Fr. Leake who was Administrator at St. George's Cathedral, his favourite novel was Charles Dickens 'Barnaby Rudge.' This novel contains a graphic account of the Gordon Riots which took place in London in 1780 just after the passing of the first Catholic Relief Act. These riots actually started at St. George's Fields almost on the spot where St. George's Cathedral now stands.

To conclude this chapter I quote from Canon Preedy writing at the time of his Golden Jubilee.

"He could of course have carried his throne about with him, but his natural unaffected dignity provided the counterpoise to that innocent badinage which he very obviously enjoys. So approachable is he that simple men and women unimportant and lowly in the social structure can invariably find in him the same direct encouraging fatherly Priest of God, while that phenomenal memory of his for faces and names commends him to those who like to be recognised and who does not?"

Chapter 14
The Final Years,
Last Illness and Death

The war years took their toll of the Archbishop's health. In May 1945 after some months of increasing pain, patiently borne, he was taken seriously ill while at Wonersh for the Pentecost ordinations. On the Friday afternoon 24th, he realised he could not carry on with the ceremonies of the following day and Bishop Brown was summoned to perform the ordinations. Meanwhile the doctor was called and ordered him to hospital. The Bishop in his diary describes the journey as being painfully slow. It took about four hours to reach St. Andrew's, Dollis Hill. He was then operated on for a prostate condition. The operation was successful and the Bishop was back at his desk on 28th June. But two days later his condition deteriorated. He had tried to come back too soon. His appearance was such that Bishop Brown thought it advisable to call together the Chapter and administer the last rites. A letter was sent out to all priests asking for prayers. However he pulled through quite well and continued to administer the Diocese from his bed. By the 28th August he was again back at his desk and was able to carry out his annual visit to the hop-fields. However he was now very old and very frail. He was often in pain from the prostate condition and needed much nursing. His sight was beginning to fail and he became hard of hearing. Yet he would allow himself no respite whatever. The rounds of visitations, interviews, letter writing, continued unabated right up to two days before he died. The only concession he made was to have an official car. His faithful secretary, Mgr. Reynolds would often drive him out to visit some presbytery or other in South London without any warning to the clergy from the Archbishop that he was coming. Often the diary simply records that the priests concerned were "out."

In 1946 he held the final synod of his episcopate. The 57th Synod of Southwark was held on Wednesday 15th May, eleven years after the last synod. A synod was planned for 1945 but had to be abandoned owing to the illness of the Archbishop. This final synod was held at St. Anne's, Vauxhall. Owing to the difficulties attendant on providing a meal for a large number of priests in the aftermath of war, only a limited number attended, one hundred and forty-six priests in all. No new decrees were passed but the Archbishop reminded his clergy particularly about their need for sanctification and also pointed out the dangers faced by priests in their lives. He was also very worried about the numbers of mixed marriages (over three thousand) that had been contracted in Southwark that year.

On the 16th July he was a guest at the Royal Garden Party at Buckingham Palace and his Autumn engagements included the annual pilgrimage to West Grinstead and Canterbury, together with the regular trip to the hop-fields. On the 22nd November he slipped and fell at Bishop's House and wrenched his leg quite badly. He was in severe pain for many weeks with a badly swollen leg.

The year 1947 saw the Archbishop make his final visit to Rome. This was the first and only time that he travelled by air. His health was now so poor that he stayed with the Blue Nuns in Rome instead of at the English College as they had an adjacent hospital. The Chaplain there was a Southwark Priest, Fr. Benedict Williamson, himself nearly 80, who died shortly afterwards.

The Archbishop stayed in Rome from 30th October until 12th November. He was accompanied by Fr. Leake, then Administrator of St. George's Cathedral. He made the usual round of visits to the Basilicas and met the Holy Father Pius XII, although his diary does not record a summary of their meeting as it did with his visits to previous Popes. He also visited the Beda College, the English and Irish Colleges, several convents and most of the curial offices. The diary mentions that he had trouble from his catheter on several days during his stay. The trouble became rather more acute on his return journey. The plane left Rome at 10.30 and stopped at Marseilles at 1.00pm. Here he was seen by a doctor. The plane continued its flight at 2.00pm and reached Northolt at 4.54pm, where again a doctor was in attendance. He eventually arrived back about 7.00pm at Archbishop's House. So ended his final visit to Rome, his thirtieth visit to the Eternal city during his Episcopate.

The year 1948 was to be the last full year of the Archbishop's life. There were two grand events to mark the year. On the 25th February he celebrated the 60th anniversary of his ordination as a priest, the last of the great jubilees. Behind the scenes Mgr. Cowderoy as Chancellor was arranging that he should receive a special message from the King, George VI. To enable this to become a reality, the Chancellor contacted the Duke of Norfolk. He wrote on 5th February 1948:

> "... I know Your Grace is well aware of his indefatigable labours and how dearly he is held in the esteem of clergy and laity.
>
> I happen to know that it would give His Grace very great happiness to receive a message from His Majesty the King on the coming anniversary. I am venturing to approach you in this matter to ask you whether it could possibly be arranged. During his serious illness in 1945 he was touched by a gracious message from the Queen, and he has always enjoined upon his flock the duty of loyalty and affection towards the Sovereign and Royal Family...."

The Duke used his influence with success. The following account is taken from the April 1948 'Southwark Record.' (25th February 1948).

"Sixty years ago today Peter Emmanual Amigo received the Sacred Order of Priesthood; he was ordained at the Pro Cathedral, Kensington on 25 February 1888.... Today on the 60th anniversary of his Ordination, His Grace the Archbishop returned once again to Walworth, to the Church he himself had built during his Rectorship there; a Church dedicated to the English Martyrs, two of them since canonised in a cause in which the Archbishop played a leading part; and there he celebrated with fitting pomp this most joyful anniversary. Catholic School children were on the route to cheer him on his way, a happy tribute to a Bishop who has always had at heart the education of our children and the preservation of our schools. His Grace arrived at the Church at 11 o'clock. A large gathering of clergy had already taken their places. ... Every place was taken.... The music was under the direction of the Rev. Desmond Coffey with the Reverend Peter Farmer at the organ. The whole body of the clergy joined in the singing of the Mass led by the special Priests choir which also sang with great effect under the skilful direction of Father Coffey, the 'Ecce Sacerdos Magnus' at His Grace's entry and a fine motet 'Cantate Domino' at the offertory.

At the end of the Mass the following gracious message was read: 'The Holy Father sends your Grace cordial felicitations on the occasion of the 60th anniversary of your priestly ordination and lovingly imparts to yourself, clergy and faithful of the Diocese of

Southwark his paternal apostolic blessing...' After the 'Te Deum' was sung it was announced that congratulations had been received from His Majesty the King.

'The King has heard with interest that you are celebrating tomorrow the 60th anniversary of your ordination as a priest. His Majesty wishes me to send you his sincere congratulations on this remarkable record, together with an expression of his hopes that you may be long spared to continue the devoted work which you have carried on in South London for so many years.'"

The Archbishop sent the following reply to the Royal Greeting:

"I was deeply touched by your gracious congratulations on the sixtieth anniversary of my ordination to the priesthood. I offer Your Majesty my most humble thanks. May God abundantly bless You and the Royal Family. May He spare you to reign over the Empire for many years."

In July 1948 came the 100th anniversary of the building of St. George's Cathedral. Although the Cathedral had been in ruins since 1941 the Archbishop had said an open air Mass there on several occasions. But for the centenary it was decided that every effort should be made to make the event as splendid as circumstances would allow. A firm of tent makers was called in to provide a huge awning over the entire sanctuary area and a large carpet was laid down.

On Saturday 3rd July there was a special Mass for the children of the Diocese and over two thousand youngsters packed in to the ruins. The Archbishop thanked them all for coming and urged them to pray for the restoration work. The children sang the hymn to St. George, 'Leader Now on Earth no longer,' with great gusto as the Archbishop passed down the aisle on his way out.

That day had been fine and warm but the celebrations on the Sunday were marred by heavy rain which meant many of the congregation were soaked through. Besides a great number of priests and laity, the Mass was attended by the students from both Wonersh and Mark Cross Seminaries and the guest of honour was His Excellency John Dulanty C.B. C.B.E. the High Commissioner for Eire. This was to be a ceremony on the grandest possible scale. Luckily the rain eased off as the procession came down the aisle with the Archbishop preceded by a mace bearer, a Cross bearer with two acolytes and eight torch bearers, an arch-priest (Fr. Leake) and the Master of Ceremonies (Fr. Farrell). His

Grace was accompanied by eight Knights of St. Columba holding the canopy. As they arrived at the sanctuary extra floodlights were switched on to reveal a scene of glittering magnificence while the choir sang the Antiphon 'Haec Dies' and the Psalm 'Quam dilecta tabernacula tua' to the same setting that had been used one hundred years before on the day that Cardinal Wiseman had come to open St. George's.

A short message from Pope Pius XII was read in which he hoped that restoration would soon be completed. The Archbishop again urged personally that all present should pray for the restoration and pointed out the monument to the great Canon Thomas Doyle who played such a large role in the building of the Cathedral which he served so loyally for many years.

During the afternoon there was a large rally of Catholic Youth held at Battersea Town Hall, during which the Cathedral Youth Club presented a 'Cavalcade of the Centenary.'

At 6.00pm came the final event of the day, a special service with sermon by the Archbishop and Benediction. During his sermon the Archbishop reminded his listeners that the infamous Gordon Riots had started out from the very spot where the Cathedral was built. He dwelt on the fire which had destroyed the building and went on to say that the Cathedral must be re-built and that "greater will be the glory of the new house, greater than the old one." Everyone had to make sacrifices, must do something to help, then: "St. George the martyr, whom we honour, will not forget us if we strive with earnestness to re-build this Cathedral dedicated to him."

The final year of the Archbishop's life was marked by a serious deterioration in both sight and hearing. The entries in the daily diary indicate the weakness of sight. Often the entries wander from one line to another. Yet still he carried on as before with the usual round of engagements. In May he had the pleasure of welcoming the great Irish leader Mr. De Valera, to Southwark. 'Dev' praised the Archbishop for his work for Ireland while the Archbishop thanked the leader for the generosity of the Irish in helping towards the cost of re-building St. George's. One may wonder if they mentioned the time when 'Dev' was a prisoner of the British Government, and the incident at Portland Prison referred to earlier.

The Archbishop knew his days were numbered. In March he had taken steps to have a co-adjutor Bishop appointed with right of succession. However he died before the appointment was made in Rome. Still there was no let up in his activity. He performed the ordinations to the Priesthood at Pentecost as usual and these were featured in the magazine 'Picture Post' in an article by Antonia White dealing with the training of future priests. At the start of September he made his final visit to his beloved hop-pickers in Kent and at the end of the month he was back at Wonersh to ordain the deacons. Within a week of these ordinations he was dead. The writing in the diaries shows a marked deterioration for the last two weeks, but the Archbishop continued his usual round of visits and interviews to within two days of his death.

He became ill during the night of the 28th September and called for assistance at 4.00am on the morning of the 29th. He was then annointed by Fr. Bernard Bogan, Administrator of St. George's Cathedral. Later that morning Bishop Brown and Archbishop Godfrey, the Apostolic Delegate, both called to see their sick brother Bishop. Cardinal Griffin was unwell at the time. Archbishop Amigo was able to dictate two letters to his secretary. The last letter he wrote in his own hand according to the diary was to the Rector of Mark Cross, Monsignor Corbishley asking for the names of the new boys who had entered the college that September. The author of this work was in fact one of these new boys.

The condition of His Grace continued to deteriorate and at 7.00pm on 30th September the death agony started. Prayers were constantly recited by the Priests attached to the House and by the Sisters who looked after him. His Grace's lips moved in prayer almost without ceasing. He grasped his crucifix firmly right to the end and remained conscious although unable to speak and with eyes closed. At 2.00am Monsignor Cowderoy started to say the Mass for a Happy Death in a corner of the bedroom where an altar had been erected. The Archbishop stirred a little at the Sanctus Bell and was clearly praying. He listened for the consecration bell but as Mgr. Cowderoy elevated the chalice after the consecration Archbishop Peter Emmanuel Amigo passed to his Creator. Mgr. Cowderoy was notified and named him in the Memento for the Dead, just as a few minutes earlier he was named in the Memento for the Living. It was about 2.30am and a thunderstorm was raging outside.

Epilogue

Before the funeral took place it was agreed that there should be a period of lying in state so that the Archbishop's many friends could take a last look at their beloved priest. The lying in state took place in the Amigo Memorial Hall, then serving as the pro-Cathedral. The Archbishop was arrayed with full pontificals, a crozier and a white mitre. Among those who filed past was a venerable old gentleman, Mr. Dan Quinlan, who had been baptised at the Cathedral, sung as choirboy there and was one of the four guards of honour at Cardinal Manning's funeral.

The watch started at 4.00pm on Tuesday 4th October with the body guarded by the Knights of St. Columba who went on duty in relays throughout the night. Hundreds of people came to file past the coffin and even during the night hours there was a constant trickle of mourners. In the morning this trickle became a flood and the people were filing past at the rate of one thousand an hour. Nuns from the various convents, children from the local schools mingled with the East Enders whom he used to meet in the hop-fields, former parishioners from Walworth and even Commercial Road, plus the many friends he had made over the years. When the watching ceased at 4.00pm hundreds were turned away.

Then came a solemn procession to Westminster Cathedral preceded by a Cross bearer and twenty acolytes. The hearse was followed by many Knights of St. Columba and members of the Guild of the Blessed Sacrament, plus members of other sodalities and societies. Following them came nearly two thousand laypeople.

The cortege was met at the doors of Westminster Cathedral by the Vicar General, Mgr. Hubert Gibney accompanied by Bishop Craven and Bishop Myers, auxiliaries of Westminster and Bishop Fitzgerald of Gibraltar. Inside the Chapters of both Southwark and Westminster were present as a solemn dirge was sung with the Cathedral packed to capacity.

The following morning the 6th October saw the Solemn High Mass of Requiem for the Archbishop. Cardinal Griffin was unwell so the Mass was sung by Bishop King of Portsmouth under the presidency of Archbishop Godfrey, then Apostolic Delegate. The penegyric was given by Bishop Beck, then co-adjutor Bishop of Brentwood. His sermon will be found in an Appendix to this volume. The Archbishop was permitted five absolutions by a kind gesture of Cardinal Griffin who allowed that Westminster Cathedral be held to be "territorially part of Southwark Diocese" for the Mass. Normally this privilege applied only if the funeral of a Bishop took place in his own Diocese. At the ceremony there were twenty-two Archbishops and Bishops and nearly eight hundred priests. From Ireland came the Primate, Archbishop D'Alton, and the Bishops of Limerick, Ferns, Derry and Dromore. The Irish Premier, Mr. De Valera was present with Mr. Sean McBrdige and Mr. Frank Aiken. Bishop Scanlan of Dunkeld represented the Scottish Hierarchy. In the congregation were many distinguished personages including the Duke of Norfolk, Mr. George Isaacs, the Minister of Labour, together with the Spanish Charge d'Affaires, the Belgian Ambassador, Catholic peers and members of Parliament, civic dignatories and a vast assembly of rich and poor, all united in their mourning. The absolutions were given by Bishop Scanlan, the Archbishop of Cardiff, Cardinal D'Alton, the Archbishop of Liverpool and the Apostolic Delegate.

The funeral cortege then left Westminster and passing through great crowds, many of them in tears, proceeded to St. George's Cathedral, Southwark where in accordance with his own wish, the Body of the Archbishop was interred in the Crypt where the bodies of many famous clerics associated with St. George's lie buried.

The committal service was taken by Bishop Brown of Pella. At this service only the clergy were present together with the more distinguished guests plus the remaining members of the Archbishop's family, his nephews Mr. James and Mr. Leo Haywood and Captain Savignon. On the following Sunday the Administrator opened the Cathedral ruins to the public and all day long crowds of the faithful visited the spot beneath which His Grace's Body now lies and prayed for his soul. The Holy Father Pope Pius XII sent a message.

"The Holy Father learns with great grief of the demise of the worthy

Archbishop Amigo and lovingly imparts to your Lordship to the Chapter, Clergy and Faithful of the Diocese, his paternal Apostolic Blessing as a pledge of comforting divine grace."

So the Body of the Archbishop now rests in his beloved Cathedral restored and re-built ten years after his death.

Appendix I
Spain and the War
(Dublin Review—April 1916)

A rough channel crossing in rainy weather was not a good beginning for a holiday, but how could we expect comfort in travel during this war? The sight of English soldiers in French territory, the darkness of the streets of Paris, the deep mourning of many persons in France, the continual demand for our passports, reminded my two companions and myself, if we needed reminding, that we were engaged in war. Still, the journey was not so difficult as we anticipated, thanks to a letter which the French Ambassador in London had most kindly given us; and Mgr. Ottley, Fr. Lawton and myself found ourselves across the Bidasoa, which divides Spain from France, within 25 hours of leaving Folkestone.

Spain is more than twice the size of Great Britain, and railway travelling is not so easy as in this country. There was not time in the five weeks at my disposal to visit the whole country, and we therefore contented ourselves with the "circular ticket," which enabled us to go to San Sebastian, Valladolid, Madrid, Saragossa and Barcelona, entering Spain by the western side of the Pyrenees and leaving it by the coast of the Mediterranean. It was convenient to go to other places from these as centres. Thus from San Sebastian we motored to the famous house of the Jesuits at Loyola, where the Rector gave us a most hearty welcome, and seemed genuinely disappointed that we did not accept his hospitality for the night in order to say Mass at the birthplace of St. Ignatius on the morrow. The narrow-gauge railway, unusual in Spain, took us from San Sebastian to Bilbao, the capital of the Basque province of Biscay and a very busy and important town, but through the kindness of a friend we made the return journey of 100 miles by motor, passing through magnificent scenery. We did not realize our hopes of going from

Valladolid to Salamanca, because we were informed that the professors and students of the Irish College of Salamanca were spending their summer holidays in Galicia; so we prolonged our stay at the English College of Valladolid, which Father Parsons founded in the reign of Queen Elizabeth. From Madrid, our next stopping-place, we went for a day to the great Royal Monastery of the Escorial, built by Philip II after the battle of St. Quentin, and it was also from the Capital that we arranged to visit the Cardinal Primate in his cathedral city of Toledo.

My object in going to Spain last September was not, however, to take a holiday, but to combine pleasure with work for England, utilising my familiarity with the Spanish language and habits of thought in order to find out the attitude of our fellow Catholics towards the Allies. Their pro-German sympathies had so often been asserted in my hearing that I considered it worth while to ascertain the truth for myself, and, if possible, to let them know our side of the dispute. In a war such as this is we cannot afford to affect indifference to hostile opinion where such exists, and it is no small achievement to increase the number of our well-wishers or even to correct the misunderstandings of those we cannot altogether win. My own experiences were completely different from those of the Abbe Lugan, recorded in the *'Tablet'* last November, and nothing could have surpassed the kindness and courtesy with which I was everywhere received; while as a Catholic Bishop with a knowledge of Spanish I had unique opportunities of meeting many distinguished ecclesiastics, whose views could not fail to be worthy of consideration.

In San Sebastian, the fashionable seaside place at which the Court was staying in September, I met the Papal Nuncio, Monsignor Ragonesi, who, during the three years in which he has represented the Holy See in Spain, has won golden opinions by his sympathetic understanding of the Spanish nation. At Toledo, the primatial city, once so mighty and always so interesting, Cardinal Guisasola received us. Many will remember the gracious presence of Cardinal Sancha at our Eucharistic Congress in London, and will be surprised to learn that Cardinal Guisasola is not his immediate successor. Two Spanish Primates have died since 1908. As a rule a Bishop has been in several Dioceses before he is made Primate, and the last one went to Toledo at the age of 74. The present Archbishop of Toledo and Patriarch of West Indies is 63 years old. He is full of energy and exercises great influence over the whole of Spain. After luncheon at his Palace I was privileged to have a long conversation with his Eminence. I had already spoken to another Spanish

Cardinal, the Archbishop of Valladolid, a true friend to the English and Scotch Colleges in that city where Columbus breathed his last and where Philip II first saw the light. Spain has nine Archbishoprics, but time did not allow me to call on any other Archbishop besides those just mentioned and the Archbishop of Saragossa. Saragossa owes its religious importance chiefly to the shrine of our Lady del Pilar, the most renowned in the whole peninsula. The Archbishop there was deeply interested in what I related to him about England, and I did not omit to point out to his Grace, as to others when occasion arose, the harm which may easily be done by Spanish Catholics writing or speaking publicly against England or France. It was out of the question to go to all the Bishops of Spain, as there are more than 40, but I saw three of their number. The Bishop of Madrid was most friendly on the two occasions on which we conversed on England. He has a diocese of the first importance, though established only 30 years ago, and the three Cardinals whom I have mentioned were all at some time Bishops of Madrid. While in the capital it was also my good fortune to meet the Bishop of Sion. He has no diocese, but his jurisdiction extends over the Army and Navy, and he is the Dean of the Court Chaplains and Ordinary of all the Institutes under Royal patronage. He is now ageing very much, but in speaking with me he manifested a great deal of the vigour for which he was known in his prime. The information which I obtained from a much younger Bishop, commonly called the Bishop of Ciudad Real but in fact Prior of the Four Military Orders of Spain, proved very useful on several occasions. Among the priests, too, there was much to be done. It would be hard to say what is the number of secular priests in Spain, but it is certainly very large. They have two influential organisations at least. The "Liga de la defensa del clero," with its headquarters in Madrid, comprises some 14,000 members in different parts of the country, and at Barcelona we found a more local association of 600 priests, whose object is the apostolate among the people. It was a very great pleasure to make the acquaintance of the able directors of these two important works.

The Religious Orders of the Church are always powerful, and in Catholic Spain this is specially the case. They suffered terrible persecution in the first half of the last century, but freedom was restored to them under Alfonso XII, and now they are once more in power, notwithstanding certain critical periods while Canalejas was Premier. The Society of Jesus has houses in every place in which we stayed, and I made a point of visiting them all; at Bilbao and Saragossa we enjoyed the hospitality of the Fathers. There are three provinces of the Society in Spain, and I spoke to two of the Provincials. They were pleased to know that we had many Jesuits in the diocese of Southwark and that England had generously given a home to their brethren from France and from Belgium. Through the 'Messenger of the Sacred Heart', through 'Razon y Fe' and through 'Lectura Dominical', the Fathers are able to exercise an influence which is perhaps even more extensive than that of their colleges and churches. It was, however, very wonderful to see what a centre of religious activity the church of the Jesuits had become at Bilbao, and I was very pleased to address more than 500 men of their Sodality at Barcelona. I also saw the two Provincials of the Augustinians: one at Valladolid and the other in Madrid. The Augustinians from their Monastery of the Escorial publish a review called 'Ciudad de Dios' and in Madrid they have 'Espana y America.' Both of these reviews have, unfortunately, printed articles against us, and it is important to make them more friendly. I called on Franciscans and Dominicans also whenever I was able, and I explained to them my desire of preventing any attacks from Catholics in Spain which might afterwards prove detrimental to religion amongst us. The Escolapios, founded by St. Joseph Calasanctius and devoting themselves to education, have more than 5,000 boys under their care in Barcelona alone. Speaking to one of their Assistant Generals, he reminded me of the words of the late Lord Salisbury, at the Guildhall Banquet, showing that the allusion to the dying nations, made many years ago by an English Prime Minister, had deeply hurt Spanish sentiment. I wish it had been possible to make the favourite pilgrimage from Barcelona to our Lady of Montserrat, especially as this is the only important monastery at present of the Spanish sons of St. Benedict in the Peninsula.

It would not have been wise to neglect the convents, as the nuns, too, and particularly the teaching Orders, have large circles of friends in that Catholic land. The Communities of the Sacred Heart welcomed us as their guests at San Sebastian and Barcelona, and in Madrid we stayed in the Assumption Convent. We called wherever we found convents of these two Orders, and I was able to address the community on the spread of the Catholic Church in England and on the liberty given to persecuted religious to find a home in our midst. They were surprised to hear that we could have processions of Our Lady in the streets of London. Visits to the Convents of Marie Reparatrice and of the Esclavas formed part of my programme, and the religious were always most interested. When any asked about Belgium I told them how Monsignor Dewachter, who has lived with me since the fall of Antwerp, had related to me atrocities committed by Germans in Belgium. But, having been warned, by persons in Spain who were in a position to know, that it was better not to insist too greatly on the crimes of Germany as I should only irritate without convincing my audience, I followed the good advice and confined myself to an account of what was being done for the Catholic Church here, and pointing out the danger of any public attack on our Government by the Catholics of Spain, just answering briefly any questions in regard to our enemies.

Though my work was thus chiefly in ecclesiastical circles it was not exclusively so. My aim was to collect as perfect ideas as possible of the nation's opinion, and to this end my companions and myself listened most willingly to the views of many lay persons as well.

It would have been thought strange if I had not asked for an audience with his Catholic Majesty when, as a Catholic Bishop, I was staying at San Sebastian, and, through the kindness of Sir Arthur Hardinge, our Ambassador, we had the honour of being received at the Miramar Palace on September 15th at noon. Monsignor Ottley and Father Lawton accompanied me, but His Majesty was graciously pleased to speak to me for 45 minutes before he allowed me to present to him my two companions. I was certainly charmed with the Spanish Monarch, and he impressed me as one who thoroughly knows and loves his people and understands the European situation to perfection. As the audience had lasted much longer than was expected we were commanded to return the following day to pay our respects to the Queen. We were thus privileged to have an audience with the Queen, who was naturally most interested in hearing news about England, and we were afterwards received by the Queen Mother, whose long regency gained her the admiration and the esteem of the whole world, and who, though herself an Austrian Archduchess, spoke most kindly of the good relations up to now between England and the land of her birth.

Among the laity we found many who were invaluable to us but whose names it is better not to give in this article. We saw many prominent persons and especially several important writers. The journalists, of course, were only too anxious to interview us, to ascertain whether we had any special mission, but we thought it better to see only those who were recommended to us by the many excellent and prudent friends whom we met in the course of our visit. Thus we gathered all the information that we could, and all three of us were well pleased with what we saw and heard, although it was inevitable that we should come in contact with a certain number whose sympathies were definitely against us.

I have related all this in order to make it clear that our opinion on the situation in Spain is at least entitled to a hearing. We certainly came to the conclusion that the people of Spain, as a body, wish to keep out of the European conflict, and do not intend to be dragged into it. The country has had wars and civil difficulties as its portion for a century, and peace is absolutely necessary for the development of its many resources, while the ceaseless struggle round Melilla drains the nation quite sufficiently. It would be extremely hard to speak with accuracy as to the sympathy of Spain with one side or the other. You cannot have the issue put clearly and plainly, and the political conditions are very complicated. The history of Spain shows us how different kingdoms were gradually brought under one king, and Castile, Aragon and Navarre still preserve their characteristics, widely different from Andalusia. The Basque provinces are quite distinct from the rest of the kingdom, and the Carlists still have many adherents there. Barcelona, with its ever increasing commerce, is always resentful of the authority of Madrid. There are to be found persons who would do or say anything to embarrass the dynasty, though the King is deservedly very popular with the greater part of his subjects. Speaking generally, however, the military admire German methods of training: the clergy resent the French treatment of the Church, and religiously-minded persons fear that the Allies may be hostile to the Catholic religion: while, on the other hand, many believe that we grossly exaggerate the atrocities in Belgium and they still have a very high opinion of the Germans because they do not know them. France and England are near but Germany is too far off.

In my letter to 'The Times' of November 20 last, I stated that there seemed to be a prejudice against England arising from several reasons. Prominent among these is the possession of Gibraltar by the British, a grievance with which the Carlist orator, Sr. Vasquez Mella, made great play last May at a meeting in Madrid. It is not forgotten, moreover, that in the Cuban War of 1898, Great Britain, as reflected at any rate by the Press, sided with the United States, and thus contributed to the loss of the Spanish colonies. Worst of all, many Spaniards, with all their reason for justifiable pride on account of the nation's splendid history, imagine that they are looked upon by England with contempt. Even the want of strenuous propaganda for our side at the beginning of the present war was interpreted as meaning that we do not care in the least whether they are with us or against us, and all the time Germany is extremely busy procuring the good will of Spain.

I was told, however, that nothing would be said to me against England, but I was warned not to flatter myself that this was a sign of benevolence towards us. It would simply be to avoid giving me personal offence. In speaking to me, very often the grievances against France would be mentioned, and our alliance was given as the cause for any unfriendly attitude. A hundred years have passed since the Peninsular War, but the memory of the French invasion still survives, and some who blamed Belgium for resisting the German army are nevertheless proud of the defence of Saragossa. Fresh cause of resentment is the French protectorate of Morocco, which Spain has wanted since her war with the Moors in 1859. They say that, though Tangier is international, most of the inhabitants there speak Spanish and the Spanish schools educate some 1,500 children without distinction of creed, and that, if France and England were friendly, it could be easily given over to Spain. Another great obstacle to a favourable view of our case among the fervent Catholics of the country, and these are many, is the legislation against the Church in France. This appeared to have a great effect, as the Spaniards have seen crowds of exiled religious taking refuge in their country, and they have an ever present fear that the example of France may be followed by their own Government, and that their own religious men and women may be turned adrift to find an exile's home as best they can. Lovers of the Holy See, they have read with sorrow that the Concordat was broken and the relations between the Vatican and the eldest daughter of the Church ended.

On the other hand, in Spain the Kaiser is reported to be well disposed to Catholics, and some, strange to say, imagine that he will restore the Temporal Power to the Pope. The Kaiser may have promised this, as well as the restoration of Gibraltar, knowing that he will never be able to carry out his promise. His utterances are thought to be sincere, though we know that deeds do not very often correspond with words. Again, Spaniards have a very high opinion of German Catholics, but they do not realise that there are no Jesuit Colleges or Sacred Heart Convents in Prussia, and that Germany opposed the Holy See when the Encyclical on St. Charles Borromeo was issued by Pius X, when the same Pope required the oath against Modernism to be taken by priests, and also when the 'Ne Temere' Decree on marriage and that on the early Communion of children were published. Spaniards who admire Germany do not know her, but their admiration must not surprise us as many amongst us, too, had great esteem for the Germans till they violated the neutrality of Belgium; and since then the destruction of Aerschot, Termonde, Louvain and many other places; the sinking without reason or warning of the 'Lusitania,' the 'Arabic,' the 'Persia' and countless others; the bombardment of unfortified towns like Scarborough and the numerous Zeppelin raids on defenceless places have made us think that the culture of twentieth-century Germans is not unlike the barbarity of fifth-century Huns. These facts have either not been brought before the notice of Spain or have been strongly denied by the numberless German agents in that country.

The Germans have made a good use of the Spanish Press to hide or explain what tells against them and to misrepresent the Allies.

We cannot but deplore that some excellent Catholics should be in favour of our enemies in this war. The vast majority of the people of Spain are on our side, but we feel deeply the tendency of the clergy and religious to be hostile to us. We wish to win them and to make them see the justice of our cause. It is worth while making every effort to show them for what principles we are fighting, and that we were not prepared for the war because we did not want it, whereas Germany had been ready and forced the war upon us by her invasion of Belgium. I am sure that any mark of good will shown by us will be gratefully appreciated by the Spaniards. Only a short time back I learnt that the leading article in '*The Times*' in connection with my letter on Spain had rejoiced many persons in that country, and the praise of Spain's benevolent neutrality by Lord Robert Cecil in the House of Commons last November was also gladly noted and will be remembered. It would be well if the Press in this country, and public men, too, sometimes spoke in praise of Spain, and the more we have of this friendly feeling the better it will be. England cannot afford to lose the friendship of Spain, and Germany for that reason is doing all in her power to prejudice Spain against England. There are powerful motives for being grateful to Spain. Thus, in consequence of her friendly neutrality from the beginning of the war, France has been able to withdraw many troops from her frontier and to utilize them against the enemy. Besides, how many a mother has been able to obtain information about her missing son, or a wife about her husband, through the good offices of the King of Spain who spares no pains in order to find out the whereabouts of the prisoners in Germany? Our papers say little of this huge work, yet it entails a multitude of letters day by day for the benefit of the sufferers, as a special department has been opened in Spain by the King for that sole object. Spain has also been most patient with us over her great losses through the war. Her trade has suffered enormously, as what England is doing cannot fully compensate her for the trade formerly carried on with Germany, Austria, Belgium and Holland. It is not our fault, but we ought to make the sufferings of a friendly neutral as little as circumstances permit. I believe that the fruit trade alone stands to lose £2,000,000 a year, an enormous sum even for a very wealthy country. We shall be wise to help Spain in every way we can. The effect will be seen not merely during the present war, but more still afterwards when Germany will try and extend her power in Spain and capture all the trade. A very practical way of showing our friendship would be by working with our great Ally across the Channel for the thorough consideration of the question of Tangier in the light of what must necessarily become a reconstructed map of the world. Though the Spaniards wish to have Tangier, they perfectly understand that this cannot be arranged while we are all fighting. It is, of course, a matter which concerns France more than ourselves, but if we were fully convinced of its utility, our French friends would assuredly not decline to unite themselves with us in the undertaking. I am certain that if a definite promise were now made that both France and England will join with Spain in a comprehensive and unbiased reconsideration of this international question when peace comes to be restored, an excellent effect would be produced in a country where we have many warm friends already, and where we earnestly hope to have many more still.

PETER, BISHOP OF SOUTHWARK.

Appendix II
The Fake Pastoral of 1929

Confidential
(copy)

BISHOP'S HOUSE,
ST. GEORGE'S ROAD,
SOUTHWARK, S.E.
Eve of Corpus Christi 1929

Secret, not to be shown, but for the general guidance of Parish Priests
who number Italian nationals amongst their communicants.
Beloved;

Great misapprehension having existed as to the relations between
the Holy See and the Fascist State, primarily as to the attitude to be
adopted by Catholics generally towards the government of Benito
Mussolini, the Holy Father has thought fit to issue the Diocesan
Bishops an encyclical of a necessarily private nature. From this encyclical I propose to draw some general and, I hope, simple instructions for
your guidance.

First, understand beyond doubt, that between Holy Church and the
Fascist State there is an unbridgeable gulf fixed! The attitude of the
Holy See towards the Fascist State is the acceptance of the lesser of a
choice of undoubted evils. A rapid survey of the history of the last few
years will convince you that there was a time of crisis when the
alternatives were the acceptance of Mussolini and his remarkably and
unexpectedly successful patriotic movement and on the other hand
acceptance of the forces of confusion, disorder and Anti-Christ directed
from Moscow, who have torn down the altars of God and put his priests
and bishops to the sword!

But the faults of Fascism were always very evident. It was accepted
as a temporary emergency expedient. His Holiness hopes then that in

the fulness of time it would please Almighty God to give a Government to Italy that would rule justly without oppression, recognize the claims of Holy Church and be acceptable to the people and the Nations of the world.

There is no reason to believe that the time is coming when such a government will appear.

It is therefore for reason of expediency most necessary that in the eyes of the children of Holy Church, She is not confused with the Fascist State! The Eastern Church in Russia suffered most of all in the hour of trial because the people considered that the priests had been linked inseparably with the old regime. This must not happen in Italy.

The Secretary of State has received absolute guarantees from certain eminent statesmen, including Nitti, that the Vatican Agreement will be acceptable to the Constitutional Party shortly to emerge and that the treaty will be extended and enriched in the favour of the Holy See!

But the encyclical of His Holiness is not merely concerned with policies of expediency. It definitely and irrevocably condemns the Fascist ideals, which are based upon an exaggerated Nationalism, well-nigh intolerable self-aggrandisement, are fraught with dangers of wars in the future and make for the separation and division of peoples.

Let that be clearly understood. Fascism is at heart as anti-Catholic as Free-masonry which it very properly desires to suppress.

The dangers of the future, should Fascism not in the Providence of God be overthrown, can be realized by the glimpse the Prime Minister of Italy gave us a few days ago when he, speaking in the Grand Council, stated that Holy Church owed its existence to establishment with the Roman Empire—that without Imperial contact it would have gradually disappeared like many another Eastern Faith! This is HERESY! A MAN THAT CAN STATE THAT IS A HERETIC!

Very well then, Fascism is heretical!

The attitude of the Holy Father towards the Fascist State is one of tolerance—at present! His children cannot do better than follow the Holy Father's lead.

What then must be our attitude?

The Doctors of the Church have, through the ages, left no doubts as to the attitude of Christians towards tyrannical governors and rulers. Authority must be accepted where there is no alternative. On the questions of oaths of loyalty, you will advise any of your flock who are in the position of having to take a Fascist oath of allegience, it may be against their conscience, that the nature of any oath depends upon the circumstances of its taking. I would advise you to read St. Ignatious upon Justifiable Casuistry!

There you will read that a seeming untruth is not necessarily a sinful lie, that a lie is sometimes excusable and certainly a half truth or a part-truth is frequently justifiable.

For instance, in the fourth century in Alexandria, at the time of the Arian persecution, when the followers of St. Athanasius were hounded to their deaths by the thousand, the Patriarch laid it down that when a Christian was asked "How many Gods do you believe in?" he was to reply—"I believe in One God"—That satisfied the Arian persecutor. It was a part-truth. If the Christian had said—"I believe in One God—in three Persons"—he would have been condemned to death. Likewise St. Ignatius rules that if a man gives an oath under duress or pressure, it is invalid; he makes "a mouthing with his mouth but the words he utters are not the thoughts of his heart, he has made a mental reservation."

That is the policy to be adapted towards the Fascist State. Let Catholics avoid taking oaths of allegience to it if possible but if they make them, let them do so with a mental reservation that whatever be the nature of their oath their duty to Holy Church comes first and the oath, so called, to the Fascist State must be set aside immediately Holy Church dictates.

So likewise with secret Societies. Many priests in this Diocese have felt difficulties in the sense that they know many good sons of Holy Church in their Parishes are banding themselves together in societies of what might be described an anti-Fascist nature.

Holy Church condemns secret Societies. But I am persuaded—and I am guided by the Holy Father's encyclical—that a band of good men, meeting together to take counsel, having the good of their fellows at heart, loving their country, loyal to Holy Church, are not necessarily a secret society within the meaning of the Church's condemnation.

True they meet in secret, but that may be because by oppression they are driven from their native land! If the object aimed at is altogether righteous, the establishment of Justice, Peace, Godly Government, then I am persuaded Holy Church would interpret the secrecy of their meeting as merely "discreet"! It is good test to apply if a priest is invited into the Counsels of these men and I know of course that in this Diocese many priests share in these counsels without consciousness of sin against the Church of Christ.

Finally, beloved, I would counsel you to be discreet. Take the example of the Irish Priests, who, through the long fight for freedom led the van, but were able to do so, so wisely, that the treaties were signed and the victory substantially won without Holy Church being stigmatised as leading a revolutionary movement!

Be wise then in your actions. Remember that as Catholic priests you are by the very nature of your high calling anti-Fascists. But remember also the Holy Father's necessity to tolerate a present evil is also yours. Act with discretion so as to bring no discredit upon Holy Church. Use the confessional and the study rather than the public meetings.

And I know it is not necessary for me to tell you that in offering the Holy Sacrifice, special intention ought frequently to be made for the troubled people of Italy, that it might please almighty God soon to establish there a government founded on righteousness, a Government Constitutional, liberty-loving and Catholic.

My blessing rests with you.

In the name of the Father, of the Son and of the Holy Ghost.

(Signed)
AMIGO Southwark.

Appendix III
"Faith in These Dark Times" (Evening Standard 14 May 1941)

War has always been one of the greatest scourges of humanity but it is exceedingly sad to think of the thousands who have already died in this present conflict. Precious lives have been lost, not only in the air, not only on the battlefield and at sea, but also during the air-raids throughout the Country and in the perils of the darkened streets after nightfall. The toll of death among men, women and children increases daily, and yet we cannot see the end of this fearful trial. We pity the mothers who mourn their sons, the wives who have lost their husbands, the children orphaned by the cruel hand of war and all who are stricken and bereaved. Certain it is that the enemy has not confined his attacks to military objectives. Numberless churches have been badly damaged or completely destroyed, and my own beautiful Cathedral is now a charred ruin. Schools and hospitals have not been spared in this merciless war. Rich and residential districts have been attacked, and very many poor people have lost their homes and all that they possessed. The whole Nation is united in common suffering. Again, parents and children have been separated by the necessity of evacuating schools to safer areas, and it is heart-rending to see hundreds of those that remain spending their nights and even part of the day in air-raid shelters. There, where they thought at least they would be safe, some have met their death. There has been some relief to this tale of woe, but undoubtedly we can speak of our times as "these dark days."

If we were to think of this world only we should indeed be of all men most miserable, as St. Paul tells us, but do not let us forget those other words of his "that which is at present light and momentary of our tribulation worketh for us above measure exceedingly an eternal weight of glory." We are made by God to be happy with Him for ever hereafter.

God Himself showed the immensity of His love for us when He took our nature and came on earth for our salvation. He suffered and died for us and we draw strength from His Passion and inspiration from the wonderful example of patience given us by Our Divine Master Jesus Christ. All grace comes to us from Him. He does not try us above that which we are able to bear, for His grace is sufficient for us. He is almighty. He loves us and knows what we are enduring. We can do nothing of ourselves but all things through Him. We have every hope and trust in God our Saviour, and we know that if we suffer we shall also reign with Him. We have St. Paul's word for that. We have no lasting city here, and we look for an eternal reward after this life. Therefore, however great our sorrows may be in these dark days, we must never be discouraged.

Our faith, moreover, gives us the greatest confidence for our final victory. We may be very far from the end of the war, and at times when we hear of one country after another being successfully invaded by Hitler we are inclined to lose heart unless we turn to God. Our King has told us to put our trust in God as he does. Our sailors, soldiers and airmen, our men and women in the civil defence services, all have done a splendid work and deserve our heartfelt gratitude, but there is one particular work in which all must play their part and that is to turn to God and beg His Blessing. We must make friends with God whom we have so often outraged by sin. With contrite and humble hearts we should beg His pardon. Many do not realise that the present calamity may be a punishment for sin and that God is waiting for us to acknowledge our faults. "There is no man that sinneth not." But God is compassionate and merciful and desires not the death of the wicked but that the wicked turn from his way and live. As we wish to win the war, we should first humble ourselves under the Mighty Hand of God. Remember the words of Judas Machabeus, that valiant captain, to his soldiers: that success in war is not in the multitude of the army, but strength cometh from heaven. Our King has repeatedly asked us to have special days of intercession, and most people have loyally responded, but we must continue unfalteringly to storm heaven with our prayers. Our enemies are most powerful. During the long years, while most of us did not seem to realise the danger, they have been preparing to strike us. They made themselves the masters of Austria and Czechoslovakia, but not until they cruelly attacked Poland did we realise that the situation was intolerable and that it was our duty to take up arms. Since then they have invaded Norway and Denmark; Belgium, Holland and Luxemburg, unprovocative and peace-loving, have been overwhelmed. Most of France is writhing beneath the conqueror's yoke. The Balkans were next over-run and we have seen with agony the defeat of the heroic Greeks. The Nazis seem to have multitudes of men in the field, and to be crunchingly superior in the number of their tanks and aircraft. Their submarines have inflicted heavy losses upon us. True, we have met them in the air and in spite of inferior numbers we have been able to defeat the massed attacks of the enemy, but unless we ask God's help we may yet be overpowered. This will never happen if we follow the lead of our King and put our trust in God. Filled with the confidence He alone can give, we shall use every means in our power to attain to victory. Thoroughly patriotic, we shall make every sacrifice demanded of us and cheerfully and bravely endure every trial. But we must never forget that we depend ultimately on God and on nothing else. Our help is in the Name of the Lord Who made heaven and earth. "In Thee, O Lord, I have hoped: let me never be put to confusion."

Letter of R. A. Butler
to Amigo 16th September 1942

I am obliged to Your Grace and to your deputation for giving me the opportunity of an informal consideration of methods by which we can ensure progress, while at the same time preserving the essential features of the denominational schools in which you have a particular interest. What I set out below is tentative, and does not represent considered Government policy. This I explained when we met. We have two main objectives: first that the schools of the country should reach a reasonably high standard, both physically and educationally, so that all children have equivalent opportunities in respect of secular instruction.

Second, we regard it as essential that the scheme of Reorganisation, under which children over 11 are taught in separate schools, should be rapidly completed and made nationwide. Indeed there is little doubt that we shall require the completion of Reorganisation within a reasonable time after the day appointed for raising the school age to 15. We recognise that the raising of the school leaving age, as suggested, and the achievement of the standards to which I have referred will impose heavy burdens upon all concerned. Our aim is, therefore to work out a plan which will overcome this difficulty, and will help all the interests concerned without giving any one denomination preferential treatment. We must, at the same time, evolve a plan which will be acceptable to the Government, to Parliament, to the many educational interests concerned and also to public opinion.

Let me turn to your own particular problems. You, Your Grace, stressed a point which His Eminence Cardinal Hinsley had previously made when I met him, namely your desire that the Catholic schools should be within the national system of education. I respect and welcome this view but I hold that it is not consistent with the claim that might be advanced that the Roman Catholic schools should receive exceptional treatment.

I have not only borne in mind your desire that your schools should be associated with the national system but also believe from what I have heard and read, that you would not desire the duality and diversity of our present educational system to be destroyed. I have accordingly attempted to work out a homogenous plan comprising the following two alternatives. Under the first alternative the arrangements would be on the following lines:

(a) The obligation of the managers in regard to repairs, alterations and improvements to pass to the local Education Authority.

(b) The appointment of teachers to pass from the Managers to the local Education Authority, subject to what is said below about the appointment of reserved teachers and of Head teachers.

(c) Agreed syllabus instruction to be given.

(d) Agreed syllabus instruction to be supplemented by not more than two periods a week of denominational instruction to be given by reserved teachers to those children whose parents desire it.

(e) Reserved teachers to be appointed to such an extent as may be necessary for the denominational teaching referred to in (d) it being remembered that it will be permissible to give religious instruction at any hour of the day, instead of, as at present at the beginning or end of the school meeting.

(f) The Head Teacher should not normally be a reserved teacher but the Managers should be consulted; such consultation might take the form of the selection of the Head Teacher by a Committee of five persons, three representing the local Education Authority and two of the Managers.

Under the second alternative, the plan would be as follows:

In cases where the Managers desire to retain their existing powers in regard to the appointment of teachers and the giving of denominational religious instruction, they should be allowed to do, provided that they are able and willing to meet within a strictly limited time 50% of the cost of repairs and such alterations and improvements as may reasonably be required by the local Education Authority. In such a case the remaining 50% would be met by a direct Exchequer grant to the Managers. I realised at our meeting that your needs and desires could not be met under Alternative 1.

The second alternative is however a considerable improvement on existing conditions, and is a generous offer, adapted to existing circumstances, under which State aid can be given towards expenditure on the fabric of schools which are to retain full liberty in the matter of denominational religious teaching, and of the religious belief and observance of *all* their teachers. I derived from our meeting a clear impression that these are in fact your essential claims.

I am anxious as I hope you will realise from our talk to do all I can to assist the Catholic community to further the interests of the children in their schools and to meet what I recognise to be very real difficulties. But we are bound to take a realist view of the present situation. This leaves no hope, in my considered view of negotiating or carrying through a policy which would place on public funds, the full cost of providing and bringing up to standard, all denominational schools, while leaving the individual school Managers the full liberties they now enjoy.

I have therefore, made the proposal as it stands in alternative 2. We discussed together how liberal an interpretation can be given to the phrase 'alterations and improvements'.

And here we need, I think, to draw a clear distinction between the replacement of existing schools and the provision of new schools. I should myself see no difficulty in so construing the words 'alterations and improvements' as to enable the 50% grant to be made in respect of the provision of school buildings designed to replace existing ones, provided that a material increase in the number of school places was not involved. On the other hand, the words clearly do not cover the provision of new schools designed to meet the needs of new centres of population or of new schools for substantially more children than are already in existing schools. Nor would I be prepared to ask Parliament to vote money for the erection of such new schools for any denomination.

I am prepared however, to discuss how far the terms of the offer in alternative 2 would meet the calls of Reorganisation and how far this offer would need to be supplemented by two specific suggestions which I should hope would be of great value to you. These are first that agreements under the 1936 Act, which because of the War have legally lapsed, should be revived and second that proposals, of which there is some documentary evidence—even though they did not reach the stage of a formal agreement to provide a new school or to extend an existing one with the aid of a grant from the Local Education Authority under the provisions of the 1936 Act—should also be revived.

Both these suggestions, to be effective, call for the co-operation and assent of the Local Authority concerned. It only remains for me to repeat what I said on the subject of the Scottish solution, namely that denominational instruction has been given in their schools for 70 years and in this respect conditions in that country differ completely from those prevailing here. Moreover, there are in Scotland far fewer non-provided schools, both numerically and proportionately, than in England and fewer denominations to consider. I think you yourself felt that the application of the Scottish solution to our English schools would be impracticable, much as many of us might like to adopt it.

It will be clear that further discussion between us will be very profitable as soon as you are able to give me the reactions of those whom you may wish to consult. I need not stress the importance of meeting the needs of the children by coming to some satisfactory agreement upon a subject which has vexed the world of education for so long. I have been very conscious in putting forward the proposals above, that they constitute *l'art du possible* in the world in which we live.

Yours Sincerely
(signed) R. Butler.

Appendix V

8th September, 1949

The Last Pastoral

PETER, by the Grace of God and the Favour of the Apostolic See, *Archbishop, Bishop of Southwark,*

To the Clergy, Secular and Regular, and to the Faithful of our Diocese, Health and Benediction in the Lord.

Dearly beloved brethren and dear children in Jesus Christ.

The Vicar of Christ calls upon all Catholics to pray in the month of October very specially. The October Devotions were started by Pope Leo XIII at a time which he called most turbulent, and it is hard to imagine that the world is any better at present. There are troubles in the East, especially from the Soviet Government of Russia which has an evil influence on several other states. We wish you to make the first Sunday of October a special day of prayer. Many of our churches have exposition of the Blessed Sacrament on that day every year. Make a point of spending some time in Adoration and ask Our Lord to bless us all. Assist at the October Devotions if you can every day. If, however, circumstances prevent you, try to say the Rosary daily at home, with the Litany of Our Lady and the special prayers in honour of St. Joseph.

We have already had Missions in many churches during this year, and we have been glad to see them well attended. Let there be special efforts during this month in attending the October Devotions. It would help those who actually take part in the public recitation of the Rosary, and it would be a source of edification to many, if they saw our churches filled during this month of special prayer. God will hear our prayers. "A contrite and humbled heart He will not despise."

215

It has been our custom for many years to tell you in the Rosary Sunday Pastoral of the progress made in building churches and schools. Two disastrous wars have prevented our continuing much of the work. We have had to tell you, instead, of damage done to churches, schools and convents. We have thought it best this year to remind you of what has been achieved in our Episcopate of more than 45 years, and to exhort you to thank God for what has been done. "The mercies of the Lord I will sing for ever."

In 1904 we could count only 92 churches in the Diocese: the Rosary Sunday collection then amounted to £511. This year we have to thank you under God for over £3,000 in the Rosary Sunday collection: we have 194 churches registered for marriages, besides the many chapels of convents and institutions. We owe a deep debt of gratitude to Bishop Brown for the valuable help he has given to us from the beginning of our Episcopate, and we are deeply grateful to all the officials of the Diocese. We have been served faithfully, loyally and well. We are proud of our clergy, of our religious, both men and women, and of our devoted laity. Our Finance Committee has met regularly every week and given us their services gladly. The Southwark Rescue Society, which was founded by Bishop John Butt in 1887, continues its great work, and we thank the Directors of the Society, the Sisters of Mercy and the Sisters of Charity, as also the Presentation Brothers, because through their services thousands of boys and girls have kept the Faith. Bishop Grant had done pioneer work with the Sisters of Norwood, who have kept their Centenary lately. Since 1905 we have had the Franciscan Capuchins providing Mass and other religious help for the thousands who come to the hop gardens of Kent for a few weeks in the Summer. We thank them and those who assist them.

Our predecessors built for us the Seminary of St. John at Wonersh, which has been so successful in training priests for the Diocese. We have added a junior Seminary under the protection of St. Joseph at Mark Cross, and this College celebrates this year the 25th year of its opening. We have succeeded in establishing two Secondary Schools for boys; one at Purley under the Patronage of St. John Fisher, and another near Guildford under the Patronage of St. Peter the Apostle. When we started the John Fisher School in the Croydon Parish it was thought we should never be able to have enough boys who would need it. Now, however, there are over 400 boys attending there, and the school has educated at least 800 Catholic men, including 4 who have been ordained priests. St. Peter's, Guildford, which started only two years ago, promises to do extremely well. The parish priest at Sevenoaks, who has himself opened a new school there recently, already has 40 boys attending. We hope that the Carmelite Fathers will be able to open another school for boys at Aylesford, the cradle of their order in England. We cannot be grateful enough for the work done by the many religious communities of women in their convent schools. We do not know what may be the future of Catholic education, but we deplore the act of 1944 with all the vast expense of reorganization of schools.

In 1908 we found ourselves heavily crippled with debts, and we set up a Commission under the presidency of the late Henry, Duke of Norfolk, with several priests and lay people to enquire into our financial position. Their report gave us confidence and interested our people in the progress of our diocese. The debts amounted to over £350,000 and we thank God that this huge debt has been paid off. Unless a special benefactor builds a church we have still to borrow money when starting new churches and schools, but these debts are not unbearable, and last year we were able to pay off some £20,000. Last year the debts were paid off at Morden, Tenterden, Biggin Hill, Downham and Broadstairs, being cleared by splendid efforts in face of great difficulty. Although a church cannot be consecrated until it is free of debt, over 50 churches have been consecrated in our Episcopate. We have been delighted to start new centres for Mass, and the work of the Travelling Mission has given people who live too far from an existing church, the opportunity to hear Mass and receive the Sacraments, and these centres have led to the foundation of 22 new parishes and missions.

We are still without a Cathedral. It has been sad to see before us during more than 8 years the ruins of St. George's, where we loved to pontificate; and although the Irish people and others have been most generous in their contributions, delays prevent us from starting the restoration we long for. An excellent improvement has been made in the adjoining hall which was erected for our Golden Jubilee of the Priesthood, and over 1,600 are thus able to hear Mass on Sundays in the district. We are most grateful. Bermondsey, Camberwell, Sydenham and St. Mary Cray are also waiting to have their churches restored.

In the many years of our Episcopate we have promoted many to the different orders leading to the Priesthood, and we have had the happiness of ordaining 1,150 priests, many of them of the Society of Jesus from their provinces of Paris and Lyons while they were studying at Canterbury and Ore Place, Hastings; some of whom were killed fighting in the French Army in the first world war and others are now scattered in different parts of the world. We are greatly indebted to the Society for helping us with late vocations in their house at Osterley. We ourselves had established St. Augustine's, at Walworth, to help young men who while still at business tried their vocations, living with the priests at Walworth and studying there after business hours, and several excellent priests have had their first preparation for the priesthood in this way.

It has been our pleasant duty as your Bishop to promote devotion to the Blessed Sacrament. Churches are built for Mass and the Blessed Sacrament is reserved there. We rejoiced in starting the men's Guild of the Blessed Sacrament in 1908, and we were able to join in the outdoor procession which, apart from the war years, has become an annual event, with some 3,000 men walking in it. This is a great demonstration of Faith which must do much good to those who take part and to those who see it. The Knights of St. Columba have an annual pilgrimage to Canterbury.

It has been our earnest wish too, to encourage our people to honour Our Blessed Lady, and with that object we have led no less than 15 diocesan pilgrimages to the Shrine of our Lady at Lourdes, although we ourselves could not lead the pilgrimage which went this year. The name of the first Bishop of Southwark is at St. Peter's in Rome on the list of Bishops who were present there when Pope Pius IX defined the Dogma of the Immaculate Conception in December, 1854, and our Diocese from the very beginning was dedicated to Our Lady Immaculate. Until this year we were always present at the annual pilgrimage at West Grinstead, and we wish that many will go year by year to honour Our Lady in this place where the Faith was kept up through the days of persecution.

We were very glad to take a Southwark contingent for the Canonization in Rome of our two great martyrs St. John Fisher and St. Thomas More in 1935, and at other times Southwark has gone to pay homage to the Vicar of Christ, especially for the Holy Years. We wish that we ourselves could go personally next year for the Jubilee Year of 1950, but at the age of 85 we feel it to be impossible. We hope, however, that Southwark will be well represented among the Catholics of the whole world who will journey to Rome on that occasion for the great Jubilee Indulgence.

We thank God with all our heart for what has been done in our long episcopate. We can never forget the help which we have had from you all. For this reason, in addition to the Mass which we are bound to say for our people on Sundays and Feasts, we say a Mass every week for all our benefactors.

St. Paul told the Corinthians, in his first Epistle to them, "I have planted, Apollo watered, but God gave the increase." We also must, while realising a great work has been done, always be deeply grateful to God. To Him be honour and glory.

"Grace be with you. Amen."

Given at Southwark on the Feast of the Birthday of Our Lady, 8 September 1949, and appointed to be read in all our churches and public chapels on Sunday, 2 October, Rosary Sunday, when the annual collection will be made for the needs of the Diocese.

PETER, Archbishop, Bishop of Southwark.

Appendix VI
And so this Man also Died

(The Sermon preached in Westminster Cathedral, 6-10-49, at the Requiem Mass for Archbishop Amigo by the Rt Rev. Mgr George Andrew Beck, Bishop of Tigia)
"And so this man also died, undefiled, wholly trusting in the Lord"
(2 Macc. VII. 40)
Your Grace, my Lords, dear brethren in Christ,

The figure of a great priest, the pastor, for forty-five years, of the diocese of Southwark, has passed from us. With his death, an era in the history of the Diocese of Southwark has come to an end; and it is proper that we should pause in the midst of the Church's solemn prayer for the repose of his soul, in order that we may pay some tribute to his memory.

Forty-five years ago, by a Brief dated 8 March, 1904, Father Peter Emmanuel Amigo, Rector of the Church of the English Martyrs, Walworth, late Vicar-General of the diocese, was appointed Bishop of Southwark, in succession to Bishop Bourne, who, shortly before, had been transferred to the Metropolitan See of Westminster. In the same year on 25 March Bishop Amigo was consecrated and enthroned in St. George's Cathedral.

After early studies at St. Edmund's Ware, Father Amigo had completed his studies for the priesthood at the seminary at Hammersmith, and was ordained priest in the Pro-Cathedral at Kensington, on 25 February, 1888. He returned, for a time, as professor, to St. Edmund's, but in 1892 began that long life of the priestly care of souls, which finished in the early hours of last Saturday morning, as the consecration of the chalice was completed by the priest who was saying Mass at his bedside.

He came to the See of Southwark with an already wide experience of parish life in London. He had served on the mission at Stoke Newington in the north, Brook Green in the west, Commercial Road in the east, and Walworth in the south. The care of souls entrusted to his charge, a concern with the spiritual well-being of his people, remained the characteristic of his life.

Only a few weeks before his appointment, a writer in 'The Shield', the then organ of the Southwark Catholic Rescue Society, had written: "The new bishop, whoever he may be, will receive the heartiest possible welcome, loyalty, co-operation, and obedience, from all the Catholics in the diocese—Chapter, clergy, and laity alike, and the one prayer of all will be that he may be the best bishop that Southwark ever had, and have a more successful and more fruitful episcopate than any of his great and venerated predecessors." How well has that prayer been answered in the course of forty-five years.

The Archbishop himself—you know that this title was conferred on him personally, by Pope Pius XI, in 1938, on the occasion of the fiftieth anniversary of his ordination to the priesthood—the Archbishop himself has left to his own people, the clergy and faithful of the diocese of Southwark, a moving summary, written almost as a testament, and read in the churches and chapels of the diocese last Sunday, of what has been accomplished during that successful and fruitful episcopate. It is an astonishing record of apostolic achievement—more than one hundred churches opened in the diocese in the last forty-five years, over fifty churches consecrated, the establishment of a motor mission from which twenty-two new missions and parishes were founded, the setting-up of a junior seminary twenty-five years ago at Mark Cross, the provision of two secondary schools for boys, and the extension of numerous primary schools. During that time too the number of Catholics in this diocese has doubled itself from just over 100,000 in 1904 to 220,000 at the present time. You will have sensed, as you heard the words read to you last Sunday, the joy, the pride, the gratitude, of a bishop, in those lines of his last pastoral in which he says: "We have had the joy of ordaining 1,150 priests."

Yet the mere record, great as it is, and magnificently as the diocese has developed under his care, is not what is in your minds at the present moment. These things were incidental to the over-riding sense of pastoral duty, ever upmost in the mind of Bishop Amigo—the provision, for the ordinary people, the Catholics of South London, of Kent and Surrey and Sussex, of the means of grace, and the opportunity to go to Mass and to practise their religion. I am sure that the picture which you, Catholics of the diocese of Southwark, have most vividly in your minds, is not so much that of the great pontiff in his episcopal vestments, much as he rejoiced to fulfil that part of his office, but the figure of your Father in God, surrounded by the children, the mothers and the fathers, at the door of a church, or in a parish hall in the suburbs of London, or in the hop-fields, giving you his ring to kiss, chiding you, teasing you perhaps, with the glint of humour in his eyes under their bushy brows and the engaging smile of his full-lipped generous mouth while he remembered so astonishingly those many details of your names, your lives and your families, never forgetting to underline the lesson that you must love our Divine Lord and His Blessed Mother, and be good and loyal children of the Church. You will not need me to remind you how much he encouraged, especially among the men, devotion to the Blessed Sacrament.

But for the grim destruction of war, the ceremony to-day would have been taking place within the walls of Pugin's great cathedral on the other side of the Thames, which he loved so well, and the loss of which was such a heavy blow to him in his last years. May I speak, therefore, to you, the clergy and people of the diocese of Southwark, for though we gather here to join in the mourning, from every part of these Islands, and, indeed, from beyond the sea, yours is the greatest loss, as yours must be the greatest pride in the memory of all that he did for you—for you have lost the shepherd and father of your souls.

You, the clergy of the diocese, must mourn for him. You may have smiled, at times, at his ways, his foibles and mannerisms, at the devastating comments he made on your persons and your work, at the appearance and the trappings of severity; but, underneath, you knew as few others could know, the great heart of this "golden priest." You, before all others, were in his love and his prayers, and each of you must undoubtedly preserve some precious memory of his fatherly interest in your priesthood and your priestly work. This was his constant concern, from the moment of his consecration. In his first pastoral letter, in 1904, he wrote of what he described as "this most important work, the training of future priests. We have a duty," he said, "not only to those of the Fold, but to those thousands and thousands who know naught of the Church of the Living God, the pillar and ground of the Truth." And he went on to add: "We are anxious that the diocese now entrusted to our care should always have a clergy noted for their learning no less than for their zeal and piety." He wrote, too,.in 1916, during the first world war on the occasion of the Jubilee of St. John's Seminary: "Priests have a most important national work at present, as well as in times of peace, and no substitute can take their place. The Nation has to acknowledge that without God we can do nothing, and that 'with God all things are possible.' All must be stirred up to do their part. Even now we have hardly begun to pray. Yet our prayers alone can bring down God's blessing on our Arms; our Masses and Communions are needed to secure for the wounded and the afflicted the graces which they look for from the bountiful Hand of the Almighty. Just as in the Penal Times not every priest was called upon to face a violent death for the faith, but every one without exception had to spend and be spent in the wearisome and prosaic effort of seeking out and saving the sheep of Christ, in obscurity and unremitting toil, so it is now. The priest is not his own, but he is at the service of his people." Do we not sense that here, all unconsciously, he was revealing something of his own priesthood and priestly ideals? And I suppose that the last time he addressed any great number of you publicly, was at St. John's, Wonersh, last August, on the occasion of the Clergy Retreat, when he spoke to you on that subject to which he so often referred, and which was so close to his heart—the charity of priests one towards the other. You can bear testimony, far better than I, of that singular quality of his own priestly zeal.

People of the diocese of Southwark, you have lost a great father. You will long remember, and hand on the memory to your children, of that striking figure, bent a little in these last years, with his lined and yellowing face, leaning on a stick since his last illness, but indomitable in the greatness of his heart, coming to your parishes for Visitation or Confirmation, sharing your sufferings and sorrows in the dark and ugly days of war, appearing at the Mission Services, to bless and encourage you, or among your families in the hop-fields in the summer—knowing you all with that extraordinary memory, truly patriarchal in his bearing, the Father of a great family in God, to which you all belong.

It was characteristic of him that he should think of you all in the last words he wrote to you, with the shadow of death over him. His words must be sounding still in your memories. "We owe a deep debt of gratitude to Bishop Brown for the valuable help he has given to us from the beginning of our Episcopate, and we are deeply grateful to all the officials of the Diocese. We have been served faithfully, loyally and well. We are proud of our clergy, of our religious, both men and women, and of our devoted laity." And again, at the end of his Pastoral: "We thank God with all our heart for what has been done in our long episcopate. We can never forget the help which we have had from you all. For this reason, in addition to the Mass which we are bound to say for our people on Sundays and Feasts, we say a Mass every week for all our benefac-

tors." In some ways the territory which he governed must have seemed
to him not so much a diocese as a very extensive parish every part of
which he knew so well, which he cherished with the diligent attention
of a priest persevering zealously in his pastoral visiting.

He has gone from you now, but his memory will remain, and you will
pray, and continue in prayer, that God may quickly give him the reward
of these long and arduous labours, which he drove himself to undertake
to the last, for your sakes, and for love of you. If anyone lived up to St
Paul's words, to spend himself and be spent for souls, it was the great
bishop who ruled you for forty-five years, and whose body we are shortly
to commit to the crypt of his ruined cathedral. Above all, as you know,
he loved the poor and the destitute and how keenly he watched the work
of the Southwark Rescue Society. The poorest among you will give him,
I know, the richness of your affection and your prayers.

But you will allow others to join with you in your mourning and in
your pride. For the greatness of his heart, which is now stilled, won for
him friends and admirers all over the world. His love for the ordinary
people, for the poor, for the oppressed, was a glowing thing that, at
times, could rage into flame; he hated anything which seemed to him to
savour of injustice, pettiness, pretentiousness, or double-dealing, and he
spoke trenchantly, even disconcertingly, in defence of his views, no
matter how unpopular might be the cause which he espoused.

You will allow the people of Belgium to join with you in your
mourning. The days of the first world war seem remote enough to us
now, but the children of many a Belgian family have the right to look
with thankfulness to the memory of the bishop of these southern
counties, who did so much to bring them comfort, temporal and
spiritual, in the dark days when their country was under the heel of the
invader.

You will allow the people of Ireland to join with you in mourning,
and in gratitude to your Father in God. Whatever differences there may
have been amongst us, however hard and cruel the road of freedom may
have been, the Irish people have always known that support and
encouragement, defence and affection, were theirs in the diocese of
Southwark under its magnanimous pastor. They will never forget all
that was implied in the Requiem Mass which was celebrated at St.
George's Cathedral on 28 October, 1920, in the presence of the Bishop
of the diocese—an incident and a story which are enshrined for ever in
the pages of their history.

Catholics of Southwark, you will allow the Spanish people to join with you in mourning, for they remember, too, the voice which was raised in defence of Catholic Spain, not only in the dreadful hour of martyrdom, but in the long, tiring years of re-building, in spite of a campaign of denigration and calumny which has remained a disgrace to the intelligence of the western world.

You will allow your fellow-Catholics of this country to share with you this tribute to the memory of a bishop whose stature towered far above his own diocese, and whose influence has been felt by us all. A fatherly counsellor to a younger generation of clergy—and of Bishops, unflinching in his devotion to duty and principles, undaunted in utterance where the defence of Catholic rights or teaching was concerned, zealous for the well-being of ordinary people everywhere, he endeared himself to the Catholics of this Island with a quality which evokes from us all, something more than admiration and respect, something more personal in its loyalty, more affectionate in its tenderness. You will allow the Catholics of England and Wales to join with you in paying tribute to his patriarchal greatness.

The whole Church, too, must mourn his passing, for his outlook and his affections were truly Catholic and Apostolic, expressed so significantly in his intense devotion to the See of Rome, the See of St Peter, his Patron, and to the person of the Holy Father.

You will want a word of deep gratitude joined to our wishes and prayers for his speedy recovery, to be addressed to his Eminence the Cardinal Archbishop of Westminster, for allowing this Cathedral to be considered for today as territorially part of the diocese of Southwark, so that the traditional rite of the five-fold Absolution may be performed.

There is a providential symbolism in the fact that the diocese of Southwark, joined by us all, has come to the Metropolitan Cathedral, his own being in ruins, as is also the church where he was ordained, to pray for the repose of the soul of the Archbishop—Bishop of the diocese. You will allow us all to join with you in that prayer. We think of him in the words applied to a much younger man, in the Book of the Macchabees: "This man also died, undefiled, trusting in the Lord." He has fought the good fight, he has finished his course, and we pray, with both proud and sorrowful hearts, that the Lord, the Just Judge, will now render to him, in this day, that which is laid up for him, the crown of justice.

Bibliography

GENERAL

The English Catholics 1850–1950. Edited by Rt. Rev George Andrew Beck AA London, Burns Oates 1950

Catholicism in England by David Matthew, 3rd Edition, London Eyre and Spottiswoode, 1955

Francis Cardinal Bourne by Ernest Oldmeadow, Burns Oates & Washbourne, Vol. 1 1940 Vol. 2 1944, London

Westminster, Whitehall and the Vatican, by Thomas Moloney, Burns and Oates 1985

The Life of Baron Von Hugel by Michael de la Bedoyere, London J.M. Dent 1950

Cardinal Gasquet, A Memoir, by Shane Leslie, London, Burns Oates 1953

The Life of Rt. Rev Ronald Knox by Evelyn Waugh, Chapman and Hall 1959

SPECIFIC TO SOUTHWARK

A Seminary in the Making, Being a History of the Foundation and Early Years of St. John's Diocesan Seminary, Wonersh 1889–1903. Compiled by Rev Thomas Hooley, London, Longmans Green, 1927.

Through Windows of Memory, by William Francis Brown, Bishop of Pella, Sands & Co. Limited, London 1946

A History of the Diocese of Southwark by Fr. Bernard Kelly, Sands & Co. Limited, London 1927. (Exists in proof-copy only, never printed).

The Shield. The Magazine of the Southwark Rescue Society Monthly.

The Southwark Record. The Magazine of the Diocese of Southwark 1922 to 1939 and 1945 onwards. Monthly.

Sources

Chapter One
Information on the Bishop's family is taken from researches made by Bishop Raymund Fitzgerald of Gibraltar and conveyed to Mgr. Reynolds in 1950. Information on affairs in Gibraltar is taken from the 'Gibraltar Chronicle' and Mgr. Caruana's researches. Information on the Bishop's career at St. Edmund's as a student is taken from the Archives of St. Edmund's Ware, now at Archbishop's House, Westminster.

Chapter Two
The information on the Bishop's career as a Priest is taken entirely from Southwark Archive Sources, File entitled "Biographical Materials Early." Fr. Hubert Rochford had already prepared a lengthy account which he put into this file. The letter of 'excommunication' is from Westminster Archdiocesan Archives. W.A.A. B. 3/56/1

Chapter Three
Information on the events leading up to the appointment of Fr. Amigo as Bishop are to be found in a file marked "Interregnum" while the letters of congratulation and description on the consecration are kept in the "Biographical Materials Early" file.

The information that Canon St. John was suggested as a candidate by Archbishop Bourne is from a note in Westminster Archives. W.A.A. B/3/29/4

Chapter Four
The story of the accusation against Cardinal Bourne of modernism is in the "Wonersh Seminary File" at Southwark and much of the material is also to be found at Westminster Archdiocesan Archives under "Bourne and Modernism."

The entire series of letters dealing with Fr. Tyrell and Maud Petre are in the Southwark Archive "Modernism" file.

The sad story of Fr. Hammersley, the affair of 'Pastoralia' and the suspect articles, are to be found in the "Vigilance Committee" File.

Chapter Five
The story of the break between Archbishop Bourne and Bishop Amigo over the Seminary Rectorship is to be found in the "Wonersh Seminary File." The difficulties over finance and over Division of the Dioceses is to be found in six large box files entitled "The Consistorial Case." This is partially indexed up to 1911 only. In all there are well over 1,000 letters or documents or extracts from newspapers. The only additional materials not found in this file are the "Letters of Cardinal Gasquet" which are kept in a separate file, and the letters from the Consistorial which are kept in the file marked "Roman Documents." (A separate file of these exists for each group of three years).

Chapter Six
There are separate files of letters relating to each Jubilee the Bishop celebrated. The information of the Bishop's activities at home during the first world war are to be found in the file marked "First World War."

The story of the Bishop's visits to Spain are documented fully in a large file which is indeed entitled "Amigo and Spain." There is also a separate file on "Belgian Refugees" and the award of the Commander of King Leopold II is to be found in a separate folder.

Chapter Seven
The entire chapter is based on a very large file entitled "Amigo and Ireland" which is indexed. This contains all the letters and press cuttings used. The description of the funeral of Terence McSwiney is taken from "The Great Link," the History of St. George's Cathedral by Fr. Bernard Bogan.

Chapter Eight
The Education files are grouped together for every five years or so. The material in each box is not in order. The account of the events surrounding the Scurr Amendment is taken from the copies of the *"Tablet"* for the weeks in question. Canon Mahoney OBE provided the information about the forming of the Diocesan Schools Commission.

Chapter Nine
Separate files deal with the Bishop's dealings over membership of the Labour Party, Parish councils and Mgr. Ronald Knox. The rest of the material describing the various events is taken from the "Southwark Record" for the relevant months. The material relating to the appointment of an Apostolic Delegate and the question of the Papal Legates being received at Dover is kept with the Roman Documents for the period.

Chapter Ten
The entire material for this chapter is taken from a file entitled "Sts John Fisher and Thomas More" except for the introduction which is based on the C.T.S. pamphlet, "The Martyrs of England and Wales, 1535 to 1680." H.469.

Chapter Eleven
The material for the chapter on the Fascist Regimes was extracted from various files and old boxes. In future all this material will be kept together in one file to be entitled "Fascist Regimes of the 1930's."

Chapter Twelve
Separate files exist for the questions of the Exemption of Church Students from Military Service, the Sword of the Spirit, War Damage Claims, Gibraltarian Refugees and St. George's Cathedral. The Information on Civil Defence, Black Out, Bombing in general etc., is taken from a file entitled "Second World War."

Chapter Thirteen
Apart from the personal recollections told to me personally, most of the information about the character of the Archbishop is drawn from the '*Southwark Record*' for June 1948 which reviewed his life and from the '*Universe*' for 7th October 1949 which gave several further insights into his career. The '*Tablet*' also published a good account of his life.

Chapter Fourteen
The events of the Archbishop's final years are taken from the '*Southwark Record.*' Again the accounts of the last illness and funeral are from both the '*Southwark Record*' and the '*Universe.*'

Index

233